Solving the World's Titanic Struggles

Kudo's for the Essays from BahaiTeachings.org Readers

This is another deeply thought-provoking article. Sometimes I think, we need to remember that this is not a cookie-cutter life.
– Melanie Black

Outstanding Mr. Richards, just very well stated!
– Dennis Pettyjohn

A lovely article Rodney, that made me giggle and my heart smile! I loved the story of you and your wife Janet, as well! Thank you!
-- Kathleen Roman

This was very well written and very well expressed!
-- Patricia Bastani

Good meditation! Helpful self-discipline, actually-- Thank you, Rodney
– Charlotte Solarz

What a fine personal account and lessons permanently learned through experience, thought, and time!
– Steve Eaton

Wonderful how you have linked the Writings with the thought you have shared. Looking forward to reading more.
– Mary Jo Schroeder

Also from Rodney Richards

Coffee, Cigarettes, Death & Mania — A survivor's bipolar romp through the world and life

Published by ABLiA Media LLC, available on Amazon

Solving the World's Titanic Struggles

Answers from Bahá'í Philosophy and Spirituality

From

Rodney Richards

ABLiA Media LLC
Trenton NJ 08690

IMPORTANT NOTICES

Solving the World's Titanic Struggles Volume 1
Copyright 2018 Rodney Richards

All rights reserved.

A few brief passages may only be used in a review when noting the author and source. Send other requests in writing to 1950ablia@gmail.com

Published by ABLiA Media LLC in the USA. This edition available from Amazon.com and other outlets. Kindle edition available.

ISBN-13: 978-0-692-30664-2

ISBN-10: 0692306641

Library of Congress **LCCN: 2017918821**

Covers: Designed by author

Some photos including front cover used from Pixaby; others used from Creative Commons Open licenses and the public domain.

Illustrations by Robert W. Quinn

Excerpts from Bahá'í texts used with permission of the copyright holder, the National Spiritual Assembly of the Bahá'ís of the United States. These essays originally published online in bahaiteachings.org and are published/printed herein with their knowledge as they hold no publishing or other rights to the material per their own policies.

ABLiA Media LLC
PO Box 2536
Trenton NJ 08619

Solving the World's Titanic Struggles

Page	Contents
i	Preface
iii	Dedications
iv	Acknowledgements
v	Introduction
1	Opening Essay: A Bahá'í Vision for the Future
6	The Prospect of an Ideal Government, Part 1
9	World Government, Parliament, World Unity, Part 2
12	Can Religion Unify the Planet?
15	Can Science and Religion Ever Agree?
18	Why Science is Reality
21	Discovering the Life of the Spirit
24	The Creation Story – Balancing Mind and Spirit
27	Passing Mental Tests on the Way to Self
30	The Seat of the Self – The Human Heart
33	Are We Truly Descended from the Apes?
36	Finding Faith and Finding Yourself Too
39	Inspired by the Glory of God
42	The Intelligence of the Rational Soul, Part 1
45	The Source of the Rational Soul, Part 2
48	The Meaning Behind Mankind's Salvation
52	One Thankful, Grateful Apostrophe to God
55	Giving Back Our Fair Share
58	How Can We Escape Our Existential Hell?

Page	Contents
61	Mutual Paradise – The Love Between Husband and Wife
64	Philosophy and Religion – Comprehending the Realities, Part 1
67	Philosophy and Spirituality Today, Part 2
71	Investigating Reality – and Philosophy, Part 3
74	Can We End War? Part 1
78	A Democratic Upsurge: Wars of Civil Unrest, Part 2
82	How Can We End Terrorism? Part 3
85	How Can We Stop Killing Each Other? Part 4
88	The Concept of Federalism Applied to the Whole World
92	How to De-weaponize Your Words
95	Do You Have a Kindly Tongue?
97	Order in the Universe, First and Foremost
100	To Progress Spiritually, Humanity Needs a Divine Educator
103	Tyrants, Fighting for Their Own Tombs
106	We Can Solve the Ills of Humanity
109	Prosperous? Be Generous. Troubled? Be Thankful.
111	Woodrow Wison: Racist or Peacemaker? Part 1
115	Wilson's Points: The Dawn of Universal Peace, Part 2
119	The 14th Point: How to Create a Peaceful World, Part 3

Page	Contents
122	How to Recognize the Truth
125	Christians Should Thank Muslims
128	What Religion Are You?
130	Act Locally, But Think Big
133	Why Do Prophets Suffer?
136	How Hard Is It, Really, To Be Kind?
138	Religion in Film: Making a Leap of Faith, Part 1
140	Looking For the Lord -- at the Cinema, Part 2
143	How Does Wealth Get Us to Peace?
146	The Human Will and the Will of God
149	Gambling: To Wager Or Work?
152	The Law: Are You a Conformer, Reformer or Rationalizer?
155	What If You Wore A Badge Of Your Belief?
158	Green Acre: Where Happiness and Peace Live
162	Are We Meant To Kill Each Other?
166	Why Do We Blame God For Our Suffering?
168	Why Does God Still Pick On Me?
172	Who Do We Talk to When We Talk to Ourselves?
175	Do You Believe in Miracles?
177	Marriage for the 21st Century
180	Earth: The Original Magic Kingdom
183	What Will Make Me Happy?
186	Giving in to Temptation
189	What Cause Should I Join?
192	Beating Swords into Words

Page	Contents
195	The Power of the Prophet's Words
198	Scripture, Facebook, and the Impact of the Written Word
201	The Mystical, Mythic Name of 'Abdu'l-Bahá
204	Who Really Raises Our Children?
206	Does God Really Help (Me)?
208	Brexit, Nationalism and World Unity
211	How to Delve Deeper into Your Soul
214	How to Consult About Reality – Lovingly
217	National Sovereignty: A Blight on Humanity
221	How Do Words Become Holy?
224	Love Songs: All About God?
227	Do You Believe in Fate or Destiny?
230	Building True Global Security
234	How to Build a Strong Nation with Consultation
238	Where is God When We Need Him?
241	Power, Authority and Systems – Balancing "The Man"
245	Who Is God Anyway?
248	How to Maintain a "Bright and Friendly Face"
251	Why this Myth of White, Red, Black, Yellow Persists
255	Gandhi and King: Nonviolence and Change
259	Are There Any Accidents in this World?
262	Investigating Reality: The First Principle of Life and Love

Page	Contents
265	5 Fatal Thinking Errors, and How to Fix Them, Part 1
269	Fixing 4 More Fatal Thinking Errors, Part 2
272	Aesop's Fables: More than Just Stories
276	So What? It's Just Another Day
279	How to Change the World in 3 Easy Steps
282	What's the Difference Between an Error and a Sin?
285	To Everyone on the Planet: Have a Great Day!
287	Courtesy: The Virtue that Precedes All Others
290	Water, Water Everywhere, But Nary a Drop to Drink
293	Do You Believe in Angels? Part 1
296	Do Angels Really Exist? Part 2
299	5 Ways to Become an Angel, Part 3
302	Why Do We Do Bad Things?
305	Why Do We Think of People as Strangers?
308	Last Essay: Why Do We Need Religion?
311	Closing Remarks: The Meaning of True Religion
317	Appendix: The Seven Candles of Unity
319	Endnotes
320	Bibliography
322	Resources

PREFACE

You'll find the topics covered in this book varied, thought-provoking, and easy to read. Primarily this is a work of non-fiction by a longtime member of a worldwide religion who desires to see the viable solutions that it offers understood more widely.
 I promise, the import of the concepts shown will astound you in their clarity and efficacy, forthrightness and candor, power and authority. Common sense but not simplistic.

This book comprises 100 short essays on social, religious, personal, community and universal themes written in conversational tones. They appeared sequentially as published between July 2014 -- May 2017 in the popular online Blog **BahaiTeachings.org,** which kicked off in December 2012.
 The essays herein are reprinted with the knowledge of that professionally-edited online publication, who holds no rights to their publication. The author's byline appeared on each essay when published.
 Pertinent quotations from the extensive Bahá'í Writings, comprising hundreds of books and thousands of letters of its central leaders, gave me impetus to write my views and raise my voice with others. **I want to make it clear however, that my thoughts and words are entirely my own, and do not necessarily reflect the opinion of BahaiTeachings.org or any institution of the Bahá'í Faith.**
 These essays project my understandings of the Bahá'í Faith as a member in good standing since 1969, and are based on my own research, feelings and experiences.
 My wife Janet and I married as Bahá'ís in 1971, and have two grown children with successful careers. Janet and I served many decades in public service, she with our school district as an elementary school educator, and I as an IT and Energy contracts manager for our home State. I was a trained municipal court mediator for 24 years, and now volunteer on our community's Environmental Commission. I maintain a

Blog for writers titled *Write with Authority* and facilitate two weekly creative writing classes and a business writing class.

Although writing as an American, you'll find world topics and views expressed herein as well.

The answers to what many people consider intractable problems do exist, as I think you'll agree upon reading. It's up to those concerned with the state of current affairs, in whatever fair ways they and we can muster, to implement divine yet practical solutions to the problems all of us face.

It's always been that way and will continue to be so.

My hope is that you will enjoy these essays and will also consider their meaning and purpose – to shine a light on new teachings for humanity.

A word about the look and feel of the book.

Although these essays first appeared online, BahaiTeachings.org, formatting herein differs from that source to fit page layouts used in the version you are reading.

Updated notes and changes are contained in **[brackets]**.

Almost all quotations are in **BOLD**.

The correct transliterations of Bahá'í names (pronounced Ba-HIGH), are as follows: Báb (pronounced Bahb), Bahá'u'lláh (Ba-ha-ul-LAH), and 'Abdu'l-Bahá (Abdul ba-HAH), with accent marks. Such marks did not appear in the original blog essays but appear herein.

The 84 pictures, sketches, and graphics used throughout are the author's choice. Many appeared in similar form on the BahaiTeachings.org Blog. Actual colors were too expensive to reproduce.

One other thing.

Please feel free to let me know if this content or any views connect with you. If you have a comment write me c/o ABLiA Media LLC, or email me at 1950ablia@gmail.com

For more on the Prophet/Founder Bahá'u'lláh and the Bahá'í Faith, visit **www.bahai.org** or call **1-800-22-UNITE**

Best always, Rod

DEDICATION TO MY MENTORS

To David Langness, past Managing Editor and writer for **BahaiTeachings.org,** also a journalist and literary critic for Paste Magazine, who has meticulously edited and improved my writing since our first meeting at Green Acre Bahá'í School in 2014.

To the memory of Maria Okros, "Mariposa" (Butterfly), past leader and mentor at our memoir writing classes at Lawrence Headquarters Branch of the public library. She and the group urged me to "Show don't Tell" until I finally got it through my thick hide — from their example — to practice writing how I truly felt.

To Dr. Michael P. Riccards, friend, author of over 25 books and plays, three-time college president, and past Executive Director of the Hall Institute, a New Jersey think tank. His experience and example these past years in writing compelling and interesting stories and prose has been invaluable.

To Tony Athmejvar, friend and writing budding in weekly memoir and creative writing classes since 2011; writing enthusiast and inveterate reader, leader and facilitator, cheerleader and promotor; ever-reliable and dedicated to the very best writing; a fine gentleman with a rich past.

And to William R. "Bill" Foster, a Knight of Bahá'u'lláh before there were Knights. A life coach who educated and mentored me and others in the deeper meanings contained in the Bahá'í Writings, particularly those of Shoghi Effendi, the appointed Interpreter of those writings for the Bahá'í communities of his time and into the future.

ACKNOWLEDGMENTS

Thank you to Robert "Bob" Quinn for his excellent sketches used throughout the book and to Doug Masim at Prime Photo for their digitization.

INTRODUCTION

BahaiTeachings.org has had over 2,000,000 views from people of all walks of life from around the world.[1]

The articles that follow contain the views of one among millions anxious for peace and prosperity in a world gone mad in too many ways to list.

But the world has not gone totally insane yet, nor will it.

Changes in hearts and minds, beliefs and practices on humongous scales are occurring every moment. People of their own volition are transforming "satanic fancies" into "heavenly virtues" daily, and those become concrete, inevitable, and positive changes—solutions—to a lamentable system that fights every progressive step.

In 2016-2018 there was/is Black Lives Matter/All Lives Matter, the #MeToo exposés, the youthful MarchForOurLives movements, and dozens more. Necessary criticism for the old ways we once accepted as the status quo is steadily building, along with new ideas and methods toward a better citizenry and world.

Our race is experiencing the twin processes of Disintegration of the old and Integration with the new, expressed by Bahá'í leader Shoghi Effendi in the 1930s:

"A titanic, a spiritual struggle, unparalleled in its magnitude yet unspeakably glorious in its ultimate consequences, is being waged as a result of these opposing tendencies, in this age of transition through which the organized community of the followers of Bahá'u'lláh and mankind as a whole are passing."[2]

Over five million Bahá'ís are caught in this mesh of a travailing age, are not immune to its effects, and also struggle to actively bring about positive change and prevent more setbacks. Their chariot is God's Plan for humankind, revealed in every age by divine Messengers who changed the course of history. Their charioteer in this new age is Bahá'u'lláh, the

Prophet-Founder of the Bahá'í Faith, and His universal and progressive solutions for a modern society. Their steed is personal transformation.

Shoghi Effendi also called this "age of transition" the Age of Frustration, and we see why every day on the news.

Despite steps backward and missteps, Bahá'ís are optimistic and are actively solving human problems and societal difficulties in hundreds of thousands of localities globally by demonstrating love, fellowship, consultation and acceptance.

I sum it up this way:

"If we fully utilize our soul, containing those inward powers of spirit and mind, especially our collective love as one human family, we can discover and implement solutions to the most intractable global problems. With time, firmness of will, unity of thought, and undivided purpose, everything is not only possible, but probable.

If we rely upon God, He will bolster our efforts and we will succeed."

Although it appears that humanity is irreparably destroying our environment, our social relationships, our religious tolerances and our families, there are reasons for the madness.

Humankind, like an ill patient, is gripped by a spiritual disease. The following essays and quotations offer remedies both personal and collective.

I encourage you to add your voice to the millions of others who are speaking and acting in favor of true welfare and peace, felicity and security—in all their aspects—for all children, teens, youth, adults, and seniors that make up the human race.

ESSAYS

On

Solving the World's Titanic Struggles

Opening Essay:

A BAHÁ'Í VISION FOR THE FUTURE

PART ONE IN A SERIES | GLOBAL CHANGE FOR THE NEXT GENERATION

...if every clan, tribe, community, every nation, country, territory on earth should come together under the single-hued pavilion of the oneness of mankind, and by the dazzling rays of the Sun of Truth should proclaim the universality of man; if they should cause all nations and all creeds to open wide their arms to one another, establish a World Council, and proceed to bind the members of society one to another by strong mutual ties, what would happen then?
– 'Abdu'l-Bahá, Selections from the Writings of 'Abdu'l-Bahá, pp. 279-280.

This series of articles takes the futuristic vision of the movement called the Bahá'í Faith, founded by the Persian nobleman Bahá'u'lláh in the middle of the 19th century, [a Prophet of God subjected to exile and imprisonment]. [These articles] apply that vision toward imagining what our global society could look like a generation from now. The Bahá'í Faith, a rapidly-expanding, recognized independent worldwide religion with more than five million adherents in almost every country and principality on the planet, has one simple (but not simplistic) watchword from Bahá'u'lláh: "The earth is but one country, and mankind its citizens."

Let us try to visualize [or imagine, an optimistic scenario]: Twenty-five years have passed, and much of the world has now achieved conscious adulthood, finally climbing out of its turbulent period of adolescence–but only after severe trials and tribulations that affect[ed] all peoples and all of their institutions

[In this scenario,] the old politics of polarization and divisiveness, corrupt and preferential governmental policies, deep indifference to the poor and uneducated, and the pursuit of wealth as a means to an end at all costs have been exposed as vacuous and destructive.

The combined efforts of citizens and [just] governments have relegated them to the dustbin of history.

Collective global security guaranteed by a democratically-elected World Council provides peace and stability at all levels of society. Most of the world's governments have now based their structures on the principles of federalism and democracy and have agreed on definitive national borders and a steep voluntary reduction in their armaments and armies. Nation building has ended, and the era of a unified world has begun.

As documented in those farsighted early 21st-Century books *The Secret Peace* [by Jesse Richards] and T*he Better Angels of Our Nature: Why Violence Has Declined [by Steven Pinker]*, human conditions have steadily improved, and fairer policies and practices have been instituted in many aspects of life.

We still have work to do, but violence has declined even more significantly than before, and global governance has begun to prevent wars.

[Using our imagination, we see that] over time, as peace spreads across more of the earth, a moderating influence has started to positively affect human relations, based on noble human values such as love, justice, equity, and social welfare. Governments increasingly heed the voices of their previously silent masses, silent no longer. Because freedom of expression, consultation and consensus now govern social relationships, we have achieved more timely and effective problem-solving, which has led to increased social good in all regions of the world and continues to benefit the world's poorest people.

The demilitarization of the world's nations, and the World Council's largely successful peacemaking efforts in regions where conflict has reigned, have both brought about a steep decline in the enormous amounts of money previously spent on war and defense.

Those funds now go to feed, clothe, and educate all the world's children.

In this [imagined] new world a generation from now, men and women are increasingly equal, and have equal rights, equal pay, and equal representation in government. Human prejudices—racial, religious, national, and all others—are disappearing.

Moderate policies across many sectors of society have created organizational stability and reliability in free markets. The new global currency and a universally-agreed-upon system of weights and measures have made worldwide trade more efficient, fairer, and more possible.

As the peoples of the world learn the international auxiliary language along with their own native language, ease of communication increases, and misunder-standings and foreignness decrease.

The earth's pressing environmental problems, although still acute, have finally begun to reverse themselves [because of] national and global cooperation—rather than the infighting, rivalries and blaming that hampered progress In past decades.

[In this new world] from a personal perspective, people have noticed that a kindly tongue increasingly replaces invective, backbiting, gossip, and verbal violence in all their forms. With national and regional peace treaties proliferating and all forms of violence and conflict declining rapidly, individual conflict and criminality has also diminished greatly.

The world has seen a great upsurge in the number of people conducting their own independent investigation of the truth; going beyond tradition and deciding on their spiritual paths themselves. Increasingly, the goal of all human interaction leans toward agreement based on truthfulness and equity....

Does this sound possible—or does it seem like a pipe dream?

The Bahá'í teachings say that humanity has the ability, the power, and the inspiration to reach these lofty goals:

Unification of the whole of mankind is the hallmark of the stage which human society is now approaching.

Unity of family, of tribe, of city-state, and nation have been successively attempted and fully established.

World unity is the goal towards which a harassed humanity is striving.

Nation-building has come to an end. The anarchy inherent in state sovereignty is moving towards a climax.

A world, growing to maturity, must abandon this fetish, recognize the oneness and wholeness of human relationships, and establish once for all the machinery that can best incarnate this fundamental principle of its life.

– Shoghi Effendi, The World Order of Bahá'u'lláh, p. 202.

#

[Author's update to the first-time reader of Bahá'í religious philosophy and tenets:

The following statement by Shoghi Effendi, great-grandson of the founder Bahá'u'lláh, and the Guardian of the Bahá'í Faith and its leader for 36 years from 1921-1957, clarifies the Bahá'í position:

Let there be no misgivings as to the animating purpose of the world-wide Law of Bahá'u'lláh. Far from aiming at the subversion of the existing foundations of society, it seeks to broaden its basis, to remold its institutions in a manner consonant with the needs of an ever-changing world.

It can conflict with no legitimate allegiances, nor can it undermine essential loyalties.

Its purpose is neither to stifle the flame of a sane and intelligent patriotism in men's hearts, nor to abolish the system of national autonomy so essential if the evils of excessive centralization are to be avoided.

It does not ignore, nor does it attempt to suppress, the diversity of ethnical origins, of climate, of history, of language and tradition, of thought and habit, that differentiate the peoples and nations of the world.

It calls for a wider loyalty, for a larger aspiration than any that has animated the human race, It insists upon the subordination of national impulses and interests to the imperative claims of a unified world.

It repudiates excessive centralization on one hand, and disclaims all attempts at uniformity on the other. Its watchword is unity in diversity . . . .

--The World Order of Bahá'u'lláh, p. 41]

#

The Prospect of an Ideal Government

PART 2 IN SERIES | **GLOBAL CHANGE FOR THE NEXT GENERATION**

In the first part of this [imagined] series of essays on the potential of our world a generation from now, we looked at the possibility of a democratic World Council and a universal peace treaty, and at all the powerful, positive impacts those changes could make for the people of the earth. Let us consider, in this part of our exploration, what a future government, both national and global, could possibly aspire to become.

Flag of the EU (Actual flag is yellow stars and dark blue background)

[Imagine,] A generation from now, the federal system has evolved, and nation-states have now become a federated union across the entire planet. Much like the current states in the United States or the individual nations in the European Union, the world's nation-states now belong to one global federal system.

Born out of the realization that the old model of national sovereignty led inevitably to conflict, the [countries in the] new world federation, a Parliament of Humanity, [have willingly ceded their] ability to declare war. Instead, each country maintains a military force sufficient to deal with its internal needs, and all governments agree that consultation, diplomacy, mediation and arbitration have replaced the destruction and devastation of war.

Most of the world's nations now have strong, non-arbitrary and non-preferential laws and regulations universally applied, and state laws cannot trump or conflict with federal laws, which now cover lower levels of human and business interactions. Government serves all its constituents, at six basic levels: global, federal, state, county, township, and city. Three branches of government still apply: Executive, Legislative and Judiciary, with clear separation of duties, powers, and responsibilities, and without internecine strife.

As opposed to the infighting and political gridlock of a generation ago, those three branches of government increasingly cooperate and support each other to the extent that the general public's [welfare] and security are always the primary goals of all governmental operations.

As [imagined] individuals, citizens voluntarily cede some of their personal rights and resources for the common good of the majority.

Likewise, the States have ceded some of their sovereignty to make laws and collect taxes in favor of national standards, just as the nations have in pursuit of international unity.

All people have access to good health care and competitive medical programs, where the user knows all costs and prices in advance, and archaic state laws restricting many insurance sales and programs are now administered globally, with regional influences allowed for and incorporated. Taxation, which previously favored those with the most financial resources, is now more progressive, equitable and fair for all, with very limited exemptions.

The [possible] Executive branch at the global level administers and maximizes stewardship of the world's vast resources and production, provides for common defense and emergency responses, as well as social services; maintains foreign relations, and enforces laws and regulations.

The [possible] Legislative branch is composed of a bicameral legislature (i.e. senate, assembly), and flourishes based on compromise and consensus at the planetary, national, and state levels. Legislators discuss proposed laws in public forums before passage, and online access to all bills and ordinances provides multiple opportunities for public comment, opinion, and debate.

Elected representatives vote their conscience and are not responsible to vote the way any individual, political party, cabal, industry, or lobbying group would wish.

[In an iterim political system 25 years from now more] than two parties coexist to accomplish solutions to societal problems, and the influence of [enormous] amounts of money on the electoral system is minimized.

Elected representatives must adhere to the highest ethical standards and rules of conduct in order to retain their position. For example: all campaign contributions have limits, and influence-peddling and lobbying are restricted to information and fact-sharing.

In the [imaginary] Judiciary system, municipal, county, state, national and international court systems remain, but are coordinated and supplemented by citizen volunteers for certain criminal and civil issues, such as impartial mediation to adjudicate disputes. All laws and regulations are easily accessible and searchable online by any citizen or organization, both well before and after passage, and there is an easy online process for commenting. Laws are reviewed every three to five years for applicability and modified or abolished to fit the needs and requirements of the times.

[Increasingly,] taxes at every level of government will pay for what the public welfare and safety necessitates, and allow government to provide for such needs. Increasingly, taxation promotes the social good and better social behaviors, education at all levels, clean air and water and land.

[In this new world environment] As the global need for huge military budgets drastically diminishes, the unfair burden of taxes on all people drops enormously:

Implements of war and death are multiplied and increased to an inconceivable degree, and the burden of military maintenance is taxing the various countries beyond the point of endurance. Armies and navies devour the substance and possessions of the people; the toiling poor, the innocent and helpless are forced by taxation to provide munitions and armament for governments bent upon conquest of territory and defense against powerful rival nations.
– 'Abdu'l-Bahá, The Promulgation of Universal Peace, p. 317.

#

WORLD GOVERNMENT, WORLD PARLIAMENT, WORLD UNITY

PART 3 IN SERIES: GLOBAL CHANGE FOR THE NEXT GENERATION

What kind of world will we leave our children and grandchildren? This question plagues every parent, and because we love our offspring, we want them to have a better world than the one we have now.

In this series of essays, we've looked at the 'potential [of] global cooperation and unity a generation from now. The Bahá'í teachings, which include a very well-developed vision for that future world our children and grandchildren will inherit, promise humanity that we can achieve such a vision. Although the state of the world today may not look very promising to most people, [or even 25 years from now] and the unification of the planet's nations may seem too ambitious a goal, Bahá'u'lláh assures the world that if we unify we can achieve international harmony, cooperation and peace.

These next paragraphs from the Guardian of the Bahá'í Faith contain a succinct summary of the overarching goals of [a Bahá'í] future world order:

The unity of the human race, as envisaged by Bahá'u'lláh, implies the establishment of a world commonwealth in which all nations, races, creeds and classes are closely and permanently united, and in which the autonomy of its state members and the personal freedom and initiative of the individuals that compose them are definitely and completely safeguarded.

This commonwealth must, as far as we can visualize it, consist of a world legislature, whose members will, as the trustees of the whole of mankind, ultimately control the entire resources of all the component nations, and will enact such laws as shall be required to regulate the life, satisfy the needs and adjust the relationships of all races and peoples.

A world executive, backed by an international Force, will carry out the decisions arrived at, and apply the laws enacted by, this world legislature, and will safeguard the organic unity of the whole commonwealth.

A world tribunal will adjudicate and deliver its compulsory and final verdict in all and any disputes that may arise between the various elements constituting this universal system.

A mechanism of world inter-communication will be devised, embracing the whole planet, freed from national hindrances and restrictions, and functioning with marvelous swiftness and perfect regularity.

A world metropolis will act as the nerve center of a world civilization, the focus towards which the unifying forces of life will converge and from which its energizing influences will radiate.

A world language will either be invented or chosen from among the existing languages and will be taught in the schools of all the federated nations as an auxiliary to their mother tongue.

A world script, a world literature, a uniform and universal system of currency, of weights and measures, will simplify and facilitate intercourse and understanding among the nations and races of mankind.

In such a world society, science and religion, the two most potent forces in human life, will be reconciled, will cooperate, and will harmoniously develop.

The press will, under such a system, while giving full scope to the expression of the diversified views and convictions of mankind, cease to be mischievously manipulated by vested interests, whether private or public, and will be liberated from the influence of contending governments and peoples.

The economic resources of the world will be organized, its sources of raw materials will be tapped and fully utilized, its markets will be coordinated and developed, and the distribution of its products will be equitably regulated.

National rivalries, hatreds, and intrigues will cease, and racial animosity and prejudice will be replaced by racial amity, understanding and cooperation.

The causes of religious strife will be permanently removed, economic barriers and restrictions will be completely abolished, and the inordinate distinction between classes will be obliterated.

Destitution on the one hand, and gross accumulation of ownership on the other, will disappear.

The enormous energy dissipated and wasted on war, whether economic or political, will be consecrated to such ends as will extend the range of human inventions and technical development,

to the increase of the productivity of mankind,

to the extermination of disease,

to the extension of scientific research,

to the raising of the standard of physical health,

to the sharpening and refinement of the human brain,

to the exploitation of the unused and unsuspected resources of the planet,

to the prolongation of human life,

and to the furtherance of any other agency that can stimulate the intellectual, the moral, and spiritual life of the entire human race.

— The World Order of Bahá'u'lláh, pp. 202-204.

The worldwide Bahá'í community, and each individual Bahá'í, works for the establishment of this far-sighted vision of the future every day.

But Bahá'ís do not believe that humanity can achieve such a massive and monumental change in our fortunes without a unifying force to guide, assist and inspire us. In the next and final iteration of this series, let us look at the power of religion and see if it can possibly fill that role.

#

Can Religion Unify the Planet?

PART 4 IN SERIES: GLOBAL CHANGE FOR THE NEXT GENERATION

The endowments which distinguish the human race from all other forms of life are summed up in what is known as the human spirit; the mind is its essential quality. These endowments have enabled humanity to build civilizations and to prosper materially.

But such accomplishments alone have never satisfied the human spirit, whose mysterious nature inclines it towards transcendence, a reaching towards an invisible realm, towards the ultimate reality, that unknowable essence of essences called God.

The religions brought to mankind by a succession of spiritual luminaries have been the primary link between humanity and that ultimate reality, and have galvanized and refined mankind's capacity to achieve spiritual success together with social progress....

No serious attempt to set human affairs aright, to achieve world peace, can ignore religion.
– The Universal House of Justice, October 1985, Address to The Peoples of the World

Historians recognize religion, one of the most potent forces guiding human conduct and promoting social good, for its [significant] role in helping everyone's] moral and spiritual development—but also for controlling materialism and advancing civilization.

Just like human development, which has incrementally and steadily matured over the past thousands of years, religion has also reached adulthood.

Many people now recognize all the Prophets and Founders of the world's great Faiths for what and who they are: progressive messengers of the same God, a God of love. In the Bahá'í view of a systematic, unified and sequential development of faith, each religion plays a required and legitimate role in a single divine, continuing, perpetual religion.

Bahá'ís believe the Messengers of God will continue to succeed one another "until the end that hath no end," each bringing in turn a fuller measure of God's unending guidance to humankind.

In the Bahá'í teachings, we learn that God has given us an unfolding plan for happiness and social order, based on spiritual principles of love, service to others, and personal conduct.

In the Bahá'í teachings, the twin goals of every religion, unity and freedom of worship, are blended and harmonized for the modern age.

In the Bahá'í teachings, the religions agree on spiritual and moral principles, although internal social laws differ in major and minor aspects, [temporarily].

In the Bahá'í teachings, science and religion agree.

Bahá'ís believe that the Golden Rule applies universally and serves as the foundation of civilization. The Bahá'í teachings uphold the sanctity of life, with consideration for the mother's [health at birth]. Bahá'ís have no clergy. The Bahá'í teachings encourage marriage and family life and consider the raising of children a parental and societal duty.

Bahá'í House of Worship in Wilmette (outside Chicago)

Bahá'í houses of worship are open to everyone. They [may be associated with] schools, dispensaries, homes for the aged, medical facilities, social services, and other charitable efforts.

Bahá'ís teach and respect shared religious values universally. Bahá'ís do not proselytize or forcibly convert people to their faith. Sane reasoning replaces superstition, outworn rituals, blind dogma, and restrictive traditions, without sacrificing the influence of the heart.

The Bahá'í teachings encourage each individual to discover a personal reality based on an independent investigation of the truth, and not through the knowledge or traditions of others.

In the Bahá'í teachings, the religious distortions, disagreements and intolerance of the past, a main source of disunity, have been reconciled. Hatred, verbal or physical violence, and fanaticism have been replaced by acceptance, unity and understanding.

Could the Bahá'í Faith be that universal religion of the future, the missing cohesive element that leads humanity to a unified and peaceful world? The Bahá'í teachings encourage everyone to investigate and answer that question for themselves:

Now is the beginning of the manifestation of the spiritual power, and inevitably the potency of its life forces will assume greater and greater proportions.

…it is evident that day by day it will advance. It will reach such a degree that spiritual effulgences will overcome the physical, so that divine susceptibilities will overpower material intelligence and the heavenly light dispel and banish earthly darkness.

Divine healing shall purify all ills, and the cloud of mercy will pour down its rain. The Sun of Reality will shine, and all the earth shall put on its beautiful green carpet.

Among the results of the manifestation of spiritual forces will be that the human world will adapt itself to a new social form, the justice of God will become manifest throughout human affairs, and human equality will be universally established.

– 'Abdu'l-Bahá, The Promulgation of Universal Peace, p. 131.

#

Can Science and Religion Ever Agree?

PART 5 IN SERIES | GLOBAL CHANGE FOR THE NEXT GENERATION

Can science and religion ever agree?
[Here is] the better question: When did science and religion not agree?

Religion has stayed its course for 10,000 years that we know of, from the religion of Abraham through all the prophets up to Bahá'u'lláh in the 19th century. The Bahá'í teachings promise many more revelations to come in the glorious future of the human race. At no time did these divine messengers forbid the investigation of reality, and in fact, since the revelation of the Bahá'í Faith, the independent investigation of truth has been its number one principle.

But man is imperfect, and so some leaders who want power and control over others have produced blind imitations, which obscure and totally blot out the truth:

Alas! that humanity is completely submerged in imitations and unrealities notwithstanding the truth of divine religion has ever remained the same.

Superstitions have obscured the fundamental reality, the world is darkened and the light of religion is not apparent. This darkness is conducive to differences and dissensions; rites and dogmas are many and various; therefore discord has arisen among the religious systems whereas religion is for the unification of mankind.

True religion is the source of love and agreement amongst men, the cause of the development of praiseworthy qualities; but the people are holding to the counterfeit and imitation, negligent of the reality which unifies; so they are bereft and deprived of the radiance of religion. They follow superstitions inherited from their fathers and ancestors.

To such an extent has this prevailed that they have taken away the heavenly light of divine truth and sit in the darkness of imitations and imaginations.

That which was meant to be conducive to life has become the cause of death; that which should have been an evidence of knowledge is now a proof of ignorance;

that which was a factor in the sublimity of human nature has proved to be its degradation.
– 'Abdu'l-Bahá, Foundations of World Unity, p. 71.

We have one united scientific truth, and the Bahá'í teachings say that we also have one unified religious truth.

Both discover the realities, one in humanity's inner life and the other in the natural world. The Bahá'í writings say that true religion unlocks and uncovers **"that which is beyond the range of the senses, that realm of phenomena through which the conscious pathway to the Kingdom of God leads . . ."**
- ibid, p. 49.

The Bahá'í writings say that true science **"discovers latent realities within the bosom of the earth, uncovers treasures, penetrates secrets and mysteries of the phenomenal world . . ."**
– ibid, p. 49.

According to Forrester Research, over one billion PCs existed worldwide by the end of 2008; two billion will exist by 2015. As Silicon India recently reported, the number of active cell phones will reach 7.3 billion by 2014. That's the world's population–right now. We can thank science and logic and human intelligence for perfecting these and a myriad of amazing technologies.

Man did not magically climb out of the primordial mud and immediately create fire, nor computers, nor cell phones. These realities took years to nurture and develop, just as spiritual principles take years to nurture and develop in a human heart. They can be discovered by trial and error, testing hypotheses, or yet again, in an instant of inspiration and change of viewpoint.

True religion and science have never disagreed—instead, they both became the discoverers, unlockers and uncoverers of reality.

Only humans, in our imperfection, have created these disagreements:

Religion is the outer expression of the divine reality. Therefore it must be living, vitalized, moving and progressive. If it be without motion and non-progressive it is without the divine life; it is dead.

The divine institutes are continuously active and evolutionary; therefore the revelation of them must be progressive and continuous. All things are subject to reformation. This is a century of life and renewal. Sciences and arts, industry and invention have been reformed. Law and ethics have been reconstituted, reorganized.

The world of thought has been regenerated. Sciences of former ages and philosophies of the past are useless today. Present exigencies demand new methods of solution; world problems are without precedent.

Old ideas and modes of thought are fast becoming obsolete.

Ancient laws and archaic ethical systems will not meet the requirements of modern conditions, for this is clearly the century of a new life, the century of the revelation of reality and therefore the greatest of all centuries.

Consider how the scientific developments of fifty years have surpassed and eclipsed the knowledge and achievements of all the former ages combined.

—ibid, p. 84.

#

Why Science Is Reality

PART 6 IN SERIES | GLOBAL CHANGE FOR THE NEXT GENERATION

Religious institutions have often reviled and denied scientific facts, and even severely punished those who discovered them.

Original Galileo Galilei portrait by Giusto Sustermans

In the famous case of Galileo in 1633, the Holy Office of the Catholic Pope put him on trial for his scientific theory that the Earth revolved around the Sun. The trial verdict found Galileo "vehemently suspect of heresy", and the Church forced him to publicly recant his theory.

Famously, he said about the Earth immediately after his trial, "And yet it moves."

For his crime of discovery, Galileo spent nine years, the rest of his life, under house arrest.

Science discovers reality, as does religion, in its own way. Now, in the 21st century, scientific views have undergone a 180-degree revolution. Today scientific theories have become so numerous and so ubiquitous that we tend to regard them as fact instead of hoax until proven otherwise. And religious truth has become secular in [too] many instances, to adapt.

Another example, my beloved three cups of coffee per day, according to Leslie Stahl's reporting last month on 60 Minutes, could prolong my life into the 90's and beyond. At one time the prevalent science recommended against drinking coffee, yet now, research has shown that coffee gives us more than just a morning jolt; that steaming cup of java also provides the number one source of antioxidants in the U.S. diet, according to a new study by researchers at the University of Scranton in Pennsylvania.

Every created thing, including us, reflects the reality of the moment we live in. Some scientific truths and religious dogmas have been proven wrong or right, years after technologists or scientists or sociologists first report their findings. The single truth underlying all science, and indeed, all of life itself, is that discovering reality never ends.

The Bahá'í principle of the agreement of science and religion says that truth, whether spiritual or scientific, has one source and one reality:

It is evident then that each elemental atom of the universe is possessed of a capacity to express all the virtues of the universe.

This is a subtle and abstract realization.

Meditate upon it, for within it lies the true explanation of pantheism. From this point of view and perception, pantheism is a truth, for every atom in the universe possesses or reflects all the virtues of life, the manifestation of which is effected through change and transformation.

Therefore the origin and outcome of phenomena is verily the omnipresent God for the reality of all phenomenal existence is through Him.

There is neither reality nor the manifestation of reality without the instrumentality of God.

Existence is realized and possible through the bounty of God, just as the ray or flame emanating from this lamp is realized through the bounty of the lamp from which it originates.

Even so all phenomena are realized through the divine bounty, and the explanation of true pantheistic statement and principle is that the phenomena of the universe find realization through the one power animating and dominating all things; and all things are but manifestations of its energy and bounty.

The virtue of being and existence is through no other agency.
Therefore in the words of Bahá'u'lláh the first teaching is the oneness of the world of humanity...."
– *Foundations of World Unity*, p.59

As rational human beings, we realize through the truth of religion that God gives us the faculty of reason to discover both material and spiritual and reality:

Religion and science are the two wings upon which man's intelligence can soar into the heights, with which the human soul can progress. It is not possible to fly with one wing alone!
Should a man try to fly with the wing of religion alone he would quickly fall into the quagmire of superstition, whilst on the other hand, with the wing of science alone he would also make no progress, but fall into the despairing slough of materialism.... But the religion which does not walk hand in hand with science is itself in the darkness of superstition and ignorance.
Much of the discord and disunion of the world is created by these man-made oppositions and contradictions. If religion were in harmony with science and they walked together, much of the hatred and bitterness now bringing misery to the human race would be at an end. Consider what it is that singles man out from among created beings, and makes of him a creature apart. Is it not his reasoning power, his intelligence? Shall he not make use of these in his study of religion?
I say unto you: weigh carefully in the balance of reason and science everything that is presented to you as religion.
If it passes this test, then accept it, for it is truth!
If, however, it does not so conform, then reject it, for it is ignorance!
– 'Abdu'l-Bahá, *Paris Talks*, pp. 143-144.

Reality, like fantasy and imagination, goes on forever.
With its billions of galaxies, so does the universe. That unimaginable vastness means we have an enormous amount left to discover, if we can unite the spiritual and the scientific in the pursuit of truth.

#

Discovering the Life of the Spirit

PART 7 IN SERIES: **GLOBAL CHANGE FOR THE NEXT GENERATION**

The great Liberator of Science, Rene Descartes (31 March 1596 – 11 February 1650), was a French philosopher, mathematician and writer who spent most of his life in the Dutch Republic. Dubbed the "father of modern philosophy" his work is studied carefully even today. Much of subsequent Western philosophy simply responds to Descartes' writings.

René Descartes

Descartes arrived at a single foundational principle: *thought exists*.

He said, "Thought cannot be separated from me; therefore, I exist." Most famously, we know this as *cogito ergo sum* in Latin, or in English: "I think, therefore I am."

The philosophy and realities of Descartes exposed and liberated science from the chains of religious dogma common in Europe and elsewhere at the time. Another way of understanding his profound insight into humankind [is his]

"I am body and I am mind," [that] he labeled "dualism." These ideas still prevail today—many people, especially in the western world, define themselves this way.

Dualism does not go far enough, however, in describing human beings. It excludes the most important aspect of human existence–our spirit. Many people have pointed out this glaring omission in Descartes' philosophy, but George Williams, a British draper, did something about it. Appalled by the terrible conditions in London of young working men in the 19th Century, he gathered a group of his fellow drapers together to create a place that would not tempt young men into sin–the YMCA, which he founded in June of 1844.

I still remember as a nine-year-old boy in 1959, wearing my white beginner's Gi (uniform), learning Jujitsu at the [Trenton] Y from a master teacher. The Young Men's Christian Association, now a worldwide organization, has more than 57 million beneficiaries from 125 national associations.

It aims to put Christian principles into practice by developing a healthy "body, mind, and spirit," reflected in the sides of its (red) triangle, part of all YMCA logos:

If Descartes called his mind/body dichotomy dualism, you could call this belief in all three human realities "Triism."

Billions of people would agree wholeheartedly with the presence of these three realities in all of us. However, physical science has not yet discovered "hard" evidence of what most of the world's people already know. Faith in a human spirit leads not just to discovering one's full, true self, but also discovering the best in humankind, as exemplified by the saints, prophets and major messengers of God– manifestations such as Buddha, Krishna, Zoroaster, Moses, Christ, Muhammad and more recently, the Báb and Bahá'u'lláh.

These revelators, along with many more whose names are lost to history, named spirit as the foundational component of humanity. In all their teachings, the prophets of God and the founders of the world's great Faiths say the human spirit defines our reality. When we search for our own spiritual core, our soul, these divine educators and messengers say we embark on the true search for our deepest being.

Our own spirit, our soul, gives us life.

How could it be otherwise?

What animates a human being in the embryo to begin with?

In other words, we all live the life of the spirit. In the creation stories and myths of most cultures, we learn that God created man in His own image—which doesn't refer to a physical image, but a spiritual one.

These beautiful passages from the Bahá'í writings illustrate that mystical truth:

O Son of Man! Veiled in my immemorial being and in the ancient eternity of My essence, I knew My love for thee; therefore I created thee, have engraved on thee My image and revealed to thee My beauty.
– Bahá'u'lláh, The Hidden Words, p. 4.

O Son of Being! Thy heart is my home; sanctify it for My descent. Thy spirit is My place of Revelation; cleanse it for My manifestation.
– Bahá'u'lláh, The Hidden Words, p. 17.

The ancients, philosophers, prophets, and manifestations, one and all, have taught and written volumes upon volumes on this powerful theme. They knew that humans will always search for our own spirit, for what makes us who we are.

Life, internal in our minds, or external in our bodies and in the world, impels us on a journey toward the discovery of the most important thing that exists—knowledge of our own selves, and the life of the spirit.

#

The Creation Story – Balancing Mind and Spirit

PART 8 IN SERIES Global Change for the Next Generation

Every culture has a creation myth, and many of them have striking similarities—they typically feature the story of the first man and woman and tell us about the symbolism and meaning of their spiritual universe.

Most of the world's peoples know the Biblical creation story of Adam and Eve from Genesis. In it, after the seventh day, God first creates the body of Adam, breathes into his nostrils the spirit of life, "and man became a living soul."

Then God created a garden, and the tree of knowledge of good and evil.

God then took one of Adam's ribs and created the first woman, Eve.

At first all seemed idyllic eastward of Eden, and God gave them every good thing, and one command, "thou shalt not eat" of the fruit of the Tree of Knowledge.

But the subtle serpent tempted Eve into eating the fruit, saying, "For God doth know that in the day that ye eat thereof, then your eyes shall be opened, and ye shall be as gods, knowing good and evil."

And Eve ate of it and shared it with Adam who ate also. Upon which God was very displeased and cast them from the Garden into the wilderness. He even placed cherubim and a flaming sword at the garden's gate, to make sure Adam and Eve stayed out.

As God had told them, the day they ate the forbidden fruit they died. Beguiled by the world, Adam and Eve's "fall" metaphorically represented human beings putting their own wills before God's.

Genesis explains why God has sent us his prophets and messengers ever since, to teach us respect, humility, kindness once again–all the virtues we symbolically tossed aside to eat the forbidden fruit, with or without knowing the true implications of that action. In my view, the story symbolizes humanity throwing away our original trust in God.

In the Bahá'í teachings, 'Abdu'l-Bahá explains the deep symbolism of the Creation story:

…by "Adam" is meant the spirit of Adam and by "Eve" is meant His self. For in certain passages of the Sacred Scriptures where women are mentioned, the intended meaning is the human self.

By "the tree of good and evil" is meant the material world, for the heavenly realm of the spirit is pure goodness and absolute radiance, but in the material world light and darkness, good and evil, and all manner of opposing realities are to be found.

The meaning of the serpent is attachment to the material world.

This attachment of the spirit to the material world led to the banishment of the self and spirit of Adam from the realm of freedom to the world of bondage and caused Him to turn from the kingdom of Divine Unity to the world of human existence.

When once the self and spirit of Adam entered the material world, He departed from the paradise of freedom and descended into the realm of bondage.

He had abided in the heights of sanctity absolute goodness, and set forth thereafter in the world of good and evil.
-- 'Abdu'l-Bahá, Some Answered Questions, newly revised, pp. 138-139

I bring up the Creation story, one I learned so well as a Catholic boy, because of the sequence of Adam's creation. First God created his body from dust, then breathed the "spirit of the Lord" into him, and subsequently God made Eve. They ate of the tree of knowledge and discovered their nakedness, as well as good and evil.

The philosopher in me can't help but think those symbols mean that the creation of the human body comes first, forever, infused with spirit, giving the body its life-force. This occurs both scientifically and spiritually when egg meets sperm.

Our binary nature, both the lower animal instincts and our higher spiritual yearnings, may have led to Descartes' concept of mind and body in dualism.

Progress in the physical sciences, and today in technology, have impelled individual and societal developments of the powers of the mind. Just as Freud, Jung and Adler proved with advances in psychiatry and psychology– giving birth to the modern raft of therapies for individuals, couples, families and even organize- tions–revelations of the mind will continue indefinitely.

But the search for our inner selves, the discovery of the reality of the self, requires more than just a mind. Without the proper tools, the job of finding one's self becomes practically impossible if we only rely on one of our human components– body or spirit or mind alone.

That spiritual search requires interaction and integration of our reasoning and caring abilities, and the proper balance between all three elements of our nature.

We have entered an era of great expansion in humanity's mental abilities—and now our greatest task is balancing our intellectual powers with our spiritual development.

To truly know ourselves, we need all of our powers.

#

Passing Mental Tests on the Path to Self

PART 9 IN SERIES: **GLOBAL CHANGE FOR THE NEXT GENERATION**

In previous parts of this series I have attempted to lead up to the most challenging question of life for a human being, an innate question built into our very core:
"Who am I?"
This fundamental question comes with many variations:
"What do I want to do" or "want to be," or "should I be?"
When we ask ourselves this important question, our minds can inform our bodies and spirits in confidently choosing a direction in life. We will, each one of us, decide to make our own path, follow another's, or choose none, letting happenstance guide our lives.
Regardless of our direction, we need our mind to help direct us. Mental illnesses don't make it any easier—just look at Wikipedia's [extensive] list of them under "mental disorders:"

One in five Americans experienced some sort of mental illness in 2010, according to a new report from the Substance Abuse and Mental Health Services Administration. About 5 percent of Americans have suffered from such severe mental illness that it interfered with day-to-day school, work, or family. [Source: ABC News, Jan. 19, 2012]

Being bipolar myself for more than 35 years, I can attest to the suffering mental illness can cause—but also to the progress medicine has made in effective treatments, both chemical and behavioral.
One of those effective behavioral approaches—mindfulness meditation, which I discovered during a six-week class during my mental illness treatments—
helped provide a key to my own self-awareness. I found that a regular practice of mindfulness not only aids treatment, but also allows fuller expansion of normal life activities and brain functioning.
Often, we only think about pleasing our outer senses: touch, taste, smell, hearing, and vision. Yet even comas and REM states prove the mind and spirit still works without them. The

Bahá'í teachings also name five intellectual, spiritual, or inner senses:

**...imagination, which forms a mental image of things;
...thought, which reflects upon the realities of things;
...comprehension, which understands these realities;
...and memory, which retains whatever man has imagined, thought, and understood.
The intermediary between these five outward powers and the inward powers is a common faculty, a sense which mediates between them and which conveys to the inward powers whatever the outward powers have perceived. It is termed the common faculty as it is shared in common between the outward and inward powers.**
– 'Abdu'l-Bahá, *Some Answered Questions*, newly revised, p. 243.

Obviously, our bodies and minds and spirits use these structural tools for discovering the reality we call Me.

Precisely by reason of our discoveries into the realities of our own selves over the millennia, we have developed our five inward powers that are equivalent to our outward powers. Those inner powers have now far surpassed our physical powers alone. Our mental powers created technology, which gave us the ability to see inside our own brains with CAT scans and MRI's, and increasingly learn what it means to be human.

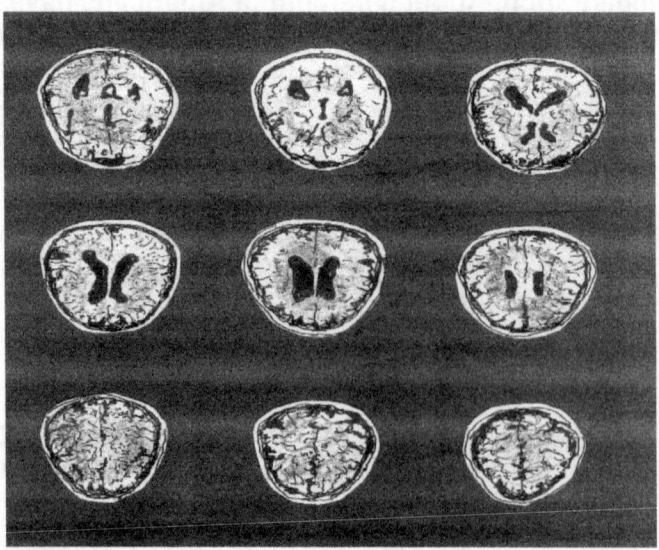

Brain scans

So–why do I exist?

The Bahá'í teachings say that we all exist to grow spiritually—to fully develop those inner senses and powers.

We can live like the animal, rely only on our outward five senses, take what we want and not care about others' feelings, or, we can utilize our inward, spiritual senses, and find ways to live in harmony and prosperity with our fellow human beings.

If we fully utilize those inward powers of mind and spirit, especially our collective minds as one human family, we can discover and implement solutions to the most intractable global problems. With time, will, and unity of thought and purpose, everything is not only possible, but probable.

#

The Seat of the Self – the Human Heart

PART 10: GLOBAL CHANGE FOR THE NEXT GENERATION

We began this series looking into the future at a peaceful world, which safeguards the rights of all people.

Can you imagine what life on Earth might look like twenty-five years from now? We will not just be going into a store and swiping our wrists over a chip reader to pay for our purchases, or routinely flying to our destinations in all fusion weightless airmobiles.

Instead we can look forward to a future when finally, across the entire face of the Earth, humanity enjoys peace and prosperity. Prosperity means jobs, for every person on earth; and peace means an end to the militarization of the world and the death of millions.

How can we all work toward this powerful vision of the future? We can start in the seat of the self, the human heart:

Briefly; we must strive with heart and soul in order that this darkness of the contingent world may be dispelled, that the lights of the Kingdom shall shine upon all the horizons, the world of humanity become illumined, the image of God become apparent in human mirrors, the law of God be well established and that all regions of the world shall enjoy peace, comfort and composure beneath the equitable protection of God.
– 'Abdu'l-Bahá, *Foundations of World Unity*, p. 73.

If we begin with the human heart, the Bahá'í teachings tell us, we can solve our vast ills and troubles.

Our hearts give us life, fueling our brains [and lungs] with oxygen. With the power to beat, the heart makes blood flow through our bodies. Those beating hearts symbolize love, refinement, hope and the grace of God.

Throughout the ages, humans have called the heart the seat of our emotions, feelings, wants and desires.

Of course, we now know that our deepest emotions and feelings emanate from our brains, [and they are also influenced greatly by our souls according to spiritual belief systems.] [Our brains are] closely attached to our limbic system, the automatic and elemental part of us said to have stemmed from the dinosaurs themselves.

Deep in our brain's cerebellum, which scientists call the arbor vitae–Latin for "tree of life"—lies the cerebral white matter, so called for its branched, tree-like appearance. Present in both hemispheres, it brings sensory and motor information to and from the larger brain, and functions as our main center of thought and communication.

This communication may be more than physical or verbal, it may be spiritual also:

There is no doubt that the forces of the higher worlds interplay with the forces of this plane. The heart of man is open to inspiration; this is spiritual communication. As in a dream one talks with a friend while the mouth is silent, so is it in the conversation of the spirit. A man may converse with the ego within him saying: "May I do this? Would it be advisable for me to do this work?" Such as this is conversation with the higher self.
– 'Abdu'l-Bahá, *Paris Talks*, p. 179.

What 'Abdu'l-Bahá refers to here could be the reality of the self, the very purpose of existence. When we open our hearts to inspiration, we learn our true emotions and thoughts, and we get in touch with our higher self.

To me, our very purpose as human beings is to find out everything about ourselves that we can, to answer the question "Who am I?"

#

Are We Descended from the Apes?

Science

Author Charles Darwin (1809-1882), the British naturalist and geologist, became famous for his pronouncement "Man descended from the apes" in his 1859 book The Origin of Species by Means of Natural Selection–right?
Well, not so much. Having read his book, in tiny print I might add, and finishing it along with Darwin's The Descent of Man (first published in 1871) this morning, I could not find those words or that phrase in their combined 924 pages.
  Here's Darwin's short biography from Wikipedia: **Charles Robert Darwin...best known for his contributions to evolutionary theory. He established that all species of life have descended over time from common ancestors, and in a joint publication with Alfred Russel Wallace introduced his scientific theory that this branching pattern of evolution resulted from a process that he called natural selection, in which the struggle for existence has a similar effect to the artificial selection involved in selective breeding.**

Darwin, through his precise observations of plants, animals, and human tribes, and citing other works as well, overcame the then-current scientific concept of "transmutation" to refer to species who have had biological changes through hybridization.

The scientists of the time had to invent terms to describe their theories, and after the publication of *Origins*—and several severe debates—the term "evolution" was coined. The scientific community and much of the public had accepted this new term by 1870. Today, in modified form, science has developed a broad consensus recognizing natural selection as the basic mechanism of evolution.

Reading Darwin's books, you can see that he became the consummate observer, recorder, and synthesizer of these important theories during his lifetime. Whereas *Origin* has 374 pages, along with a twelve-page glossary, *Descent* is written in three discrete parts for a total of 534 pages and supplemental notes, at least in my undated copy. The reading can seem somewhat tedious—yet every page brings a new discovery or insight, or more importantly, the basis for later insight and conviction.

The *Descent of Man* had a much greater influence on science than *Origin* did, especially in describing the evolutionary history of humanity. Darwin notes all the similarities humans have to animals, even to the downy hair on some of us, the vestiges of much thicker coverings in the past. He describes mating and birth and the bones and senses of man and compares them closely to all mammals.

Finally, he writes:

…that man with all his noble qualities, with sympathy which feels for the most debased, with benevolence which extends not only to other men but to the humblest living creature, with his god-like intellect which has penetrated into the movements and constitution of the solar system—with all these exalted powers—Man still bears in his bodily frame the indelible stamp of his lowly origin.
– Source: *Descent*, p. 405.

He goes on to state an important fact, on which myself and most religionists would agree, from as early as the story of Adam and Eve's creation: "If we consider all the races of man as forming a single species, his range is enormous."

This idea—the essential oneness of all humanity—came from the Bahá'í teachings, several years previous to Darwin's writings on the subject. [Note: As well as from earlier religions and sources, expressed in diverse ways.]

So, if you want to learn about Darwin's theory, I would recommend *The Descent of Man* as the better book to read regarding human evolution. While it may not answer the old question "Did Darwin say we humans descended from apes?" it does an [excellent] job of establishing the science of evolutionary theory conclusively.

What Darwin wrote on page 895 of *Descent of Man*, as I have attempted to show, is that man certainly "descended from some ape-like creature"–which makes sense, given our most recent anthropological discoveries.

As we now know, with the physical identification of the bones of pre-Neanderthal, Neanderthal and Cro-Magnon Man, the tree of human evolution has many branches, and some we have yet to find.

Bahá'ís believe that science and religion agree—so the Bahá'í teachings have a unique and very science-friendly perspective on human evolution. They maintain that although human beings at one time certainly took the form of an "ape-like creature," our uniqueness, our heritage and our spiritual destiny is much more than that of any animal, either now or in the dim past.

"Abdu'l-Bahá pointed out in the book *Some Answered Questions* that human evolution certainly occurred, but that the human species has always been human:

Just as man progresses, evolves, and is transformed from one form and appearance to another in the womb of the mother, while remaining from the beginning a human embryo, so too has man remained a distinct essence— that is, the human species—from the beginning of his formation in the matrix of the world, and has passed gradually from form to form.

– 'Abdu'l-Bahá, *Some Answered Questions*, newly revised, p. 221.

#

Finding Faith and Finding Yourself Too

SPIRITUALITY PART 11 IN SERIES: GLOBAL CHANGE FOR THE NEXT GENERATION

Do you believe, as [most] religionists do–for example 2.1 billion Christians, 1.5 billion Muslims, 900 million Hindus, 394 million Buddhists and millions of other faith adherents—that God created us in his image?

You might find it easier to believe if you think of "image" not as physical but as spiritual, revolving around our souls and spirits, and of course our hearts–the throne of love.

Whom and what do we love? With a fortunate environ-ment we love our parents, siblings, and families, which expands, if we let it, to the entire human race. We love those who educate us about ourselves and the world, helping us embark on a lifelong condition of learning. Formal schooling into our teenage years, and hopefully college or trade school beyond, can help us in this modern age to establish our identity and meet its challenges.

All of that, of course, depends on the openness of our hearts propelling us forward in our search for self and reality:

Only when the lamp of search, of earnest striving, of longing desire, of passionate devotion, of fervid love, of rapture, and ecstasy, is kindled within the seeker's heart, and the breeze of His loving-kindness is wafted upon his

soul, will the darkness of error be dispelled, the mists of doubts and misgivings be dissipated, and the lights of knowledge and certitude envelop his being.

At that hour will the Mystic Herald, bearing the joyful tidings of the Spirit, shine forth from the City of God resplendent as the morn, and, through the trumpet-blast of knowledge, will awaken the heart, the soul, and the spirit from the slumber of heedlessness.

Then will the manifold favors and outpouring grace of the holy and everlasting Spirit confer such new life upon the seeker that he will find himself endowed with a new eye, a new ear, a new heart, and a new mind.

He will contemplate the manifest signs of the universe, and will penetrate the hidden mysteries of the soul. Gazing with the eye of God, he will perceive within every atom a door that leadeth him to the stations of absolute certitude.

He will discover in all things the mysteries of Divine Revelation, and the evidences of an everlasting Manifestation.
– Bahá'u'lláh, *Gleanings From the Writings of Bahá'u'lláh*, p. 267.

The Bahá'í teachings say that "a new eye, a new ear, a new heart, and a new mind..." are the prerequisites in our search for our inner reality.

With a new heart and mind we can discover and mold our own view of ourselves and the world. We can enable the progress of our souls and unravel the mysteries of the Tree of Knowledge. For our individual and collective search to become fulfilled, the discovery of truth is itself the highest goal. We seek reality.

As we've discussed, both religion and science are also discoverers of reality:

The foundation of progress and real prosperity in the human world is reality, for reality is the divine standard and the bestowal of God.

Reality is reasonableness, and reasonableness is ever conducive to the honorable station of man.

Reality is the guidance of God. Reality is the cause of illumination of mankind.

Reality is love, ever working for the welfare of humanity.

Reality is the bond which conjoins hearts. This ever uplifts man toward higher stages of progress and attainment.

Reality is the unity of mankind, conferring everlasting life.

Reality is perfect equality, the foundation of agreement between the nations, the first step toward international peace.
– 'Abdu'l-Bahá, *The Promulgation of Universal Peace*, p. 376

Recognizing and accepting truth isn't easy, or we wouldn't have such dissension and difference of opinion in the world, too often crippling our ability to improve our individual and collective condition—and recognize reality, both inner and outer.

And the signs of positive change and raised consciousness gather more momentum every day.

Faith in ourselves and our fellow men and women of the world to do the right thing, will attain it.

#

Inspired by the Glory of God

Spirituality

The Bahá'í teachings contain enormous wisdom. For me, every time I read Bahá'u'lláh's or 'Abdu'l-Bahá's writings, I feel powerfully informed and inspired:

**Having created the world and all that liveth and moveth therein, He, through the direct operation of His unconstrained and sovereign Will, chose to confer upon man the unique distinction and capacity to know Him and to love Him—
<u>a capacity that must needs be regarded as the generating impulse and the primary purpose underlying the whole of creation</u>....**

Upon the inmost reality of each and every created thing He hath shed the light of one of His names, and made it a recipient of the glory of one of His attributes. Upon the reality of man, however, He hath focused the radiance of all of His names and attributes, and made it a mirror of His own Self.

Alone of all created things man hath been singled out for so great a favor, so enduring a bounty.

– Bahá'u'lláh, *Gleanings from the Writings of Bahá'u'lláh*, pp. 65-66. [Underline emphasis added]

Sometimes I let that inner inspiration transform itself into poetry. Reflecting on the two passages above from Bahá'u'lláh's writings, I wrote this poem at 1:30 pm on the 16th of December 2014, while sitting on a Presbyterian Church bench dedicated to the Glory of God.

It's Always There by Rodney Richards

My eyes often travel downward

I see the tuft of grass in the sidewalk crack
   and follow my urge to pluck It
I spy the dirty napkin caught on the church's lawn
   and bend down to dispose of It
Then they travel upward
I bask in Sol's glow behind the clouds and push my body
   and face into It
I meditate on His Godness
   and speak words of praise to It
Then they travel inward
I feel the wrath of ire at the speeding car
   and the dangerous driver in It
I sense the love from my own true love
   and wonder how we have held It
Then they meander the world
I find Banana Split ice cream in the fridge
   and spoon the deliciousness out of It
I watch the senseless hate turning to violence
   and wish mankind to end It

Grass, napkin, Sol, Godness, wrath, love, ice cream,
   and hate   all lay in my Path
I acknowledge them with unhesitating impulses
   to touch, feel, give way, absorb and consume them
All the essences of this life we humans experience
   every day, every wakeful moment of It
The Its of existence at our fingertips

These energies with which the Day Star of Divine bounty and Source of heavenly guidance hath endowed the reality of man lie, however, latent within him, even as the flame is hidden within the candle and the rays of light are potentially present in the lamp. The radiance of these energies may be obscured by worldly desires even as the light of the sun can be concealed beneath the dust and dross which cover the mirror.

Neither the candle nor the lamp can be lighted through their own unaided efforts, nor can it ever be possible for the mirror to free itself from its dross.

It is clear and evident that until a fire is kindled the lamp will never be ignited, and unless the dross is blotted out from the face of the mirror it can never represent the image of the sun nor reflect its light and glory.

– Bahá'u'lláh, *Gleanings from the Writings of Bahá'u'lláh*, pp. 65-66.

#

The Intelligence of the Rational Soul

Spirituality PART 1 IN SERIES: THE MEANING OF MEANING

Here in the 21st century, we know without doubt that the powers of our brains can astonish us.

The neuroscientists tell us that we probably haven't plumbed even a fraction of what our rational minds can potentially accomplish. That distinct combination of reason, intellectual discovery and the perceptual power of the human spirit, the Bahá'í teachings say, forms our rational soul:

The foremost degree of comprehension in the world of nature is that of the rational soul. This power and comprehension is shared in common by all men, whether they be heedless or aware, wayward or faithful. In the creation of God, the rational soul of man encompasses and is distinguished above all other created things; It is by virtue of its nobility and distinction that it encompasses them all.

Through the power of the rational soul, man can discover the realities of things, comprehend their properties, and penetrate the mysteries of existence. All the sciences, branches of learning, arts, invent-ions, institutions, undertakings, and discoveries have resulted from the comprehension of the rational soul.

These were once impenetrable secrets, hidden mysteries, and unknown realities, and the rational soul gradually discovered them and brought them out of the invisible plane into the realm of the visible. This is the greatest power of comprehension in the world of nature, and the uttermost limit of its flight is to comprehend the realities, signs, and properties of contingent things.
– 'Abdu'l-Bahá, *Some Answered Questions*, newly revised, p. 250-251.

Some scientists have calculated that we normally process between 20,000-70,000 thoughts in a waking day.

Here, test yourself: Count out one second in your mind without saying it aloud. Ready?

Think 'one thousand one.'

That took one second. You spend approximately 61,200 seconds awake each day!

Yes, sometimes our minds wander (often, actually), and our conscious minds draw a blank. But the unconscious mind doesn't wander.

Thoughts don't "stop."

Only sleep stops the waking mind, and we know thoughts don't stop there, either–because we dream constantly.

These thoughts our mind consistently produces insistently ask for examination. When I think or say, 'one thousand one,' my mind instantly translates my English language words into images and meaning. My mind 'pictures' the number 'one' and knows it as the first Arabic numeral, which represents a single item. It does the same for whatever comes to mind, whenever it comes into our heads.

Our minds simultaneously translate every nanosecond of what we see, feel, hear, taste, touch and smell into images, thoughts, ruminations, ideas, and internal and external sensations. That never-ending stream of human consciousness makes us intelligent, searching, spiritual beings.

In other words, your mind and mine constantly seek meaning. Our rational souls naturally search for something we can hold on to and assimilate, for something we can make 'sense' of. We crave order and meaning.

We do not thrive in chaos, in violence, and in surprises (happy ones excluded). That's why the stock market hates uncertainty.

No matter what our skin color and life experiences, our language and customs, our education or lack thereof, our views and beliefs—our minds continue to work diligently on life's puzzles and questions. Our minds continually try to fit our experiences into our own little space of comprehension and understanding. Our minds constantly try to answer the question "Why?" and by extension, "Why me?"

But do our minds ask us those perennial questions?

Or does something else?

The Bahá'í teachings say the source for the answer to these fundamental human questions is the rational soul:

The human spirit which distinguishes man from the animal, is the rational soul, and these two terms — the human spirit and the rational soul — designate one and the same thing.

The human spirit, which in the terminology of the philosophers is called the rational soul, encompasses all things and, as far as human capacity permits, discovers their realities and becomes aware of their properties and effects, the characteristics and conditions of earthly things.

But the human spirit, unless it be assisted by the spirit of faith, cannot become acquainted with the divine mysteries and the heavenly realities.

It is like a mirror which, although clear, bright, and polished, is still in need of light.

Until a sunbeam falls upon it can it discover the divine mysteries.

– 'Abdu'l-Bahá, *Some Answered Questions*, newly revised, p. 241-242.

#

The Source of the Rational Soul

Spirituality PART 2 IN SERIES: | THE MEANING OF MEANING |

In Part I of this short series of essays, we explored the source of the question many of us ask ourselves at some point in our lives: "Why me?"

But if you're like me, you often ask yourself "Why did I do that? How could I have been so stupid?!" [Or, "Where in the world did I get that idea from?]

All these deeply reflective questions have become part of the human condition, the essence of the written word, described in stories and books from time immemorial.

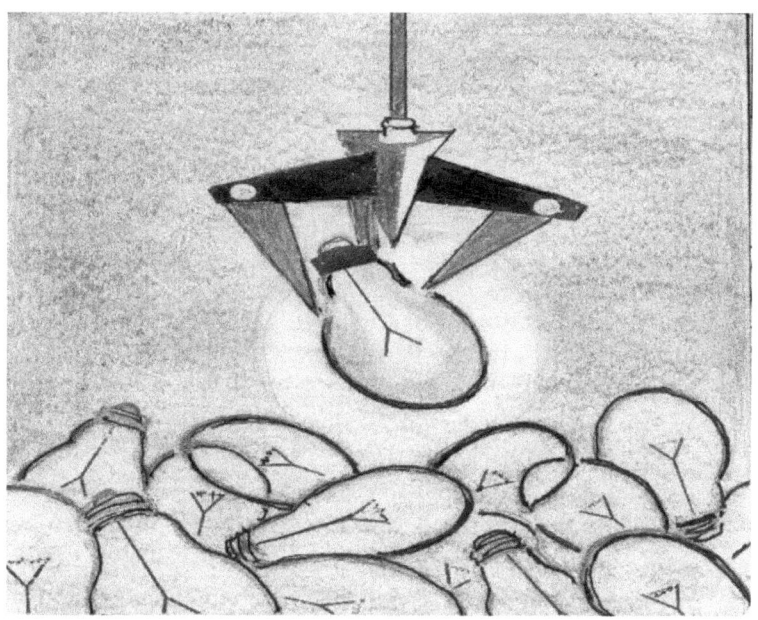

Many of us have answered these questions instinctively based on our own worldview, no matter how we came to believe what we believe or don't believe. We question neither our motives nor their premises. Most people may think naturally "This is who I am, and I am who I am," and remain perfectly satisfied and comfortable with their current existence. Others struggle with these questions, and some spend their whole lives searching out their meaning.

As an example, I think of devout Buddhist monks dedicated to finding "The One," the Tao, within themselves, within others, and within nature.

This quest, the unquenchable human thirst for meaning, is built into our psyche, as evidenced by the powers of our rational minds to ask such things of ourselves. Humans have always relied on the great religious educators — Christ, Buddha, Krishna, Abraham, Moses, Muhammad and now Bahá'u'lláh–to provide answers to these questions, as well as guidance for how to live our lives.

Once found, great truths never imply we stop our search for meaning. In fact, listening to the world's most revered teachers and following their ordinances now offers us the surest way of lifting [finally] for all time, the burden of hunger, war, and misery from humanity.

Today over seven billion people on Earth desire a harmonious peaceful society in which to live, safe and secure, with equal rights under the law, and the means to earn their living. Only the few thousands of misguided leaders who prevent age-long dreams from coming true oppose that goal. [Other preventions are racism, poverty, religios intolerance and others.] Bahá'ís believe that we continue to advance toward global unity and the efflorescence of civilization: that we will soon reach a peaceful and prosperous period in human history [if we work hard to bring it about now. Or it may take centuries.]

We constantly search for this ideal, even if only available to us in our physical home or shelter, because the human spirit strives for it, realizing it is achievable and possible if we work towards it together. We all received this true human spirit in our mother's womb.

Many have named it the soul:

In the human, worldly soul signifies the "rational being, or mind". This has a potential existence before its appearance in human life.

It is like unto the existence of a tree within the seed. The existence of the tree within the seed is potential; but when the seed is sown and watered, the signs thereof, its roots and branches, and all of its different qualities, appear.

Likewise, the "rational soul" has a potential exist-ence before its appearance in the human body, and through the mixture of elements and a wonderful combination, according to the natural order, law, conception, and birth, it appears with its identity…

Since the pure essence, whose identity is unknown, possesses the virtues of the worlds of matter and of the Kingdom, it has two sides-first, the material and physical; second, the mental and spiritual—which are attributes not found as qualities of matter. It is the same reality which is given different names, according to the different conditions wherein it becomes manifest.

Because of its attachment to matter and the phenomenal world, when it governs the physical functions of the body, it is called the human soul. When it manifests itself as the thinker, the comprehender, it is called the mind.

And when it soars into the atmosphere of God, and travels in the spiritual world, it becomes designated as spirit.
–Attributed to "Abdu'l-Bahá, *Star of the West*, Vol 4, p. 190.

History has demonstrated that our combined human spirits and the powers of reason and faith can achieve great outcomes. Look at the examples of the Prophets. The religions they founded, at the apex of their radiance, were at one point pure, educated, altruistic, progressive, kind, and unified.

But time, corruption, world-changing events, and clashes with ideals and thoughts brought by subsequent ages relegated these past institutions to the dustbin of history. Their eternal spiritual and moral principles live eternally, but the passage of time and the progress of the world ensure that their [outdated] social and material practices cannot persist.

Religion, to remain relevant, must be renewed.

As bad as things seemed yesterday, [look] today and perhaps tomorrow, Bahá'ís believe that hope has returned [through Bahá'u'lláh's Teachings].

#

The Meaning Behind Mankind's Salvation

CULTURE PART 3 IN SERIES: THE MEANING OF MEANING

The arc of the moral universe is long, but it bends toward justice. – Martin Luther King, Jr.

Humanity continues its historic march toward equality and justice.

Just as religion has propelled organized societies further, considerable advances have come from the accomplishments of a few great men of spirit and faith in modern times. The Reverend Martin Luther King Jr. in the United States, and Mohandas Gandhi in India, both stood up for human dignity through peaceful nonviolence. We've witnessed considerable leadership from America's own presidents and other heads of state, such as Mikhail Gorbachev in Russia, whose actions directly led to glasnost, and which many attribute to the tearing down of the Berlin Wall and reuniting East and West Germany.

Many courageous women have also brought us great social and spiritual progress. The female Quakers who joined with Elizabeth Cady Stanton at Seneca Falls, New York in 1848 to hold the first women's rights convention made an enormous impact on today's global movement for equality.

The world's first known peace flag was raised by Sarah Farmer, later a Bahá'í, in Eliot Maine in 1894. Abolitionist women (and men), had great effects combating slavery as early as 1820, and Sojourner Truth became known for her extemporaneous speech on racial inequality, titled "Ain't I a Woman?" delivered in 1851 at the Ohio Women's Rights Convention.

Frankly, women have been instrumental in promoting and instituting the greatest changes in the world.

Now, as always, they have constituted the [forefront] of change.

However–the celebrated, progressive leaders of humanity couldn't have accomplished much without the contributions of thousands of great people, past and present, low in station or high, of every ethnic, social, religious, and educational background, who fought for the noble principles they believed in.

No movement for social change can occur without their support, advocacy, and sacrifice. We tend to remember the names of the leaders, of course—but they only rose to prominence because the time had come for the ideas and ideals they promoted; and because those ideas struck a sympathetic chord in so many others.

The Bahá'í teachings suggest that these ideas whose time has come originate directly from the inspiration of a new divine revelation.

Whether aware of that newly-released spiritual impetus for social change or not, those who advocate for equality, justice, and peace all partake of the inspiration loosed in the world by the founders of the great Faiths:

...the divine Manifestations, the holy Mouthpieces of God, are the Collective Centers of God. These heavenly Messengers are the real Shepherds of humanity, for whenever They appear in the world They unite the scattered sheep.

The Collective Center has always appeared in the Orient. Abraham, Moses, Jesus Christ, Muhammad were Collective Centers of Their day and time, and all arose in the East.

Today Bahá'u'lláh is the Collective Center of unity for all mankind, and the splendor of His light has likewise dawned from the East. He founded the oneness of humanity in Persia. He established harmony and agreement among the various peoples of religious beliefs, denominations, sects and cults by freeing them from the fetters of past imitations and superstitions, leading them to the very foundation of the divine religions.

From this foundation shines forth the radiance of spirituality, which is unity, the love of God, the knowledge of God, praiseworthy morals and the virtues of the human world. Bahá'u'lláh renewed these principles, just as the coming of spring refreshes the earth and confers new life upon all phenomenal beings.

For the freshness of the former springtimes had waned, the vivification had ceased, the life-giving breezes were no longer wafting their fragrances, winter and the season of darkness had come. Bahá'u'lláh came to renew the life of the world with this new and divine springtime, which has pitched its tent in the countries of the Orient in the utmost power and glory.

It has refreshed the world of the Orient, and there is no doubt that if the world of the Occident should abandon dogmas of the past, turn away from empty imitations and superstitions, investigate the reality of the divine religions, holding fast to the example of Jesus Christ, acting in accordance with the teachings of God and becoming unified with the Orient, an eternal happiness and felicity would be attained.

– 'Abdu'l-Bahá, *The Promulgation of Universal Peace*, p. 164.

We are not, nor have we ever been, alone, you and me. In our hopes of realizing a gentle, loving future for ourselves and our mates, children and grandchildren, God has continually given us guidance. All around us thousands upon thousands of religious congregations, non-profit social and educational groups, corporations, and small businesses each engage in raising social consciousness, alleviating suffering and promoting goodwill in all the countries of the world. There has never been a time in human history when a collective humanity has done more good.

Wilma Rudolph, the great Olympic champion, said, "Never underestimate the power of dreams and the influence of the human spirit."

Those dreams and that spirit find expression through the rational soul, synonymous with the mind, and manifested by words and courageous actions motivated in faith. And Oh! what legions of great thinkers and doers we have in the world today, not the least of which is personified in the United Nations and its promotion of unity, peace, and world harmony. Today we have more legions working for peace and human rights than ever before.

And so, I ask myself "What am I doing? What can I do?" to both overcome my own spiritual battles, and to do my part to bring those hopes and dreams into reality.

#

One Thankful, Grateful Apostrophe to God

Spirituality

Drivin' home from a three-hour session with my banker, after tryin' to eliminate fees from my simple business accounts, my mind was very much still in a questioning mood, looking for solutions. As usual, in my inner mental sanctum closed off from the world, except for my driving persona, I began reciting my noonday prayer.

That Bahá'í prayer goes like this:

I bear witness, O my God, that Thou hast created me to know Thee and to worship Thee. I testify, at this moment, to my powerlessness and to Thy might, to my poverty and to Thy wealth. There is none other God but Thee, the Help in Peril, the Self-Subsisting.
– Bahá'u'lláh, *Bahá'í Prayers*, p. 3.

Here's my inner [and out loud] conversation:

"I bear witness," I mean, I would tell anyone I believe, "O my God," my God, Rodney Richards' God if you will, "that Thou," meanin' you, my God, "hast created me."

Well, You're the Creator, and I am those strands of DNA and genes and body and everything else that You started, "to know Thee," and how do I know Thee? through Thy prophets and their words and actions, at least what I've seen, heard, and read, "and to worship Thee."

Ah, how do I worship Thee?

I've read, God, that you are in no need of your servants, but as I just said, You desire that I "worship Thee." How can I do that?

The simplest way to worship, from my perspective, involves being a good Bahá'í, or as my wife reminds me, "Be nice."

'Abdu'l-Bahá, in one of His London talks, said that a man may be a Bahá'í even if he has never heard the name of Bahá'u'lláh.
– quoted by J.E. Esslemont, *Bahá'u'lláh and the New Order*, p. 71

"I testify," or swear again, "at this moment," on Wednesday February 11th at 1:06 pm (quick glance), "to my powerlessness," which I guess means that although I've got free will, I am only ever in total control of a little, and even then it's mostly circumstances I find myself in, "and to Thy might," and yes, just from my Bible studies I know you are the Almighty and All-Powerful, "to my poverty," and here I think that means impoverished of Thy grace unless You give me some, for I count us very lucky as far as prosperity goes.

Wish it were the same for everyone."...and to Thy wealth."

And what wealth is greater than all conceivable wealth and then some? I mean You do as You Will, and what greater wealth is there? And I know You share it, God, like in June of 2009 when I [prayed] for [good weather], so my son and his fiancée could get married outside in our back yard, and sunny it was, and even the squall passed with its dark clouds off to the west.

"There is," again, meanin' now and every moment, right? "none other God but Thee," which is to say, from Day One you and the Prophets and seers have always been telling us this, "the Help in Peril," like the time You saved my good-paying job when I should've been fired, or saved me from bein' run over by a movin' bus when my motorcycle crashed in that oil slick. I didn't even have time to ask for Your help, and you know me, I ask all the time, "the Self-Subsisting." Yeah, I wonder why You put up with us most times, when You don't need us, no matter how many, nor this planet, nor even this solar system!

Except that I know you love us. You love your creation, like I love Janet and the kids and especially grandbaby Sienna Rose now, and all thanks to You.

Thank you so much…

And then I drove through Dunkin Donuts with my gift card and got my medium coffee with cream and two Sweet-n-Low's.

O Son of Spirit!
My claim on thee is great, it cannot be forgotten.
My grace to thee is plenteous, it cannot be veiled.
My love has made in thee its home, it cannot be concealed.
My light is manifest to thee, it cannot be obscured. –
-Bahá'u'lláh, *The Hidden Words*, Arabic # 20, pp. 8-9.

#

Giving Back Our Fair Share

Culture

We receive, for free, much more than we can ever give back.

In our 1958 apartment with mom and brother Stephen, the massive tin pot of tapioca pudding on the stove, once chilled, was my favorite dessert – free. The school lunches of egg salad on Wonder Bread she used to make – free. The blue pants, white shirt, and logoed blue tie I had to wear to Catholic mass each morn, and to elementary school, all free. Growing up, I got everything for free, until age 15, when I sold magazines door-to-door all over Central Jersey. Then I had things I bought with "my money," only for myself, which somehow meant much more.

An hour ago, 5:48 a.m. at the squawk box at the new Dunkin Donuts just a mile from my house, I said, "Good morning my friend," replying to her sweet voice asking for my order.

"Oh, good morning to you... please pull up." She knew my order by heart and gave me such a good feeling to be known by just the sound of my voice. I pull up holding out my credit card, and Moha holds out my medium regular coffee... but doesn't take my card.

"That's free, for you, my customer."

Of course, I say, "Oh no, oh thanks so much!" and pull away saying aloud, "You've got to be kidding. How nice!"

This is not the first free thing she's given me completely unasked. Yesterday, for Sunday School when I ordered 50 munchkins for the kids, my girlfriend-clerk asked, "You? Why munchkins?" And I told her, and she said, "How nice, that'll be half price." So, I left the 5 dollars as part tip too. Once again, I couldn't believe how nice that was.

And now I had yet another reason for liking my Egyptian-American friends at this Dunkin, and people in general.

I think of other things we get "for free," like my Catholic grammar school, Ewing public High School, and even my California junior college education, all for free. In those years I never realized my parents' property taxes, and the property taxes of thousands of other homeowners, paid for my education. I shudder now as an adult to wonder how my parents paid for that, and food, and clothing, and Christmas and birthday presents, and everything else we all needed.

Now, as I pay my own property taxes for schools, and sales taxes for social programs, state and Federal income taxes, and gasoline taxes for highways and others, I see that everything which exists for me, for my family's ease and comfort, was mostly paid for by others, by society. I can't help but think, at least I can do my part too.

We hope our leaders do their part, to make our lives better and not miserable as too many are, not just in other countries, but here in America as well.

Free?

Earning goodwill, and peace and security where I live, and in America, and in the world, is not free. It requires some measure of wealth, enough to support a family and a home and to meaningfully contribute to the society we all live in and depend on.

The Bahá'í teachings have a unique and fascinating viewpoint on acquiring and using material wealth. This passage from Bahá'u'lláh, for example, praises those who earn their living and then devote themselves to giving back:

...man should know his own self and recognize that which leadeth unto loftiness or lowliness, glory or abasement, wealth or poverty.

Having attained the stage of fulfilment and reached his maturity, man standeth in need of wealth, and such wealth as he acquireth through crafts or professions is commendable and praiseworthy in the estimation of men

of wisdom, and especially in the eyes of servants who dedicate themselves to the education of the world and to the edification of its peoples.
– *Tablets of Bahá'u'lláh*, p. 34.

This wonderful practice of giving back doesn't have to be monetary – it also takes doing our part, being kind to all others, caring a little bit or a lot, and helping where we can. When we focus on the oneness of humanity, it's not that difficult, because we're related to every person we meet.

#

How Can We Escape Our Existential Hell?

Spirituality

Existential paradise and hell are to be found in all the worlds of God, whether in this world or in the heavenly realms of the spirit...
Similarly, ultimate retributions and punishments consist in being deprived of the special bounties and unfailing bestowals of God and sinking to the lowest degrees of existence. – 'Abdu'l-Bahá, *Some Answered Questions*, newly revised, pp. 257-259.

Each of us has our own kind of hell.

I'm not talking about an actual place of fire and brimstone—Bahá'ís believe that old conception of hell simply provides us with a metaphor for the inner, existential torment we all suffer as a result of our actions and the actions of others.

For some people hell happens every day of every year. Luckier ones suffer through it for only periods of time–whether going through severe sickness or seeing a loved one taken by cancer or car accident. Some hells come suddenly, and many last so long they strain all human endurance.

I thought about hell a lot while watching the recent film *Selma* this morning. The sole occupant of the movie theatre, I was free to cry and moan openly and loudly at the injustice and hurts, and the sheer hatred from the perpetrators. I prayed "Amen" to God, just as that black congregation did–only my prayer was that God's tears would fall on those perpetrators and burn them to dust.

Sketch of "Bloody Sunday" Selma, Alabama (1965)

That somehow, magically, as throughout the Bible, the Hand of God would strike the oppressors down.

That's one vision of hell, ground to dust without hope of heaven, and sometimes it seems well-deserved by some mortal's inhumane sins committed against our fellow human beings. When human beings act worse than animals, what chance of heaven do they deserve?

Hell can also take the form of a life of discrimination, poverty, segregation, and prejudice, as is too often the case here in America for all its law and order. We've seen that kind of hell demonstrated clearly by the murders of unarmed, some even mentally impaired, young men in the news recently, by the murderous warfare in the Middle East, and by the countless rapes of young women taking place across the world, too.

These hates and criminality arise out of dreams–dreams of sexual conquest for the pervert, dreams of wealth for the criminal, dreams of a closed society for the fanatic or terrorist, dreams of conquest and power for the tyrant. These terrible dreams, reminiscent of the Dark and Middle Ages, make it hard to tell the difference in the barbarity between then and now.

All of these living hells require every fair-minded, good-hearted persons to work for positive change. No matter which town, village, city, county, state, and nation you live in, you can do your part, joining the thousands and millions, even billions that dream of a world without hell.

If we don't all take part, it will never end.

The Bahá'í teachings tell us that hell on earth was never meant to last. We might think centuries of discontent, and greed, and demagoguery will always continue.

But they won't—the world will gradually improve as we adopt a more spiritual civilization, the Bahá'í teachings say:

If love and agreement are manifest in a single family, that family will advance, become illumined and spiritual; but if enmity and hatred exist within it destruction and dispersion are inevitable.

This is likewise true of a city. If those who dwell within it manifest a spirit of accord and fellowship it will progress steadily and human conditions become brighter whereas through enmity and strife it will be degraded and its inhabitants scattered.

In the same way the people of a nation develop and advance toward civilization and enlightenment through love and accord, and are disintegrated by war and strife.

Finally, this is true of humanity itself in the aggregate.

When love is realized and the ideal spiritual bonds unite the hearts of men, the whole human race will be uplifted, the world will continually grow more spiritual and radiant and the happiness and tranquillity of mankind be immeasurably increased. Warfare and strife will be uprooted, disagreement and dissension pass away and universal peace unite the nations and peoples of the world.

All mankind will dwell together as one family, blend as the waves of one sea, shine as stars of one firmament and appear as fruits of the same tree.

This is the happiness and felicity of humankind.

This is the illumination of man, the glory eternal and life everlasting; this is the divine bestowal.

—'Abdu'l-Bahá, *Foundations of World Unity*, p. 18.

The Bahá'í Faith assures us that the turmoil and travails we now experience are preparing us for a world of peace, safety and felicity, when the hatreds of people have been exposed, excoriated and finally eliminated.

We absolutely do not need to live in an existential hell here on this earth. We have the power in our own selves and with certitude and faith to create a world of justice and enjoyment for all.

The final hell?

It happens when we don't even try, [to alleviate] the pain of others.

It happens when we have the power to change, and don't use it.

It happens when we miss the opportunity to do something now, at this moment in history.

#

Mutual Paradise: The Love Between Husband and Wife

Culture

The love between husband and wife must not be purely physical, nay, rather, it must be spiritual and heavenly.

These two souls should be considered as one soul. How difficult it would be to divide a single soul!

Nay, great would be the difficulty!

In short, the foundation of the Kingdom of God is based upon harmony and love, oneness, relationship and union, not upon differences, especially between husband and wife...

–Attributed to "Abdu'l-Bahá in a tablet to an individual Bahá'í.

I met my soul mate during the turbulent year of 1967, in a challenging high school art class made easier by her interest in my wrestling clay creation:
"Wow, that looks cool. Wrestlers, right?" she asked.
"Well my attempt at a wrestling stance, yes. How 'bout you? What are you workin' on?"
I'm afraid to admit I remember no further.
But that short exchange laid the groundwork for our hanging out together during June's monthly Ewing High dance. Escorting her to her friend's VW bug, a peck on the cheek sealed something unforetold. Our relationship was as cemented as if we had donned wedding rings at that moment; a flirtatious brush of lips to cheek led to what would occur four years later almost to the day.
How can anyone prepare for love's dart striking true?

In these planes, the nightingale of the heart hath other songs and secrets, which make the heart to stir and the soul to clamor, but this mystery of inner meaning may be whispered only from heart to heart, confided only from breast to breast.
– Bahá'u'lláh, *The Seven Valleys*, p. 30.

We were fortunate that auspicious year to have met, solely by chance, yet solely by fate also. It must have been fate, because this grateful husband deeply appreciates God's Grace, received that day and since:

Refresh my heart, O my God, with the living waters of Thy love and give me a draught, O my Master, from the chalice of Thy tender mercy. Let me abide, O my Lord, within the habitation of Thy glory, and suffer me, O my God, to emerge from the darkness in which Thy divine obscurity is shrouded.

Enable me to partake of every good Thou hast vouchsafed unto Him Who is the Point and unto such as are the exponents of His Cause, and ordain for me that which beseemeth Thee and well becometh Thy station.

Do Thou graciously forgive me for the things that I have wrought in Thy holy presence, and look not upon me with the glance of justice, but rather deliver me through Thy grace, treat me with Thy mercy and deal with me according to Thy bountiful favours, as is worthy of Thy glory.

Thou art the Ever-Forgiving, the All-Glorious, the Bestower of favours and gifts, the Lord of grace abounding. Verily no God is there but Thee. Thou art the All-Possessing, the Most High.
– The Báb, *Selections from the Writings of the Báb*, p. 208.

And the Greater Grace, recognition of the Messenger of God for this Age, followed with two years of our meeting, again by chance, yet again by fate also.

Our outdoor wedding at Green Grove two years after that occurred on a sunny noontime with thirty guests, a few cold cuts and small chocolate icing cake, following our Bahá'í vows to each other in the presence of friendly witnesses. Blessings without end, proved by our mutual felicities and the virtuous progeny, have showered all through our 48 years together.

Certainly, longer time together is hoped for, prepared for, in the next spirit realm.

Not my purpose here to tout one couple, but rather to share the basic underlying truth expressed by this anonymous author:

"Tis better to proceed through life together than apart."

Rodney & Janet, Photo by Bob Harris, photographer, and friend

#

Philosophy and Religion – Comprehending the Realities

PART 1 IN SERIES: MODERN PHILOSOPHY AND MODERN RELIGION

Philosophy consists in comprehending, so far as human power permits, the realities of things as they are in themselves... The power of human under-standing does not encompass the reality of the divine Essence: All that man can hope to achieve is to comprehend the attributes of the Divinity, the light of which is manifest and resplendent in the world and within the souls of men.
– 'Abdu'l-Bahá, *Some Answered Questions*, newly revised edition, p. 255.

Albert Camus

If you had to pick one philosophy that best fits your outlook on life, what would it be?

I would say I'm a Humanist, like Camus—but not an Absurd Humanist. Or maybe I'm an Existentialist. I'm definitely an Analytic Philosopher, the most modern flavor. I love the philosophy of the Rational Soul and Rational Mind, which combines the thinking of the Rationalists, the Empiricists, and the Romanticists. I guess, if you combined them all, I'd call myself a Spiritual Philosopher. In a way, all these schools of thought have led me to the real purpose of all philosophy–to determine, describe and detail the meaning of life.

The Bahá'í teachings would call that the love of God:

O Son of Man! I loved thy creation, hence I created thee. Wherefore, do thou love Me, that I may name thy name and fill thy soul with the spirit of life.
– Bahá'u'lláh, *The Hidden Words*, p. 4.

Modern philosophy began with the Frenchman Rene Descartes (1596-1650), who wrote and expressed the idea that since he could think, he could question his own thinking—and that he therefore must be human, with a mind, existing in the phenomenal world of nature.

As human beings in this material world, John Locke said, we're born "a blank slate." Rather, from a Bahá'í perspective, we're each born with a purpose: "to know and to love God," according to the Bahá'í writings.

Therefore, I agree with Gottfried Leibniz (1646-1716), that "God created the best possible world" for us to learn about Him.

I understand David Hume's and the other empiricist's point (1711-1776), about material existence–that all we can know is what we experience. But that does not [consider] the mind of man and his inner powers, like imagination and thought.

Jean-Jacques Rousseau was right on target when he made the leap to believe in the "innate goodness of man." Perhaps, though, we could understand the dichotomy between innate human goodness and the evil men do by realizing that all people have dual natures:

Man is intelligent, instinctively and consciously intelligent; nature is not.

Man is fortified with memory; nature does not possess it.

Man is the discoverer of the mysteries of nature; nature is not conscious of those mysteries herself. It is evident, therefore, that man is dual in aspect: as an animal he is subject to nature, but in his spiritual or conscious being he transcends the world of material existence.
– 'Abdu'l-Bahá, *The Promulgation of Universal Peace*, p. 81.

Voltaire's ideas (1694-1778), on civil liberties and social reform helped inspire the French and American revolutions. His writings on reason superseding nature influenced the church and church doctrine, yet he remained a firm believer in the Deity. In fact, religious belief informed the thinking of all the early philosophers, because of its power to change people's hearts.

Immanuel Kant (1724-1804), the great German philosopher who built a bridge, or tried to, between the two modern camps of rationalism and empiricism, with his idea "that all knowledge comes from the senses but is filtered through our rational minds," altered current thinking and revolutionized the debate. Kant realized the difference between how things really are and [how human beings experience things.] This has become self-evident, with the advent of the scientific method and the remarkable discoveries science continues to make.

Religion has also provided the guidance to use reason and science for moral purposes, just as all the great philosophers have included [a] God-being in their treatises and philosophies, [even as a denial.]

The bottom line in my own thinking on philosophy to this point—it evolves progressively, logically, and rationally, just like science, religion, and existence itself.

#

Philosophy and Spirituality Today

PART 2 IN SERIES: MODERN PHILOSOPHY AND MODERN RELIGION

The supreme cause for creating the world and all that is therein is for man to know God.
– Bahá'u'lláh, *Tablets of Bahá'u'lláh*, p. 268.

From a Biblical perspective, it all began in the Garden of Eden with Adam and Eve eating the fruit of the Tree of Knowledge–not an apple, but the knowledge of good and evil. In another word: Nature; the physicality of existence as opposed to abstract reality.

For the most part, those who believe only in the physical creation, nature, [are called] materialists:

By materialists, whose belief with regard to Divinity hath been explained, is not meant philosophers in general, but rather that group of materialists of narrow vision who worship that which is sensed, who depend upon the five senses only, and whose criterion of knowledge is limited to that which can be perceived by the senses.
– 'Abdu'l-Bahá, *Tablet to Auguste Forel*, p. 7.

We began this series on philosophy mainly focusing from the 16th century onward with the Deistic philosophers, followed by the atheistic ones. Their words and writings, voiced by the beliefs of their hearts and minds, reveal deep insight and intelligence. That very intelligence, the Bahá'í teachings say, proves that an unseen reality exists:

In like manner the mind proveth the existence of an unseen Reality that embraceth all beings, and that existeth and revealeth itself in all stages, the essence whereof is beyond the grasp of the mind.

Thus the mineral world understandeth neither the nature nor the perfections of the vegetable world; the vegetable world understandeth not the nature of the animal world, neither the animal world the nature of the reality of man that discovereth and embraceth all things.
– *ibid*, p. 9.

The reality which created all philosophy is, according to the Bahá'í Writings, the rational soul. Here again, 'Abdu'l-Bahá explains:

The foremost degree of comprehension in the world of nature is that of the rational soul. This power and comprehension is shared in common by all men, whether they be heedless or aware, wayward or faithful. In the creation of God, the rational soul of man encompasses and is distinguished above all other created things: It is by virtue of its nobility and distinction that it encompasses them all.

Through the power of the rational soul, man can discover the realities of things, comprehend their properties, and penetrate the mysteries of existence.

All the sciences, branches of learning, arts, inventions, institutions, undertakings, and discoveries have resulted from the comprehension of the rational soul.
– *Some Answered Questions*, newly revised edition, p. 217.

That brings us to the point and purpose of philosophy itself.

After all, what is philosophy? Opinions? Rules to live by? Morals and human values meant to be expressed in acceptance and action?

At its core all philosophy rests on some moral value. Hence, true philosophy should be no different than true religion, no different than the core and essence of all religions–the human spirit and its good actions. Good thoughts result in right actions, as the Buddha's philosophy asserts—but humanity, the Bahá'í teachings say, has lost touch with that spirit:

Alas! that humanity is completely submerged in imitations and unrealities notwithstanding the truth of divine religion has ever remained the same.

Superstitions have obscured the fundamental reality, the world is darkened and the light of religion is not apparent.

This darkness is conducive to differences and dissensions; rites and dogmas are many and various; therefore discord has arisen among the religious systems whereas religion is for the unification of mankind.

True religion is the source of love and agreement amongst men, the cause of the development of praiseworthy qualities; but the people are holding to the counterfeit and imitation, negligent of the reality which unifies; so they are bereft and deprived of the radiance of religion. They follow superstitions inherited from their fathers and ancestors.
– 'Abdu'l-Bahá, *Foundations of World Unity*, p. 71.

This statement could easily apply today in the 21st century.

Manmade systems of philosophy and governance—socialism, capitalism, and communism—have tried to supplant and even replace religion. [Although humanity learns from these systems, the greatest knowledge comes from God as revealed by His Messengers.]

Those [manmade] philosophies, the Bahá'í teachings tell us, will all eventually fail based on their inadequate and unequal moral grounds, and their lack of attention to the human spirit.

Finally, lest we think that religion and philosophy belong only to the realm of the thoughts and morals of men, the foundations of men owe their origin to women, their mothers and life-givers. Even Christ, who had no physical father, was "born of woman." Women are the upholders of love and caring for the world and the first educators of every child.

Lucretia Mott

We owe a great debt in this age to women like Tahirih in mid-19th century Persia, and Elizabeth Cady Stanton and Lucretia Mott at the Seneca Falls NY Convention of 1848, for bringing to the world's attention the critical role of women in [establishing] humane values and progress.

Philosophy depends on clear thinking and right action, and religion depends on the Word of God revealed in every age by prophets and sages [as demonstrated by their faithful and honest followers].

Investigating Reality – and Philosophy

Culture PART 3 IN SERIES: MODERN PHILOSOPHY AND MODERN RELIGION

In Part One of this multi-part series we looked at the [persuasive argument] of major 17th and 18th-century philosophers, [in Part Two it was the role of philosophy and religion] —now let's turn to 19th and 20th-century thinkers.

Georg Wilhelm Friedrich Hegel (1770-1831) turned philosophical inquiry around by expounding the concepts of "thesis, antithesis and synthesis." At heart an idealist, his three theses could be said to be a scientific method for understanding thought and motivation which influenced many including Karl Marx. [Like] Hegel, Auguste Comte (1798-1857), another Frenchman like Descartes, firmly grounded sociology and positivism using the scientific method to investigate reality.

[Some} Sociologists today would agree with British philosopher John Stuart Mill (1806-1873), who revered "the greatest happiness to the greatest number of people," as the ideal. He believed that the greatest good comes from satisfying the needs of the majority. Bahá'ís would agree [that that is a worthy goal], adding protection for the rights of [every] minority, [in my opinion.]

The Dane Soren Kierkegaard [1813-1855] apprehended theistic existentialism, echoing the deistic philosophers credited with creating "western" logic-from-reality, who all receive praise from the Bahá'í writings:

As to deistic philosophers, such as Socrates, Plato and Aristotle, they are indeed worthy of esteem and of the highest praise, for they have rendered distinguished services to mankind. In like manner we regard the materialistic, accomplished, moderate philosophers, who have been of service (to mankind).

We regard knowledge and wisdom as the foundation of the progress of mankind, and extol philosophers who are endowed with broad vision.
– 'Abdu'l-Bahá, *Tablet to August Forel*, p. 7

With the publication of *Walden* by the American philosopher Henry David Thoreau (1817-1862), transcendentalism became the rage. Thoreau's philosophy centered on the inherent goodness of people and nature. Evidenced by the actions of Bahá'ís like Sarah Farmer in Eliot, Maine at the turn of the century–she founded a great center of learning, Green Acre Bahá'í School, and is [responsible] for raising the first Peace Flag.

A different view of human relations to relieve oppression was generated by Karl Marx (1818-1883) and Friedrich Engels (1820-1895) with the publication of the *Communist Manifesto* in Russia. We still watch its struggles to govern itself.

Friedrich Nietzsche, auspiciously born in 1844 in Germany (d. 1900), pinpointed the effects of secular society and science compared to religious belief with his famous statement, "God is dead…and we have killed him." It set off a revolution in philosophical thought that promoted the realities of this world over those of the world beyond, touching on nihilism.

Friedrich Nietzsche

This brings us to 20th century philosophers—I'll name only a few.

Briton Bertrand Russell (1872-1970), logician, mathematician, historian, writer, social critic, political activist, at times a liberal, a socialist, and a pacifist, founded analytic philosophy—which uses scientific methods to solve philosophical problems.

After Russell came Ludwig Wittgenstein (1889-1951), considered one of the greatest philosophers of the 20th century. Wittgenstein's philosophy, or at least a portion of it, centers around the profound idea of finding ways to reach ineffable spiritual insight. He urged everyone to investigate reality independently. Wittgenstein said, "Our life has no end in the way in which our visual field has no limits."

A different yet familiar track to Kant and Kierkegaard was laid by Jean Paul Sartre (1905-1980), who preached the merits of atheistic existentialism—still currently [a widely held belief,] especially these days as a philosophy that emphasizes individual existence, freedom, and choice. Sartre held the view that humans define their own meaning in life and try to make rational decisions despite existing in a (so-called) "irrational universe."

Rather than being specious arguments for understanding life, humanity owes a great deal to these philosophers for unveiling a crucial component of a person's makeup, as stated here by 'Abdu'l-Bahá:

The first teaching is that man should investigate reality, for reality is contrary to dogmatic interpretations and imitations of ancestral forms of belief to which all nations and peoples adhere so tenaciously. These blind imitations are contrary to the fundamental basis of the divine religions, for the divine religions in their central and essential teaching are based upon unity, love and peace, whereas these variations and imitations have ever been productive of warfare, sedition and strife.

Therefore, all souls should consider it incumbent upon them to investigate reality. Reality is one; and when found, it will unify all mankind. Reality is the love of God. Reality is the knowledge of God. Reality is justice. Reality is the oneness or solidarity of mankind. Reality is international peace. Reality is the knowledge of verities. Reality unifies humanity.
– 'Abdu'l-Bahá, *The Promulgation of Universal Peace*, p. 372.

Thanks to the philosophical beliefs of each of us, and those who spoke and wrote out their thinking against the currents of their times, [humanity] has been better for it—and continues to progress to fuller understandings of God and the truth of [existence].

#

Can We End War?

Culture PART 1 IN SERIES: **IS AN END TO HUMAN SUFFERING IN SIGHT?**

WAR noun 1. a conflict carried on by force of arms, as between nations or between parties within a nation; warfare, as by land, sea, or air. 2. a state or period of armed hostility or active military operations

Finally, humanity has begun to grow tired of war.

So far in the 21st Century, we haven't had any widespread global wars, thank God. Of course, since World War II, leaders have propagated dozens of wars: the Indo-Pakistani wars, the Korean "conflict," the Vietnam War, the Six-Day War, the Dirty War in Argentina, even the Football War in 1969. But since the turn of the century, wars have steadily dwindled and smaller "rebellions," "wars of independence," "military actions," and especially "civil unrest" have taken over.

Make no mistake, these "smaller" wars still provoke the unmitigated suffering that larger wars bring. Misery, displacement, and destruction continue, along with mass exoduses across vast distances, and death for tens of thousands. But the world has not had a war with death counts in the millions so far in this century.

There are no wars or conflicts of any kind in North America, unless you count race and class struggles or Mexico's "drug wars."

Central and South America have remained relatively calm, except for several now-settled civil wars in places like Nicaragua and El Salvador and the short-lived Falklands War back in '82.

Europe, the progenitor of most wars on earth into the 20th century, remains relatively unscathed now.

The Eastern Bloc with its clash of ideologies broke apart in '89, and many smaller clashes continue in the region, but no wider war has broken out yet.

China is mostly calm.

In Africa, several rebellions and coups have taken place, [and with the Arab Spring, the Middle East is in turmoil,] but [some] of the continent has stayed peaceful.

Why?

Bahá'ís believe that humanity is coming of age—leaving behind the six thousand years of fractious warfare and constant bloodshed and maturing into a more thoughtful, empathetic, and spiritually-minded species.

[Many internal strife's have broken out, but wars between nations have not. It is the time to abolish war:]

...it is our duty to put forth our greatest efforts and summon all our energies in order that the bonds of unity and accord may be established among mankind.

For thousands of years we have had bloodshed and strife. It is enough; it is sufficient.

Now is the time to associate together in love and harmony.

For thousands of years we have tried the sword and warfare; let mankind for a time at least live in peace.

Review history and consider how much savagery, how much bloodshed and battle the world has witnessed.

It has been either religious warfare, political warfare or some other clash of human interests. The world of humanity has never enjoyed the blessing of Universal Peace.

Year by year the implements of warfare have been increased and perfected. Consider the wars of past centuries; only ten, fifteen or twenty thousand at the most were killed but now it is possible to kill one hundred thousand in a single day.

In ancient times warfare was carried on with the sword; today it is the smokeless gun. Formerly battleships were sailing vessels; today they are dreadnoughts. Consider the increase and improvement in the weapons of war.

God has created us all human and all countries of the world are parts of the same globe. We are all his servants. He is kind and just to all. Why should we be unkind and unjust to each other? He provides for all. Why should we deprive one another? He protects and preserves all. Why should we kill our fellow-creatures?
– 'Abdu'l-Bahá, *Foundations of World Unity*, p. 50.

The wars we've put ourselves through fill thousands of bookshelves. Yet mankind can [almost] rejoice!

You and I can [almost] rejoice [also]!

Wars, in the old sense of fighting to retain or expand one country's borders against another's, are almost over. The consequences of modern warfare and atomic weapons have become too terrible to contemplate–or use--and nuclear saber-rattling by any nation should cease.

Disarmament treaties [should progress.]

The Bahá'í writings point [to the near-end of untamed state sovereignty]:

Unification of the whole of mankind is the hallmark of the stage which human society is now approaching. Unity of family, of tribe, of city-state, and nation have been successively attempted and fully established.

World unity is the goal towards which a harassed humanity is striving.

Nation-building has come to an end.

The anarchy inherent in state sovereignty is moving towards a climax.

A world, growing to maturity, must abandon this fetish, recognize the oneness and wholeness of human relationships, and establish once for all the machinery that can best incarnate this fundamental principle of its life.
– Shoghi Effendi, *The World Order of Bahá'u'lláh*, p. 282.

Yes, we've had a few wars in the 21st Century—Iraq, Afghanistan, Syria, to name three–yet they tend toward models of a new type of war fought by a coalition of multiple country's military forces. These wars protect borders rather than expanding them. [It is true that new internecine conflicts include many groups, even terrorists, and time will tell if these explode over set borders to the point of all out war between nations.]

[But huge military] wars to permanently colonize or build nations have almost ended, and now claims for land acquisition [except Russia's takeover of Ukraine's Crimea in December 2014] are predominantly fought diplomatically or in the courts.

We can be grateful for the demise of all-out global warfare. Yet, humanity's unrest grows with its discontent over the Old World Order, as clearly [shown] by citizens' [unrest] around the world through massive demonstrations.

#

A Democratic Upsurge:
Wars of Civil Unrest

Culture PART 2 IN SERIES: IS AN END TO HUMAN SUFFERING IN SIGHT?

During the past two decades, the world's peoples have both propagated and experienced groundswells of civil unrest for a multitude of reasons.

Cairo, Egypt – February 25, 2011.

One reason stands out [why]: civil disobedience used to overthrow corrupt and evil leaders and governments, [or practices,] that suppress human rights. This [new] kind of civil unrest—with names like the Arab Spring—attempts to install democracy where autocracy or theocracy has long ruled.

In the process, lives are lost in defense of human rights. These battles are fought internally, inside national borders, with the goal of establishing democratic republics. [For example countries like India throwing off colonial yokes, semi-peaceful ones like Brazil, and in modern times, a federation of nations, the EU.] .

Many of those battles have already resulted, and many more will likely result, in implementations [closer to the] model of democratic federalism that the Bahá'í teachings so strongly recommend:

You can best serve your country, was 'Abdu'l-Bahá's rejoinder to a high official in the service of the federal government of the United States of America, who had questioned Him as to the best manner in which he could promote the interests of his government and people,
if you strive,
in your capacity as a citizen of the world,
to assist in the eventual application of the principle of federalism underlying the government of your own country to the relationships now existing between the peoples and nations of the world.
– Shoghi Effendi, *The World Order of Bahá'u'lláh*, p. 37.

America's federation of colonies and later states has become a model of organization that many other nations subsequently adopted [to some degree.] In the 18th Century world of Kings and Queens and authoritarian rulers fighting to expand their territory and borders, the rise of democracy in America and France stunned the globe.

Today [most of] those autocrats are gone, just as Bahá'u'lláh promised they would be if they resisted the spirit of the age. Since then, the growth of representative democracies has outstripped any other form of government.

Here's [a graphic on] how democracy grew during the 20th Century:

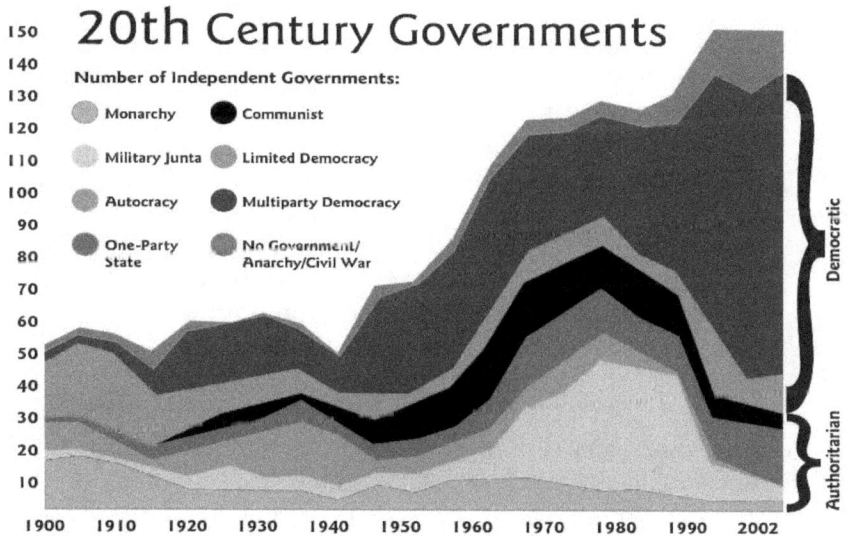

By Jesse Richards

Besides depicting the meteoric rise of democratic nations, this chart also shows clear growing unrest, anarchy, and civil wars in the countries without democratic representation.

Essentially, democratization has become the standard generic process that all nations and peoples will eventually go through. The clash of strong opinions and civil unrest seem simply unavoidable, unless authoritarian rulers voluntarily give up their power and allow the people to rule. Those kinds of peaceful revolutions have happened in several countries already—the Philippines, Poland, Czechoslovakia, Ecuador, etc.

Even after a nonviolent revolution, however, achieving democracy is difficult, takes years to stabilize, is contentious and sometimes bloody, and must provide the political means for affecting reasonable policies of any new government.

But the rewards, once achieved, are too significant to overlook.

Equal treatment under the law, free speech, freedom of assembly, the right to own property, freedom from slavery and the government-supported right to work—people have died for these since long before the American Revolution.

In a public address to an American church congregation in 1912, 'Abdu'l-Bahá said:

Consider what a vast difference exists between modern democracy and the old forms of despotism. Under an autocratic government the opinions of men are not free, and development is stifled, whereas in democracy, because thought and speech are not restricted, the greatest progress is witnessed.

It is likewise true in the world of religion. When freedom of conscience, liberty of thought and right of speech prevail—that is to say, when every man according to his own idealization may give expression to his beliefs—development and growth are inevitable.

– *The Promulgation of Universal Peace*, p. 197.

The full democratization of all 196 or more countries of our world today hasn't been fully realized—but the trend is clear. As 'Abdu'l-Bahá predicted while in the United States in 1912, the 20th Century, "this century of light," and the beginning decades of the 21st, have set the stage and put the forces in motion necessary to accomplish this gigantic task.

Civil unrest, with the goal of establishing fully independent, fully sovereign democratically elected nations, as evidenced by global outbreaks of protests and movements, is now reaching its climax.

That physical climax, unfortunately, has given rise to terrorism in our times.

Next Part: How Can We End Terrorism?

#

How Can We End Terrorism?

CULTURE PART 3 IN SERIES: IS AN END TO HUMAN SUFFERING IN SIGHT?

Terrorism, in the most widely accepted contemporary usage of the term, is fundamentally and inherently political. It is also ineluctably about power: the pursuit of power, the acquisition of power, and the use of power to achieve political change.

Terrorism is thus violence — or, equally important, the threat of violence — used and directed in pursuit of, or in service of, a political aim.

With this vital point clearly illuminated, one can appreciate the significance of the additional definition of 'terrorist' provided by the OED: 'Any one who attempts to further his views by a system of coercive intimidation'.

This definition underscores clearly the other fundamental characteristic of terrorism: that it is a planned, calculated, and indeed systematic act.

– *Inside Terrorism*, by Bruce Hoffman. [OED, Oxford English Dictionary]

Terrorism of any kind destroys world peace and world order.

Terrorism is the epitome of man's inhumanity to man. Terrorism is also the wanton taking of property and lives–of countrymen, countrywomen and country children. It uses random [or targeted] violence and threats to intimidate or coerce, especially for political or religious purposes.

Even open war, just or unjust imprisonment, and torture, hold out the hope of an end and a release—but that's not true with terrorism.

Terrorism is rooted in every human being's need to belong to a group of peers [to achieve a political, socioeconomic, or even religious, end]. In these times it has become ideologically acceptable to indiscriminately murder innocents to affect the terrorist's goal: A social order based on their sole conception of what is right for them as right for all others, no exceptions. They require instant, exact, and complete obedience to their orders and tenets, as verified by the actions of human suicide bombers. Between 1982 and January 2015, over 4,283 suicide attacks in 40 countries were documented, with untold pain and destruction the result.

Most of the terroristic acts we see today no longer fit the old saying "One man's terrorist is another man's freedom fighter." Take for example Nazi Germany's stance against resistance groups opposing Germany's occupation of their lands, labeling them "terrorists." Fighting for freedom, justice and equality is [different from] fighting for repression and subjugation.

The terrorist, like the egotist, somehow cannot consider the feelings or the life of others as important:

The man who thinks only of himself and is thoughtless of others…." "[He] … is undoubtedly inferior to the animal because the animal is not possessed of the reasoning faculty. The animal is excused; but in man there is reason, the faculty of justice, the faculty of mercifulness. Possessing all these faculties he must not leave them unused. He who is so hard-hearted as to think only of his own comfort, such an one will not be called man.
– 'Abdu'l-Bahá, *Foundations of World Unity*, p. 42.

So far, the falsities of terroristic actions and ideologies have revealed themselves as obvious and self-defeating. It's the recognized duty of good people and governments everywhere to expose their vapid philosophies and unsound justifications for killing innocents. The Bahá'í teachings say that the spread of terrorism exposes one of the deepest flaws in the way humanity has ordered its affairs:

Flaws in the prevailing order are conspicuous in the inability of sovereign states organized as United Nations to exorcize the spectre of war, the threatened collapse of the international economic order, the spread of anarchy

and terrorism, and the intense suffering which these and other afflictions are causing to increasing millions.
– The Universal House of Justice, *The Promise of World Peace*, p. 1.

Of course, governments also kill innocent people with bombs and missiles and drones. Bahá'ís believe that all such actions—whether under the guise of terrorism or government—must stop. As we've seen in the past, killing and death only produces more killing and death.

Instead, the Bahá'í teachings say, we must adopt a genuine, universal framework that can regulate, contain and eventually stop the world's violent terrorist outbursts.

That framework calls for a new way of organizing the world based on justice and unity:

Acceptance of the oneness of mankind is the first fundamental prerequisite for reorganization and administration of the world as one country, the home of humankind. Universal acceptance of this spiritual principle is essential to any successful attempt to establish world peace. It should therefore be universally proclaimed, taught in schools, and constantly asserted in every nation as preparation for the organic change in the structure of society which it implies.

In the Bahá'í view, recognition of the oneness of mankind "calls for no less than the reconstruction and the demilitarization of the whole civilized world — a world organically unified in all the essential aspects of its life, its political machinery, its spiritual aspiration, its trade and finance, its script and language, and yet infinite in the diversity of the national characteristics of its federated units."

– *ibid*, p. 4.[smaller font to fit page space]

#

How Can We Stop Killing Each Other?

Culture PART 4 IN SERIES: IS AN END TO HUMAN SUFFERING IN SIGHT?

Killing one another, even a brother, has been the human race's modus operandi since the story of mankind's genesis. Whether justified by just wars or civil unrest, unjustified by unjustified wars or civil unrest, or totally unjustified under any condition or ideology by terrorism, the Bahá'í teachings say we can find ways to stop the killing if we focus on our unity:

> However great the conqueror, however many countries he may reduce to slavery, he is unable to retain any part of these devastated lands but one tiny portion—his tomb! If more land is required for the improvement of the condition of the people, for the spread of civilization (for the substitution of just laws for brutal customs)—surely it would be possible to acquire peaceably the necessary extension of territory.
>
> But war is made for the satisfaction of men's ambition; for the sake of worldly gain to the few, terrible misery is brought to numberless homes, breaking the hearts of hundreds of men and women! How many widows mourn their husbands, how many stories of savage cruelty do we hear! How many little orphaned children are crying for their dead fathers, how many women are weeping for their slain sons!
>
> There is nothing so heart-breaking and terrible as an outburst of human savagery! I charge you all that each one of you concentrate all the thoughts of your heart on love and unity. When a thought of war comes, oppose it by a stronger thought of peace. A thought of hatred must be destroyed by a more powerful thought of love.
>
> Thoughts of war bring destruction to all harmony, well-being, restfulness and content. Thoughts of love are constructive of brotherhood, peace, friendship, and happiness.

– 'Abdu'l-Bahá, *Paris Talks*, p. 30.

In this age of transition toward a new global standard of universal peace, terrorists who murder innocents only produce senseless deaths. Some verbal terrorists also extort concessions when they demand, like children who throw a screaming tantrum, no negotiation; no consensus; no attempts at reaching compromise.

Yet these ruinous wars will pass away, Bahá'u'lláh promises us:

That all nations should become one in faith and all men as brothers; that the bonds of affection and unity between the sons of men should be strengthened; that diversity of religion should cease, and differences of race be annulled—what harm is there in this? ...Yet so it shall be; these fruitless strifes, these ruinous wars shall pass away, and the 'Most Great Peace' shall come.
– *The Proclamation of Bahá'u'lláh*, p. viii.

Every age has its exigencies and requirements, all leading to the ultimate progress of the human race. But we shouldn't be surprised, since every day of our lives in whatever age we live presents opportunities and challenges to either add to humanity's woes, do nothing, or to correct society's ills by our own actions.

Our own personal struggles to survive and thrive are [bound] up in the circumstances surrounding us and those we love.

The Bahá'í writings clearly describe this "titanic spiritual struggle" [that] we find ourselves a part of. Humanity as a race is growing into full maturity, and these stages of worldwide disruption, from autocratic rule to civil unrest to democracy, from war and terrorism to stable governments and peoples, are inevitable and to be expected.

This titanic struggle for the hearts of all people will be won if we each do our part. Bahá'u'lláh's new Faith asks us to live peaceful, humble lives dedicated to the welfare and well-being of the entire world:

Be united in counsel, be one in thought. Let each morn be better than its eve and each morrow richer than its yesterday. Men's merit lieth in service and virtue and not in the pageantry of wealth and riches.

Take heed that your words be purged from idle fancies and worldly desires and your deeds be cleansed from craftiness and suspicion. Dissipate not the wealth of your precious lives in the pursuit of evil and corrupt affection, nor let your endeavors be spent in promoting your personal interest.

Be generous in your days of plenty, and be patient in the hour of loss. Adversity is followed by success and rejoicings follow woe. Guard against idleness and sloth, and cling unto that which profiteth mankind, whether young or old, whether high or low.
– *Tablets of Bahá'u'lláh*, p. 138.

#

The Concept of Federalism Applied to the Whole World

History

America's Great Depression began quietly in August of 1929, followed by the stock market crash of October, wiping out equity for thousands of individuals and companies, throwing millions out of work overnight. Some of the very wealthy avoided its devastating effects.

Most didn't.

Franklin Roosevelt

In the deepest part of that Great Depression, Americans elected Franklin Roosevelt, who implemented his New Deal policies. The New Deal mandated a changed role for the Federal government. No longer passive, government became active and forceful in steering human behavior and the American economy.

The government-built dams along the Tennessee River. Farmers were paid not to grow crops, which ended wasteful surpluses and raised their income. Workers gained the right to unionize for better wages and conditions.

Congress and the President created the Public Works Administration to build large public-benefit projects like bridges, schools, and highways around the country, and give people jobs. The PWA employed millions, including artists. Efforts like these lifted the nation out of depression and poverty and gave America back its future.

That concept—government by and for the people—runs throughout the Bahá'í teachings. The Bahá'í vision of a just government starts with democratic representation in a federal system, and then expands that representation to every human being on Earth:

...the Supreme Tribunal which His Holiness Bahá'u'lláh has described will fulfill this sacred task with the utmost might and power. And his plan is this: that the national assemblies of each country and nation—that is to say, their parliaments—should elect two or three persons who are the choicest men of that nation, and are well informed concerning international laws and the relations between governments and aware of the essential needs of the world of humanity in this day.

The number of these representatives should be in proportion to the number of inhabitants of that country. The election of these souls who are chosen by the national assembly—that is, the parliament—must be confirmed by the upper house, the congress and the cabinet and also by the president or monarch so that these persons may be the elected ones of all the nation and the government.

From among these people the members of the Supreme Tribunal will be elected, and all mankind will thus have a share therein, for every one of these delegates is fully representative of his nation.
– 'Abdu'l-Bahá, *Foundations of World Unity*, pp. 32-33.

'Abdu'l-Bahá further endorsed such a global democratic system when he told an American [official]:

You can best serve your country if you strive, in your capacity as a citizen of the world, to assist in the eventual application of the principle of federalism, underlying the government of your own country, to the relationships now existing between the peoples and nations of the world.
– quoted by Shoghi Effendi in *The Advent of Divine Justice*, p. 87.

Bahá'ís believe that a federal system of government represents the best foundation for the ordered life of mankind on this planet, the best foundation for responding to the immediate and long-term needs of the peoples of the world.

[The] question arises: "How do we pay for such a global system?" I cite below a resource allocation from Benjamin Franklin in an 1883 letter:

What vast additions to the conveniences and comforts of living might mankind have acquired, if the money spent in wars had been employed in works of public utility; what an extension of agriculture even to the tops of our mountains; what rivers rendered navigable, or joined by canals; what bridges, aqueducts, new roads, and other public works, edifices, and improvements... might not have been obtained by spending those millions in doing good, which in the last war have been spent in doing mischief.

The Bahá'í teachings share that view:

The war expenses of each nation have increased greatly of late years. Although there has not been the physical clash and turmoil of actual war, yet in reality a financial and economic war has been going on incessantly and draining the resources of the people. For a goodly portion of what the poor labourers, farmers and artisans get with the sweat of their brows and the labour of their hands is taken from them under the name of taxes, and expended over military preparations.

Hence war is uninterrupted. This exaction breeds discontent, class feeling and group consciousness against the established order;-everyone realizing that human society is out of gear.

Now if they could employ this pugnacity, this hammer and tongs, this fists and heels spirit, this feverish haste

in the accumulation of war materials, this waste of great thoughts over the perfection of military science—

I say if they could expend this exertion and effort, this endeavour and high-mindedness, in bringing about Love among mankind, in strengthening the ties of interdependence between nations and governments and in establishing fellowship and affinity between the races—how much more efficacious it would have been!

Instead of unsheathing the sword to shed each other's blood, they should think of the perfection of each other's civilizations, sciences, arts, commerce, progress and advancement.

Is this not better? Is it not worthier for the noble station of man?
–Attributed to "Abdu'l-Bahá, *Star of the West*, Vol 4, p. 180.

Franklin also wrote: "By failing to prepare, you are preparing to fail."

[Are we only preparing for war? What about peace?]

Rather than expending all our energy and preparation on the immediate threat of hostility and war, we would all do humanity a great service if we prepared now for the inevitable extension of the concept of federalism to the entire world.

\#

How to De-weaponize Your Words

Culture PART 1 IN SERIES: WORDS FOR THE WARM HEARTED

Words can wound.

They can cut much deeper than a knife, penetrate to the core of the heart like a bullet, and leave an injury that never heals.

What ordnance do some possess in the munitions cache of their words, with sharpened tongues of knives and swords to cut down opponents midstream, bursts of verbal vitriol to put someone in their place immediately, shotgun blasts of shouted pronouncements supposed to be taken as "God's honest truths?"

Bahá'ís don't carry weapons unless absolutely necessary:

Bahá'u'lláh confirms an injunction… which makes it unlawful to carry arms, unless it is necessary to do so. With regard to circumstances under which the bearing of arms might be "essential" for an individual, 'Abdu'l-Bahá gives permission to a believer for self-protection in a dangerous environment.

Shoghi Effendi in a letter written on his behalf has also indicated that, in an emergency, when there is no legal force at hand to appeal to, a Bahá'í is justified in defending his life. There are a number of other situations in which weapons are needed and can be legitimately used; for instance, in countries where people hunt for their food and clothing, and in such sports as archery, marksmanship, and fencing.

On the societal level, the principle of collective security enunciated by Bahá'u'lláh, and elaborated by Shoghi Effendi does not presuppose the abolition of the use of force, but prescribes "a system in which Force is made the servant of Justice," and which provides for the existence of an international peace-keeping force that "will safeguard the organic unity of the whole commonwealth."

…Bahá'u'lláh expresses the hope that "weapons of war throughout the world may be converted into instruments of reconstruction and that strife and conflict may be removed from the midst of men."
– Note 173 in Bahá'u'lláh's *Most Holy Book*, p. 241, [English translation released by the Universal House of Justice in 1992].

Unarmed with physical weapons, Bahá'ís also try to de-weaponize their words. Kindness, "… the Lodestone of the heart," marks the true Bahá'í path to others' acceptance of what we have to say, and how we express ourselves:

Consort with all men, O people of Baha, in a spirit of friendliness and fellowship. If ye be aware of a certain truth, if ye possess a jewel, of which others are deprived, share it with them in a language of utmost kindliness and good-will. If it be accepted, if it fulfil its purpose, your object is attained. If any one should refuse it, leave him unto himself, and beseech God to guide him. Beware lest ye deal unkindly with him. A kindly tongue is the lodestone of the hearts of men. It is the bread of the spirit, it clotheth the words with meaning, it is the fountain of the light of wisdom and understanding….
– Bahá'u'lláh, *Gleanings from the Writings of Bahá'u'lláh*, p. 289.

This admonition resonates at the core of the Bahá'í teachings, and asks us to disarm the weapons of our words with the utmost kindness and love:

Be kind to all people, love humanity, consider all mankind as your relations and servants of the most high God.
  Strive day and night that animosity and contention may pass away from the hearts of men, that all religions shall become reconciled and the nations love each other, so that no racial, religious or political prejudice may remain and the world of humanity behold God as the beginning and end of all existence.
  God has created all and all return to God.
  Therefore love humanity with all your heart and soul. If you meet a poor man, assist him; if you see the sick, heal him; reassure the affrighted one, render the cowardly noble and courageous, educate the ignorant, associate with the stranger.
  Emulate God.
  Consider how kindly, how lovingly He deals with all and follow His example. You must treat people in accordance with the divine precepts; in other words, treat them as kindly as God treats them, for this is the greatest attainment possible for the world of humanity.
– 'Abdu'l-Bahá, *Foundations of World Unity*, p. 73.

And why shall we speak in kindnesses? So [that] our utterances and example will reach the city of men's hearts, the Throne of God Himself, before bullets do:

Should it be God's intention, there would appear out of the forests of celestial might the lion of indomitable strength whose roaring is like unto the peals of thunder reverberating in the mountains. However, since Our loving providence surpasseth all things, We have ordained that complete victory should be achieved through speech and utterance, that Our servants throughout the earth may thereby become the recipients of divine good.
– Ibid., p. 197.

Perchance all shall be the "recipients of divine good" in our own lifetimes.

#

Do You Have A Kindly Tongue?

Culture PART 2 IN SERIES: WORDS FOR THE WARM HEARTED

Sticks and stones can break my bones, but words will never harm me.

Everyone knows this children's rhyme—but do you know where it came from? It first appeared in *The Christian Recorder*, a publication of the African Methodist Episcopal Church, in 1862. Maybe it arose out of AME church members and their children defending themselves against racist taunts and verbal attacks.

I sure heard that rhyme as a kid. I said it myself multiple times, thinking of it as a consolation, but the ire and madness at the verbal slights from others welled up in my heart anyway. Then they exploded, a few times in fisticuffs, twice in knife fights—no one injured, thank goodness. A serious cutting could've landed me on probation or worse, in jail. Who knows if an ambulance would've helped?

Words, [harsh] words, or attacks on character, always sting. Not only sting, they hurt. They can hurt worse than a physical wound, and last longer. Bahá'u'lláh wrote:

He must never seek to exalt himself above any one, must wash away from the tablet of his heart every trace of pride and vainglory, must cling unto patience and resignation, observe silence, and refrain from idle talk.

For the tongue is a smouldering fire, and excess of speech a deadly poison. Material fire consumeth the body, whereas the fire of the tongue devoureth both heart and soul. The force of the former lasteth but for a time, whilst the effects of the latter endure a century.
– *The Book of Certitude*, p. 193.

Just as harsh words can injure, a kindly tongue can work miracles in human responses. For Bahá'ís, this is no mere aphorism or philosophical bon mot. Bahá'u'lláh shows us how to acquire such kindly and effective speech:

Human utterance is an essence which aspireth to exert its influence and needeth moderation. As to its influence, this is conditional upon refinement, which in turn is dependent upon hearts which are detached and pure. As to its moderation, this hath to be combined with tact

and wisdom as prescribed in the Holy Scriptures and Tablets.

O My Name! Utterance must needs possess penetrating power. For if bereft of this quality it would fail to exert influence. And this penetrating influence dependeth on the spirit being pure and the heart stainless.

Likewise it needeth moderation, without which the hearer would be unable to bear it, rather he would manifest opposition from the very outset. And moderation will be obtained by blending utterance with the tokens of divine wisdom which are recorded in the sacred Books and Tablets.

Thus when the essence of one's utterance is endowed with these two requisites it will prove highly effective and will be the prime factor in transforming the souls of men.
– Bahá'u'lláh, *Tablets of Bahá'u'lláh*, pp. 198-199.

How do we exercise this kind of kindly speech? How many times are we loathe to give up on our views, and argue what we believe is "the most correct," over another's?

Attached to our own views at the expense of listening fully to another's, of course alienates us and keeps us in our own reality, right or wrong. Tact does not emanate naturally from naturally selfish creatures. It takes knowledge and wisdom to learn and apply, just as every schoolteacher is trained to develop their pupils for the age, and capacity, and intelligence they each possess.

Tact and wisdom come from learning the world's Scriptures, which contain universal, spiritual, and life-giving purpose. Yet tact and wisdom from knowing the Scriptures, though necessary, is not enough.

Our ideas and where they belong often conflict with other's sense of their ideas. The basic spiritual rule of moderation in all things allows an exchange of thoughts, realities, and ideas; which lead to tolerance and acceptance rather than outright rejection as an opposing view. Here Bahá'u'lláh shows us he understands human nature deeply, and that he can enlighten us with the beauty and moderation of his words.

Bahá'u'lláh reminds us that only the Word of God, unlocked in the sacred Books and Tablets (the Scriptures), will provide divine wisdom.

Moderation and kindness in uttering your words, in response to the yearnings of every human heart, will indeed penetrate consciousness and can change lives.

#

Order in the Universe, First and Foremost

Science PART 1 IN SERIES: THE UNIVERSAL LAWS OF CREATION

When we gaze out into the Milky Way at night, what does it show us?

In the newly revised and re-translated Bahá'í book *Some Answered Questions*, 'Abdu'l-Bahá begins by describing nature and its adherence to universal laws, such as gravity, which maintains the planets and their moons in orbit around our life-giving sun for billions of years. Our solar system's sun and its rules govern our lives on this material plane of existence.

The principal component of the solar system, our G2 main-sequence star contains 99.86% of the system's known mass and dominates it gravitationally. For a moment, consider that amazing organizational feat—keeping these immense bodies in place or in orbit, hanging in space in a small galaxy amid billions of galaxies, providing order for billions of years:

This nature is subject to a sound organization, to inviolable laws, to a perfect order, and to a consummate design, from which it never departs. To such an extent is this true that were you to gaze with the eye of insight and discernment, you would observe that all things—

from the smallest invisible atom to the largest globes in the world of existence, such as the sun or the other great stars and luminous bodies—

are most perfectly organized, be it with regard to their order, their composition, their outward form, or their motion, and they are all subject to one universal law from which they never depart.
– 'Abdu'l-Bahá, *Some Answered Questions*, newly revised edition, p. 3.

'Abdu'l-Bahá then goes on to say:

It is certain that the entire contingent world is subject to an order and a law which it can never disobey. Even man is forced to submit to death, sleep and other conditions— that is, in certain matters he is compelled, and this very compulsion implies the existence of One Who is All-Compelling.

> So long as the contingent world is characterized by dependency, and so long as this dependency is one of its essential requirements, there must be One Who in His own Essence is independent of all things. – Ibid., p. 6.

This beautiful, intellectually cohesive proof of the existence of God demonstrates nature's and humanity's reliance on a Creator. When we look up into the skies, the universe shows us a perfect order and symmetry—which reveals the mind of the Artist who made it:

> Among the proofs and arguments for the existence of God is the fact that man has not created himself, but rather that his creator and fashioner is another than he. And it is certain and indisputable that the creator of man is not like man himself, because a powerless being cannot create another being, and an active creator must possess all perfections to produce his handiwork.
> Is it possible for the handiwork to be perfect and the craftsman imperfect? Is it possible for a painting to be a masterpiece and the painter to be deficient in his craft, notwithstanding that he is its creator?
> No: The painting cannot be like the painter, for otherwise it would have painted itself. And no matter how perfect the painting may be, in comparison with the painter it is utterly deficient.
> – Ibid., p. 5.

Next, 'Abdu'l-Bahá logically compares the two poles of existence.

He cites a range of opposites, such as poverty to wealth, wisdom to ignorance, or goodness to evil.

Then he asks: For how would we know light without the Sun? How would we know darkness without the absence of that light?

Having clearly shown how universal laws govern all existence, created and enforced by the Supreme Being, 'Abdu'l-Bahá outlines the process of divine education, and challenges us to acquire the attributes and perfections of God:

> Human education, however, consists in civilization and progress, that is, sound governance, social order, human welfare, commerce and industry, arts and sciences, momentous discoveries, and great undertakings, which

are the central features distinguishing man from the animal.

As to divine education, it is the education of the Kingdom and consists in acquiring divine perfections. This is indeed true education, for by its virtue man becomes the focal centre of divine blessings and the embodiment of the verse "Let Us make man in Our image, after Our likeness." This is the ultimate goal of the world of humanity.
– Ibid., p. 9.

The Bahá'í teachings ask us all to aspire to the highest goal of humanity: to know and love our Creator. How can we do that? How can we acquire a divine education?

We'll look at that question in the next essay in this series.

#

To Progress Spiritually, Humanity Needs A Divine Educator

Culture PART 2 IN SERIES: THE UNIVERSAL LAWS OF CREATION

Just as the sun gives life to this world, the Bahá'í teachings say, God enlivens the world of humanity by sending us the bright suns of the prophets and founders of the great Faiths.

In the first section of the Bahá'í book *Some Answered Questions*, 'Abdu'l-Bahá proceeds to describe the lives and circumstances of the great prophets. Humble and faithful men, they were inspired by God through the intermediary of the Holy Spirit and brought the teachings that enlightened the moral and spiritual life of all people.

'Abdu'l-Bahá explains why we human beings, our souls and spirits which give us life in all the worlds of God, revolve around the teachings of the divine educators. He spends the next six chapters of *Some Answered Questions* demonstrating the need for a divine educator in every age, and describing the vicissitudes the prophets of God overcame, their teachings, and the power of love they established.

That power, which attracted the hearts of millions, eventually overcome all the forces arrayed against them and established great civilizations.

'Abdu'l-Bahá cites several examples:

Among those who possessed this divine power and were assisted by it was Abraham. The proof is this: Abraham was born in Mesopotamia of a family that was ignorant of the oneness of God; He opposed His own people and government, and even His own kin; He rejected all their gods; and, alone and single-handed, He withstood a powerful nation.
– *Some Answered Questions*, newly revised edition, p. 14.

It was such a man [Moses] Who freed a great people from the fetters of captivity and persuaded them to leave Egypt and settle in the Holy Land.
That people had sunk to the depths of degradation and were lifted up to the heights of glory. They were captives and were set free. They were the most ignorant of peoples and became the most learned.
– Ibid., p. 17.

Briefly, this Man, [Christ] Who appeared lowly in the eyes of all, arose nonetheless with such power as to abrogate a fifteen-hundred-year-old Dispensation, notwithstanding that the least deviation from its laws would expose the offender to grave danger and bring about his death and annihilation.
– Ibid., 20.

What objection, then, can be directed against Muḥammad? Is it this, that He did not, with His followers and their women and children, place himself at the mercy of these lawless tribes? Moreover, to free these tribes from their bloodthirstiness was the greatest gift, and to curb and restrain them was pure bounty. It is like a man who holds in his hand a cup of poison and who is about to drink it. A loving friend would certainly shatter the cup and restrain the drinker.
– Ibid., p. 25.

As for the Báb —may my soul be His sacrifice!—it was at a young age, that is, in the twenty-fifth year of His blessed life, that He arose to proclaim His Cause. Among the Shí'ihs it is universally acknowledged that He never studied in any school, nor acquired learning from any teacher....

The government, the nation, the clergy, and prominent leaders sought to extinguish His light, but to no avail. At last His moon rose, His star shone forth, His foundation was secured, and His horizon was flooded with light.
– Ibid., pp. 30-31.

Bahá'u'lláh appeared at a time when Persia was plunged in the darkest ignorance and consumed by the blindest fanaticism...

He was put in chains and thrown into a subterranean dungeon.

His extensive hereditary possessions were entirely plundered, He was four times exiled from land to land, and in the end He came to abide In the Most Great Prison.
– Ibid., pp. 32-33.

From his prison cell Bahá'u'lláh addressed summon-ses and warnings to the great leaders of the world:

Briefly, all that was recorded in the Tablets to the Kings is being fulfilled: if from the year A.D. 1870 we compare the events that have occurred, we will find everything that has happened has appeared as predicted: only a few remain which will afterward become manifested.
– Ibid., p. 39.

All of these prophets, and more, served as the divine educators of their age, like the life-giver the sun sustains and warms the Earth. They provided humanity with spiritual sustenance, with moral guidance, with a connection to the Creator.

The greatness of these divine educators lies in the examples of their lives; the word of God shared with mankind as laws, principles, and teachings; and the civilizations that have arisen and are arising, [because] of their foreordained appearances.

The Bahá'í teachings ask us to consider them all as one.

#

Tyrants, Fighting For Their Own Tombs
Culture

If I hit my wife, does she have the right to leave me or kick me out?

If I steal corporate or government secrets and get caught, should I spend months or years in jail and ruin my career and my family's unity?

If I lie to my boss about being sick, and she finds out, will she lose trust in me?

We can't foresee the future, but in these scenarios, society increasingly says that individuals should suffer the consequences of their unjust actions.

Our societies have archetypes of acceptability, and it behooves us, if we wish to benefit from society's bounties, to follow society's mores. But those mores differ by group and are not yet universal.

Today extreme groups like ISIS and Al-Qaeda frighten rational people, with deviant views of the truth and violent, fanatical behavior. Yet tyrants who run despotic nations—the world's Hitlers and Pol Pots of the past in new clothing—[also wreak havoc]. [How] do we ameliorate these vile, vociferous killings and maiming of humanity by leaders who have such warped views of "Truth?"

In truth, our own vain imaginings cause humanity's ills. The transgressors—tyrants, political leaders, generals, and despots—[can be] liars of the worst kind. They lie to us, and to themselves. They have lost the struggle for righteousness and justice within their own minds and hearts. They have decreed, like Napoleons of the past, "Verily I am God. Obey me."

Yet they are nothing more than the foam on the ocean wave, to one day be interred in their own abominable graves covered by the very dirt they coveted. The Bahá'í teachings say that their futile plans can only have one ultimate result:

The highest of created beings fighting to obtain the lowest form of matter, earth!
Land belongs not to one people, but to all people. This earth is not man's home, but his tomb. It is for their tombs these men are fighting. There is nothing so horrible in this world as the tomb, the abode of the decaying bodies of men.

However great the conqueror, however many countries he may reduce to slavery, he is unable to retain any part of these devastated lands but one tiny portion — his tomb!
– 'Abdu'l-Bahá, *Paris Talks*, p. 29.

Bahá'ís believe that only the Sun of Truth, the Prophet of God, can dispel these dark obscuring clouds of delusion. God is merciful. Like the foam on the wave, these dictators and totalitarians and Caesars will pass, and they will inevitably suffer the consequences of their actions, in this world or the next.

It's our job not to vote nor encourage new demigods to replace them. Whether dictator, candidate or elected, let's rely on God, and our own purposeful counteractions to evil. We can use our words and deeds, minds and skills, to expose society's falsehoods by spreading the truth and healing mankind. Let's build up a new society where specious ideas and empty promises find no foothold in the hearts of humanity.

Our task is to:

Rely upon God, thy God and the Lord of thy fathers. For the people are wandering in the paths of delusion, bereft of discernment to see God with their own eyes, or hear His Melody with their own ears. Thus have We found them, as thou also dost witness.
– Bahá'u'lláh, *Bahá'í Prayers*, p. 212.

The Bahá'í teachings say that the tyrants' self-important reigns will end:

...rely not on thy glory and thy power.

Thou art even as the last trace of sunlight upon the mountaintop. Soon will it fade away, as decreed by God, the All-Possessing, the Most High.

Thy glory, and the glory of such as are like thee, have been taken away...

– Bahá'u'lláh, quoted by Shoghi Effendi in *The Promised Day Is Come*, p. 88.

#

[**Author's update:** The Bahá'í Faith takes no positions or sides in politics, and is strictly apolitical. It is cognizant of history, of world affairs and events, and does not meddle. It offers its teachings and programs as models for world unity and peace, and proclaims the oneness and wholeness of the human race. It admonishes those people acting lower than the animals, which is the antithesis of the nobility of all human beings, and recognizes, if left to themselves, such people will bring great harm to humanity.

'Abdu'l-Bahá enjoined:

I charge you all that each one of you concentrate all the thoughts of your heart on love and unity. When a thought of war comes, oppose it by a stronger thought of peace. A thought of hatred must be destroyed by a more powerful thought of love. Thoughts of war bring destruction to all harmony, well-being, restfulness and content.

Thoughts of love are constructive of brotherhood, peace, friendship, and happiness.

- Paris Talks, #6 http://www.bahai.org/r/512608651]

#

We Can Solve the Ills of Humanity

Culture

Who doesn't want to be admired, or wealthy, or worshipped?

Each of us has an innate desire to be known, appreciated, recognized, and loved. But for what purpose?

The purpose of the creation of man is the attainment of the supreme virtues of humanity through descent of the heavenly bestowals. The purpose of man's creation is, therefore, unity and harmony, not discord and separateness.
– 'Abdu'l-Bahá, *The Promulgation of Universal Peace*, p. 4.

We are born with an innate sense of self, of being, of egoism. That sense of self motivates us to become something, or someone, worthwhile. It's also why we, most of us, return the love and kindness shown to us by friends and parents and coworkers and even strangers.

But what of that childhood, the environment in which we lived and matured? Did we live peacefully, or did we struggle? Did we have full, loving parental guidance, or not? Did we have despicable parents or were we wild orphans? Did we either learn to be civilized and polite as children, or were we unruly, constantly acting out?

Those lucky enough to have had a nurturing environment when young ought not to condemn or misunderstand the search for self by those untrained or unschooled in the virtues 'Abdu'l-Bahá speaks of—virtues and morals such as courteousness, caring, trustworthiness, fairness, hope for better things and a better life, self-confidence and an appreciation for others and their condition.

What if we do feel alone, isolated, hurt by the world's cruelties, none of which we deserved?

Through no fault of their own, the impoverished children of the world, numbering almost two billion souls, are left to their own devices to survive. Of course, we want them all to thrive—but how will they thrive?

In the absence of proper training, care and supervision, egotism, [depression,] and mental illness will thrive instead, as witnessed by more than 110 U.S. school shooting attacks since 2000. We mourn the twenty innocent children and six adult staff murdered by gunshots at Sandy Hook Elementary School, but [seemingly] little has been done to prevent more [according to activists.] This sadly highlights the weakness of many current political leaders to tackle the issues involved [systematically]—unless we force them to, through our raised unified voices and concerted actions.

Despite these tragedies, the Bahá'í teachings say, we also have ample evidence that the old principles of materialism and self-interest, the old sectarian and patriotic prejudices and animosities, are perishing. [They lie discredited,] amidst the ruins they have wrought. We can see the signs of a new spirit of faith, of unity, of international cooperation, bursting the old bonds and overrunning the old boundaries.

'Abdu'l-Bahá said, **"Revolutionary changes of unprecedented magnitude have been occurring in every department of human life."**
– Bahá'u'lláh and the New Era, p. 3.

Still, humanity has a myriad of ills and perils, brought on by a relatively few self-serving and parochial individuals and interests, which rely on man's persistent animal nature and self-preservation at all costs. [But the real reason is having turned away from God's instructions relevant to today's age. That's apparent by the decline of religion and our social institutions.]

We know most people are good, and that most people understand, [like] children, [that we] need education, food, shelter, and clothing—and love.

[The word of God provides those things.]

The Guardian of the Bahá'í Faith, Shoghi Effendi, said:

The immediate future, as clearly predicted by Him ['Abdu'l-Bahá],
  must necessarily be very dark for the Cause
  as well as for the whole world,
  but the promises He has repeatedly given us
  of a glorious future for the Faith and for mankind
as a whole
  are of such character as should assuredly sustain and strengthen us
  amidst the trials and tribulations of the days ahead.

– Unfolding Destiny, p. 437.

Would you like to help [make a better world]?

Look at yourself and your doings, and then look within.

Ask yourself: am I doing enough in my own inner life and private character to alleviate these ills where I find them; and am I working to effect change? Am I a source of joy, or misery?

Let me know what differences you are making.

#

Prosperous? Be Generous. Troubled? Be Thankful.

Culture

Be someone.
 If not for yourself, for your Mom or Dad, friend or mate, stranger or foe.
 Carry down the wash Saturday morning or pick up trash you usually step over in 7/Eleven's parking lot.
 Nod and say Hello to passersby on your city street instead of keeping eyes averted or start up a conversation on the elevator with strangers.
 Volunteer as dispute resolution mediator for municipal court, or sort books for the Friends of the Library.
 Teach a literacy class for zero remuneration, just for the joy of learning the craft.
 Be early for your job instead of late because you delayed getting out of bed, as usual.
 Give a dollar tip for a change instead of nothing for that two-dollar coffee.
 Don't just hold the door open for the old couple—wish them a blessed day.
 Smile back when the Walmart or Acme clerk says Good morning and say, "How's it goin'?" and listen to their answer or offer a cheery "Good morning" to them.
 Like the movie, pay the seventy-five-cent toll forward for the car behind you.
 Try, even for a while, to be your mindful self, lose any malice in your heart, and:

Be generous in prosperity, and thankful in adversity.
 Be worthy of the trust of thy neighbor, and look upon him with a bright and friendly face.
 Be a treasure to the poor, an admonisher to the rich, an answerer to the cry of the needy, a pre-server of the sanctity of thy pledge.
 Be fair in thy judgment, and guarded in thy speech.
 Be unjust to no man, and show all meekness to all men.
 Be as a lamp unto them that walk in darkness,
a joy to the sorrowful, a sea for the thirsty, a haven for the distressed, an upholder and defender of the victim of oppression.
 Let integrity and uprightness distinguish all thine acts.

Be a home for the stranger, a balm to the suffering, a tower of strength for the fugitive.

Be eyes to the blind, and a guiding light unto the feet of the erring.

Be an ornament to the countenance of truth, a crown to the brow of fidelity, a pillar of the temple of righteousness, a breath of life to the body of mankind, an ensign of the hosts of justice, a luminary above the horizon of virtue, a dew to the soil of the human heart, an ark on the ocean of knowledge, a sun in the heaven of bounty, a gem on the diadem of wisdom, a shining light in the firmament of thy generation, a fruit upon the tree of humility.

Entreat thou the one true God to sanctify the ears, and the eyes, and the hearts of mankind, and to protect them from the desires of a corrupt inclination. For malice is a grievous malady which depriveth man from recognizing the Great Being, and debarreth him from the splendors of the sun of certitude. We pray and hope that through the grace and mercy of God He may remove this mighty obstacle.

– Bahá'u'lláh, *Epistle to the Son of the Wolf*, pp. 93-95.

#

Woodrow Wilson: Racist or Peacemaker?

History PART 1 IN SERIES: **14 POINTS FOR WORLD PEACE**

Forty-four unique men have served as President of the United States.

History shows that U.S. Presidents have achieved many good things for Americans, some great, and some not so great. All were men. All were human. Each and every one made mistakes as we look back historically, yet, all were products of their times. Some helped change the times.

One President, Woodrow Wilson, is now being called racist for his views on equality. Eighteen [presidents] gone before may just as easily have been [labelled] racist also, based on their ownership of slaves. Shall we tear down all the monuments and change the names of thousands of buildings, streets and highways, towns and cities named after them? Should we erase their notable achievements in the name of hindsight? Can we "read back" into history, and try to correct it ex post facto?

Does pointing out their flaws—which were many, as in most people—have any beneficial effect or alter what we [still] consider as great [in them, or their achievements]? Or should we consider their positive attributes and accomplishments [as the contributions they were]?

As a world leader, we should recognize President Wilson's groundbreaking attempt to establish a definitive league of nations that would address and adjudicate world problems. In this short series of essays, we'll focus on that aspect of President Wilson's life's work.

Sketch of President Woodrow Wilson

Let's start with a few excerpts from the soon-to-be-published biography of Woodrow Wilson by Michael P. Riccards. Mike has authored 25 books, including *The Ten Greatest U.S. Presidents*. A past college president three times over, Mike is also a close friend, a writing partner, and an independent observer and chronicler of history. With his permission, some of his observations on Woodrow Wilson:

"Great men or women are often described as complicated, and especially we seek to understand the threads of their early being. In his brief life span no public personality so captivated the people of America and the world in general as Woodrow Wilson. Over a century later we still feel the pull of his influence. Historians do not agree whether he was a great president or a disaster; few stake out an intelligent middle ground. All admit that he was one of the most successful domestic policy presidents only rivaled by FDR, his protégé, and Lyndon Johnson, FDR's protégé.

After being elected in 1912, Wilson hated almost clinically that… he had to spend most of his time on foreign affairs. He saw himself as a domestic reformer. But ironic it was as his term in office is most remembered by history for the Great War and the difficulties of the Treaty of Versailles, and finally America's repudiation of the League of Nations.

The trigger for war was the 28 June 1914 assassination of Archduke Franz Ferdinand of Austria, heir to the throne of Austria-Hungary, by Yugoslav nationalist Gavrilo Princip in

Sarajevo. This set off a diplomatic crisis.... Within weeks, the major powers were at war and the conflict soon spread around the world.

Diplomatically Wilson argued in May 1916 for a postwar League of Peace to uphold the rights of national sovereignty, territorial integrity, and freedom from aggression. Even TR [Theodore Roosevelt] and Taft had once supported a league and some of the more enlightened Europeans, including Pope Benedict XV, agreed. But the war leaders did not comment, preferring to fight in what each side saw as victory.

Once again, and for the last time, on December 18, 1916, the President offered again to mediate the war, and he would ask each side what it would take to terminate the war and promote future security. The Central Powers insisted that victory was certain; the Allies demanded that the enemy's empires be dismembered. Oddly enough the Second World War would be the beginning of the unraveling of empires of both European and Asian states."

The leader of that anti-colonial crusade would be a Wilson protégé—Franklin Delano Roosevelt.

In 1916, however, Wilson's peace offer went nowhere.

"The advisors to Wilson were called the "Inquiry" and headed up by a president of City College in New York City. The group provided the president with a series of objectives from Berlin to Baghdad with particular emphasis on the Slavic area.

It urged that America use its financial assets to prevail, a position that the president held.

...the Inquiry laid out a statement of peace terms, and focused on "territory, territory."

The report was released on December 23, 1917. The forces of Lenin in Russia on their own pushed for an end to forcible annexation of territory seized during the war, restoring independence, protecting minorities, safeguarding weaker nations against boycotts and blockade, and allowing national groups to determine their public future by referendum. Wilson would be impacted by those principals as well as by the Inquiry report. While the President was working on his own statement of objectives, the Fourteen Points, Prime Minister David Lloyd George was giving a speech in London supporting "self-determination," this from the guardian of the British Commonwealth."

Several days later Wilson appeared before Congress with his program of world peace. It is frequently cited in his time and in ours that Wilson was a total failure in getting his ideas accepted at the peace conference, the usual charges that Wilson sold out his principles for the establishment of a League of Nations.

But as we now know, **Wilson's Fourteen Point peace plan did not fail in the long term. Instead, it served as the basis for the Armistice and the Treaty of Versailles** [despite its reparations burdens], advancing international relations and serving as the formative document for the League of Nations, the first attempt at a world governing body that could enforce global peace. [Bold emphasis added]

Under the onslaught of the aggression of the Axis powers the League fell apart at the dawn of World War II, but then its founding international principles reasserted themselves in a new incarnation—the United Nations—at the close of that war in 1945. Wilson's Fourteen Points, which replicate Bahá'u'lláh's teachings in so many ways, still have an enormous influence on diplomacy and international relations today.

Bahá'ís believe that those lofty, essentially spiritual principles—global peace, disarmament, the rights of all and an end to colonial oppression—continued and expanded throughout the world because they represent the emerging spirit of the age.

First given to the world by Bahá'u'lláh in the middle of the previous century, Bahá'í principles call on humanity and its leaders to observe peace and justice, to disarm and to end all war. The Bahá'í writings praise President Wilson for his initial advocacy of those high aims:

The President of the Republic, Dr. Wilson, is indeed serving the Kingdom of God for he is restless and strives day and night that the rights of all men may be preserved safe and secure, that even small nations, like greater ones, may dwell in peace and comfort, under the protection of Righteousness and Justice. This purpose is indeed a lofty one. I trust that the incomparable Providence will assist and confirm such souls under all conditions.
– 'Abdu'l-Bahá, *Selections from the Writings of 'Abdu'l-Bahá*, p. 109.

Next: Wilson's Points: The Dawn of Universal Peace

#

Wilson's Points: The Dawn of Universal Peace

History PART 2 IN SERIES: | 14 POINTS FOR WORLD PEACE |

As to President Wilson, the fourteen principles which he hath enunciated are mostly found in the teachings of Bahá'u'lláh and I therefore hope that he will be confirmed and assisted. Now is the dawn of universal peace; my hope is that its morn will fully break, converting the gloom of war, of strife and of wrangling among men into the light of union, of harmony and of affection.
– 'Abdu'l-Bahá, *Selections from the Writings of 'Abdu'l-Bahá*, pp. 311-312.

President Woodrow Wilson's Fourteen Points formed a new political blueprint for world peace. He first elucidated them on January 8, 1918, in a speech on the aims of war and the terms of universal peace. In this essay, let's take a closer look at points one through five, the chiefly diplomatic terms Wilson proposed, and compare them to the Bahá'í teachings:

1. Open covenants of peace, openly arrived at, after which there shall be no private international understandings of any kind, but diplomacy shall proceed always frankly and in the public view.

Ahead of his time, Wilson advocated transparency in diplomatic efforts toward one goal: Peace.

So did the Bahá'í teachings:

...day by day strengthen the bond of love and amity to this end, — that they may become the sympathetic embodiment of one nation. — That they may extend themselves to a Universal Brotherhood to guard and protect the interests and rights of all the nations of the East, — that they may unfurl the Divine Banner of justice, — that they may treat each nation as a family composed of the individual children of God and may know that before the sight of God the rights of all are equal.
– "Abdu'l-Bahá, *"Abdu'l-Bahá in London*, p. 122.

In the second and third points, Wilson called for freedom of movement and trade around the globe:

2. Absolute freedom of navigation upon the seas, outside territorial waters, alike in peace and in war, except as the seas may be closed in whole or in part by international action for the enforcement of international covenants.

3. The removal, so far as possible, of all economic barriers and the establishment of an equality of trade conditions among all the nations consenting to the peace and associating themselves for its maintenance.

Freedom of the seas, vitally important in an age before regular air flights, highlighted the growing interdependence of all peoples on mutual trade, travel, and interchange. The Bahá'í teachings recognized that interdependence long before:

All the members of the human family, whether peoples or governments, cities or villages, have become increasingly interdependent. For none is self-sufficiency any longer possible in as much as political ties unite all peoples and nations, and the bonds of trade and industry, of agriculture and education, are being strengthened every day. Hence the unity of all mankind can in this day be achieved.
– Bahá'u'lláh, *Bahá'u'lláh and the New Era*, Dr. J. E. Esslemont, p. 249.

Next, Wilson proposed a deep reduction in armaments:

4. Adequate guarantees were given and taken that national armaments will be reduced to the lowest point consistent with domestic safety.

Bahá'u'lláh made this proposal more than half a century before, in his letters to the world's kings and rulers:

Tread ye the path of justice, for this, verily, is the straight path. Compose your differences, and reduce your armaments, that the burden of your expenditures may be lightened, and that your minds and hearts may be tranquilized. Heal the dissensions that divide you, and ye will no longer be in need of any armaments except what the protection of your cities and territories demandeth.
– *Gleanings from the Writings of Bahá'u'lláh*, p. 251.

In his fifth point, President Wilson made a valiant attempt to end the scourge of colonialism:

5. A free, open-minded, and absolutely impartial adjustment of all colonial claims, based upon a strict observance of the principle that in determining all such questions of sovereignty the interests of the populations concerned must have equal weight with the equitable claims of the government whose title is to be determined.

'Abdu'l-Bahá, who recognized the negative impact of colonization on prospects for international peace, also spoke out for the principle of self-determination and the extinction of the old colonial model:

First, the nations are rivals with each other so far as commercial advantages are concerned. Second, they are thinking of the national self-aggrandizement. Third, they are thinking of planting new colonies. Therefore, it is difficult for them to step into this field, to uphold international peace, because they are contending, warlike, victory-loving people. They cannot be instrumental in promulgating international peace.
– 'Abdu'l-Bahá, *Star of the West*, Volume 4, p. 167.

'Unity in freedom' has today, of course, become a universal aspiration of the Earth's inhabitants. Among the chief developments giving substance to it, He ['Abdu'l-Bahá] may well have had in mind the dramatic extinction of colonialism and the consequent rise of self-determination as a dominant feature of national identity at century's end.
– *Century of Light*, [as prepared under the supervision] of The Universal House of Justice.

Next, in Wilson's sixth through thirteenth points, he called for a final settlement of the territorial and border-dispute issues in Russia, Belgium, France, Alsace-Lorraine, Italy, Austro-Hungary, the Balkans, Poland and Turkey and the Ottoman Empire.

The Bahá'í teachings concur that borders and boundaries should be finally determined, and recommend what [someday will] become the basis for the eventual union of all nations in one great assemblage:

In this all-embracing Pact the limits and frontiers of each and every nation should be clearly fixed, the principles underlying the relations of governments towards one another definitely laid down, and all international agreements and obligations ascertained.

In like manner, the size of the armaments of every government should be strictly limited, for if the preparations for war and the military forces of any nation should be allowed to increase, they will arouse the suspicion of others.

The fundamental principle underlying this solemn Pact should be so fixed that if any government later violate any one of its provisions, all the governments on earth should arise to reduce it to utter submission, nay the human race as a whole should resolve, with every power at its disposal, to destroy that government.

Should this greatest of all remedies be applied to the sick body of the world, it will assuredly recover from its ills and will remain eternally safe and secure.

– 'Abdu'l-Bahá, *The Secret of Divine Civilization*, p. 64.

Next: The Fourteenth Point: How to Create a Peaceful World

#

The 14th Point: How to Create a Peaceful World

History PART 3 IN SERIES: 14 POINTS FOR WORLD PEACE

Verily, His Honour President Wilson is self-sacrificing in this path and is striving with heart and soul, with perfect good-will, in the world of humanity. Similarly the equitable government of Great Britain is expending a great deal of effort. Undoubtedly the general condition of the people and the state of small oppressed nationalities will not remain as before. Justice and Right shall be fortified but the establishment of Universal Peace will be realized fully through the power of the Word of God.
–Attributed to "Abdu'l-Bahá, *Star of the West*, Vol 5, p. 42-43.

The unity of the human race, as envisaged by Bahá'u'lláh, implies the establishment of a world commonwealth in which all nations, races, creeds and classes are closely and permanently united, and in which the autonomy of its state members and the personal freedom and initiative of the individuals that compose them are definitely and completely safeguarded.
– Shoghi Effendi, *The World Order of Bahá'u'lláh*, p. 203.

President Wilson's famous Fourteenth Point—
"A general association of nations must be formed under specific covenants for the purpose of affording mutual guarantees of political independence and territorial integrity to great and small states alike"—had a powerful impact on the world and continues to expand its influence today.

The idea of a general association of nations wasn't new— Immanuel Kant and other philosophers had dreamed and written about it for centuries. But it had not yet crystallized into a workable, feasible model until the Bahá'í teachings gave it direction, content, and force:

The Great Being, wishing to reveal the prerequisites of the peace and tranquillity of the world and the advancement of its peoples, hath written:
  The time must come when the imperative necessity for the holding of a vast, an all-embracing assemblage of men will be universally realized.

The rulers and kings of the earth must needs attend it, and, participating in its deliberations, must consider such ways and means as will lay the foundations of the world's Great Peace amongst men.

Such a peace demandeth that the Great Powers should resolve, for the sake of the tranquility of the peoples of the earth, to be fully reconciled among themselves.

Should any king take up arms against another, all should unitedly arise and prevent him. If this be done, the nations of the world will no longer require any armaments, except for the purpose of preserving the security of their realms and of maintaining internal order within their territories. This will ensure the peace and composure of every people, government and nation.

– Bahá'u'lláh, *Gleanings from the Writings of Bahá'u'lláh*, p. 248.

Bahá'u'lláh [made an early] call for a world convocation of leaders to establish global peace. Wilson had a strong advocacy of the general idea six decades later. [Based on many factors] the Great Powers and a few dozen other nations succeeded in creating the first international organization with the principal mission of establishing and maintaining world peace.

The League of Nations formed on 10 January 1920, at the Paris Peace Conference, which ended the First World War. Its Covenant attempted to prevent future wars by a mechanism of agreed-upon collective security and disarmament. It promised to prevent wars through international cooperation and negotiation.

Could it work?

It might surprise you to learn that 'Abdu'l-Bahá said no:

For example, the questions of Universal Peace, about which His Holiness Bahá'u'lláh says that the Supreme Tribunal must be established: although the League of Nations has been brought into existence, yet it is incapable of establishing Universal Peace.

But the Supreme Tribunal which His Holiness Bahá'u'lláh has described will fulfil this sacred task with the utmost might and power.

And His plan is this: that the national assemblies of each country and nation — that is to say parliaments — should elect two or three persons who are the choicest men of that nation, and are well informed concerning international laws and the relations between govern-

ments and aware of the essential needs of the world of humanity of this day.

The number of these representatives should be in proportion to the number of inhabitants of that country. The election of these souls who are chosen by the national assembly, that is, the parliament, must be confirmed by the upper house, the congress and the cabinet and also by the president or monarch so these persons may be the elected ones of all the nation and the government.

From among these people the members of the Supreme Tribunal will be elected, and all mankind will thus have a share therein, for every one of these delegates is fully representative of his nation. When the Supreme Tribunal gives a ruling on any international question, either unanimously or by majority-rule, there will no longer be any pretext for the plaintiff or ground of objection for the defendant.

In case any of the governments or nations in the execution of the irrefutable decision of the Supreme Tribunal, be negligent or dilatory, the rest of the nations will rise up against it, because all the governments and nations of the world are the supporters of this Supreme Tribunal.

Consider what a firm foundation this is! But by a limited and restricted League the purpose will not be realized as it ought and should. This is the truth about the situation, which has been stated.

– 'Abdu'l-Bahá, *Tablet to the Hague*, pp. 10-11.

Of course, 'Abdu'l-Bahá's view proved uncannily accurate. With only 58 nations as members at its peak, the League never exerted much influence, and lasted only a few decades.

Instead of a chiefly unilateral agreement imposed by a group of victorious nations on the vanquished, the Bahá'í teachings recommend a much more democratic solution—the creation of a globally-elected world parliament. Until that can happen, the Bahá'í teachings say, humanity will keep operating under the old, outmoded, inefficient and inherently warlike system of competing national sovereignties.

But without question, we continue to move toward a global system of governance that will, [for the last time,] eliminate devastating warfare and its enormous costs to humanity.

The question is: How will our own individual and collective endeavors promote that powerful goal?

#

How To Recognize the Truth

Spirituality

Did you watch the sunrise this morning?

The Sun of Reality is one Sun but it has different dawning-places, just as the phenomenal sun is one although it appears at various points of the horizon. During the time of spring the luminary of the physical world rises far to the north of the equinoctial; in summer it dawns midway and in winter it appears in the most southerly point of its zodiacal journey.

These day springs or dawning-points differ widely but the sun is ever the same sun whether it be the phenomenal or spiritual luminary.

Souls who focus their vision upon the Sun of Reality will be the recipients of light no matter from what point it rises, but those who are fettered by adoration of the dawning-point are deprived when it appears in a different station upon the spiritual horizon.
–Attributed to "Abdu'l-Bahá in *Bahá'í World Faith*, p. 255.

In this quotation 'Abdu'l-Bahá gives us a parable, a beautiful analogy of the appearance of the Divine Revelations to the physical Sun.

I'm an early riser, and have watched many stunning sunrises, breathtaking in fact, a miracle of existence. The yellows, reds, oranges, and purples; the effect of glinting off innumerable versions of cloud cover, white, dark, or gray and their shadows, all create a unique sunrise for my eyes every morning. In my view, nothing holds more absolute truth than a glorious sunrise.

Of course, every morning we see the same physical sun [as it] rises, the only one [providing] humanity with light and heat. It rises from a slightly different "dawning place" on the eastern horizon every day. We watch the sunrise, but we all know the sun doesn't really "rise," since it remains stationary. Instead, the Earth's surface rotates into its beams, and the Earth's orbit gives us the slight variation in each successive morning's dawn.

Western civilization generally credits the ancient Greek astronomer Aristarchus of Samos [310-23 B.C.] as the first person to figure that out, and to propose a Sun-centered astronomical hypothesis of the universe. At that time, however, Aristarchus's heliocentrism gained few supporters, and eighteen centuries would pass before Renaissance astronomer Nicolaus Copernicus produced a mathematical model of a heliocentric system.

Here we have classic scientific investigation of truth—or rather, reality, if you consider both to mean the same thing. It may be said that "truth" often refers to abstract rather than concrete thinking, and it can be said that "reality" deals more with concrete rather than abstract. A "mathematical model" based on observable fact [is both.]

The point the Bahá'í teachings make here? Different versions of the same truths exist, as well as the terms used to describe that truth, or reality—but the truth itself is one.

The truth is one, but our accepted concepts or beliefs change, because our viewpoint changes. We are after all fallible, imperfect humans, not gifted with perfect understanding and knowledge at any moment on any particular subject.

In other words, we make our smartest guess about truth and reality, and then direct our lives on that basis.

That's as it should be, because [our human understanding of] truth, no matter what form or reality it takes, always changes and evolves.

The insights of philosophers and scientists have shown us the changing nature of reality for ages. You and I discover or change truth and reality every moment of every day, primarily through [new] experiences and knowledges [learned].

So how do we recognize the truth? The Bahá'í teachings recommend investigating the truth for yourself and coming to your own conclusions.

God has given man the eye of investigation by which he may see and recognize truth. He has endowed man with ears that he may hear the message of reality and conferred upon him the gift of reason by which he may discover things for himself [and herself]:

This is his endowment and equipment for the investigation of reality. Man is not intended to see through the eyes of another, hear through another's ears nor comprehend with another's brain. Each human creature has individual endowment, power and responsibility in the creative plan of God.
Therefore depend upon your own reason and judgment and adhere to the outcome of your own investigation; otherwise you will be utterly submerged in the sea of ignorance and deprived of all the bounties of God. Turn to God, supplicate humbly at His threshold, seeking assistance and confirmation, that God may rend asunder the veils that obscure your vision. Then will your eyes be filled with illumination, face to face you will behold the reality of God and your heart become completely purified from the dross of ignorance, reflecting the glories and bounties of the Kingdom.
– 'Abdu'l-Bahá, *Foundations of World Unity*, p. 75.

Let me end this with a question for you: By what yardstick of truth do you judge reality?

#

Christians Should Thank Muslims

Religion

Christians owe a debt of gratitude to Muslims.

Why? Because Islam has done so much to bring belief in Christ to so many people.

I am not being facetious here, nor inflammatory. There is great historical and religious context for this sentiment.

After Muhammad died in 632 A.D.—or more correctly CE, the Common Era—a series of four Caliphs governed the new Islamic state: Abu Bakr (632-634), Umar ibn al-Khattab (Umar I, 634-644), Uthman ibn Affan (644-656), and Ali ibn Abi Talib (656-661).

These leaders are known as the "rightly guided" Caliphs in Sunni Islam. They oversaw the initial phase of the spread of Islam, advancing the new religion through the Arabian Peninsula and Persia, the eastern Mediterranean and many islands, to Egypt and North Africa by the beginning of the 8th century.

Today in European countries, Muslims number between 3 and 13% of any given country's population. In Spain today, two percent of the populace is Muslim, but at the height of early Islamic expansions into Iberia by 713, the area was entirely under Muslim control.

While the world's population is projected to grow 35% in the coming decades, the number of Muslims is expected to increase by 73 percent—from 1.6 billion in 2010 to 2.8 billion in 2050.

At this same time in early Islam's spread, Christianity had already been established throughout most of Europe and the edges of the Mediterranean well into present-day Turkey. Christ's teachings even reached the edges of China by 618 CE. According to the Pew Research Foundation:

As of 2010, Christianity was by far the world's largest religion, with an estimated 2.2 billion adherents, nearly a third (31 percent) of all 6.9 billion people on Earth. Islam was second, with 1.6 billion adherents, or 23 percent of the global population.

In 2015, Islam overtook Christianity as the world's [fastest growing] religion.

But it's not a race, and [many] people realize there is, after all, only one religion, [in one sense,] the religion of one God.

Differing names and practices relevant to the age in which the great Faiths originally appeared [only seem to make it different gods].

The Bahá'í teachings embrace [the] unity and one-ness [of one God across all faiths]:

The fundamental principle enunciated by Bahá'u'lláh... is that religious truth is not absolute but relative, that Divine Revelation is a continuous and progressive process, that all the great religions of the world are divine in origin, that their basic principles are in complete harmony, that their aims and purposes are one and the same, that their teachings are but facets of one truth, that their functions are complementary, that they differ only in the nonessential aspects of their doctrines, and that their missions represent successive stages in the spiritual evolution of human society....
– Shoghi Effendi, *The Promised Day is Come*, p. v.

In other words, I have one name, Rodney, but I wear different hats when needed: father, husband, employee, volunteer etc. No matter which hat I wear, even the title "Catholic" as I grew up, makes me no less a believer in one God, universal and indivisible, with a unified message for all humanity.

That message is simply to love and cooperate with each other. Christ taught it, and so did Muhammad.

We are forbidden to harm or kill each other.

"Thou shalt not kill [/murder]," is a mighty Commandment.

"Love thy neighbor as thyself," the Golden Rule, is common to all religions.

So [over 1.6 billion] Muslims have performed a great service [to Christianity] in the name of the prophet Muhammad, [even though specific beliefs differ].

Following his words in the Qur'an, Muslims absolutely believe in the divinity and holiness of Jesus Christ. The story of Christ's birth recited in the Qur'an is moving and wondrous. In fact, Christ is mentioned in 93 of the Qur'an's verses [called surihs].

Bloodsheds and hatreds, even age-old vendettas will cease when we realize for our own good and our continued life on this planet, that religion was meant to be the source of amity and concord:

All the teaching of the Prophets is one; one faith; one Divine light shining throughout the world. Now, under the banner of the oneness of humanity all people of all creeds should turn away from prejudice and become friends and believers in all the Prophets.

As Christians believe in Moses, so the Jews should believe in Jesus. As the Muhammadans believe in Christ and Moses, so likewise the Jews and the Christians should believe in Muhammad.

Then all disputes would disappear, all then would be united. Bahá'u'lláh came for this purpose. He has made the three religions one. He has uplifted the standard of the oneness of faith and the honour of humanity in the centre of the world.

Today we must gather round it, and try with heart and soul to bring about the union of mankind.

– 'Abdu'l-Bahá, *'Abdu'l-Bahá in London*, p. 43.

#

What Religion Are You?

Religion

We all need services and products. Needs and wants, wants to needs. Listening to my favorite local radio station this morning, I realized that I have seen and heard many millions of commercials selling everything from acne cleansers to zylophones, or tax aid from accountants to Zippity-Do-Da Cleaning during my lifetime. I've learned to listen carefully and look for good and honest value for my hard-earned dollars, and it took me years to understand that reliability and quality should be my first purchasing considerations.

So, we know what we want—the best value—but how do we distinguish which product or service gives it from the constant barrage of hype?

Really, most importantly, the buying decision comes down to two choices: impulse and convenience if you don't care too much, or belief [and conviction] based on some knowledge or experience. "Brand Loyalty," the marketers call it, that all-too-human tendency to stick with what's familiar, reliable, and comfortable. Once you buy a product or service, and it performs relatively well, you tend to remain loyal and continue down that same path.

But what about brand loyalty when "choosing" a religion?

Frankly, most of us don't "choose" our religion. Instead, we grow up in the practices and traditions and cultural interpretations of one religion or another, or of no religion. **Very few of us actively set out on a quest to choose our religion.** [Bold emphasis added] Strangely, while we compare products and services, we rarely compare belief systems.

Our religion—our deepest, most closely-held inner convictions—[is mainly] chosen for us, by our heritage or our parents or our culture. That's brand loyalty to the extreme, even to the extreme of hating or despising those who don't agree with us, or worse actually [murdering] in religion's name, as we've seen throughout history and now highly practiced by Islam's hijackers.

In this case, as I hit "like" this morning on Facebook, I agreed with the meme "If religion means hating and killing, it's better there be no religion."

I first heard this at age 22 when I read:

Religion should unite all hearts and cause wars and disputes to vanish from the face of the earth; it should give birth to spirituality, and bring light and life to every soul.

If religion becomes a cause of dislike, hatred and division it would be better to be without it, and to withdraw from such a religion would be a truly religious act.

For it is clear that the purpose of a remedy is to cure, but if the remedy only aggravates the complaint, it had better be left alone.

Any religion which is not a cause of love and unity is no religion.
– 'Abdu'l-Bahá, *Paris Talks*, p. 132.

If you're lucky, you get to choose the food you eat, where you sleep, what you drink, where you work, what you buy, what you drive, your date or mate, to have children or adopt. You even get to choose the radio station you listen to.

Can you say you've also chosen your religion?

Or has your religion chosen you?

#

Act Locally, But Think Big

Culture

I'm sure you're familiar with the still-popular bumper sticker advice: "Think Globally, Act Locally."

You may consider it a child of the '60s consciousness, along with "ecology" and black power, but the maxim is much older than you might imagine. In fact, it was the brainchild of Patrick Geddes, a 1915 town planner and social activist.

But long before Geddes and others forged their global consciousness, the Bahá'í prophet Bahá'u'lláh wrote, "**Let your vision be world-embracing, rather than confined to your own self.**"
– *Tablets of Bahá'u'lláh*, p. 87.

For thousands of years we have left the world-embracing "think globally" part of the equation up to others—the thinkers, philosophers, statesmen and world leaders. Most of us on Earth have chiefly concerned ourselves with our own town, state, and nation. In these modern times an argument could be made that big corporations think more globally than many world leaders.

So much has our attention focused on solely local issues, that it's only relatively recently that modern magazines and news sources have covered world events to a similar extent, like *The Week* and *The Economist,* providing alternative views across the globe. Today thousands of magazines, TV stations, and newspapers disseminate world news, although national issues dominate. In fact, newspapers have cut back drastically on local news and photos.

So, we find ourselves in an age of world problems affecting local, state, and national policies and politics, with huge implications for the welfare of ordinary citizens everywhere. Besides natural disasters affecting tens of thousands, civil wars displacing millions as refugees, and global poverty and lack of jobs affecting billions, now climate change affects everyone on the planet.

At times we feel like throwing up our hands and failing to get involved out of frustration or despair. Of course, that's exactly why these problems become intractable and grow steadily worse – because enough of us do not actively involve ourselves in finding and implementing global solutions. We focus solely on the local and forget the big picture.

Of course, it's easy to get confused about where to apply one's limited resources to effect change. With over one million charitable organizations in the U.S. alone, who do I help?

How can I add my voice in the most effective way?

They all have good purposes, don't they?

What can I do that will actually help the world, my country, my town, my own family?

The Bahá'í teachings ask us to focus our efforts on the betterment of the entire world:

All men have been called into being for the betterment of the world. It behoveth every soul to arise and serve his brethren for the sake of God.
– Bahá'u'lláh, *Tabernacle of Unity*, p. 5.

...if the man of moral integrity and intellectual acumen shall unite for human betterment and uplift with the man of spiritual capacity, the happiness and progress of the human race will be assured.
– 'Abdu'l-Bahá, *The Promulgation of Universal Peace*, p. 102.

O people of God! Do not busy yourselves in your own concerns; let your thoughts be fixed upon that which will rehabilitate the fortunes of mankind and sanctify the hearts and souls of men. This can best be achieved through pure and holy deeds, through a virtuous life and a goodly behaviour.
– Bahá'u'lláh, *Tablets of Bahá'u'lláh*, p. 86.

We all admire honesty, integrity, forthrightness, fairness, and equanimity in our leaders.

We can do no less in examining our own motives and purposes when we want to help ourselves and society.

Whether that means supporting a worthy charity or one or more just causes, or helping clean up our local parks and playgrounds, or serving in volunteer or paid positions for our local or state government, or merely performing honest work and providing for our families, we all have the power to do something that will help.

That local action and activism, however, can best help the entire world when it focuses on building a unified, harmonious humanity.

The Bahá'í teachings ask each of us to act locally, but also to think big, considering ourselves citizens of one world working toward a unified future.

#

[**Author's update:** This article was not meant to imply that people should only work alone and not also work in groups or organizations to promote social good and social change. For example, Bahá'ís are actively engaged on local, regional, national and global levels in diverse programs that promote unity, cooperation, understanding, education and so on. Bahá'ís serve in a multitude of organizations, and actively participate in their home communities by volunteering. Bahá'ís are also building up a Bahá'í social and administrative order in their communities as outlined in the Bahá'í Writings. All such efforts are transformative and regenerative both individually and collectively and are aimed at effecting positive change amidst all levels of society.]

#

Why Do Prophets Suffer?

Religion

God sent all His Prophets into the world with one aim, to sow in the hearts of men love and goodwill, and for this great purpose they were willing to suffer and to die. All the sacred Books were written to lead and direct man into the ways of love and unity; and yet, in spite of all this, we have the sad spectacle of war and bloodshed in our midst.

When we look into the pages of history, past and present, we see the black earth reddened by human blood. Men kill each other like the savage wolves, and forget the laws of love and tolerance.

…only if material progress goes hand in hand with spirituality can any real progress come about, and the Most Great Peace reign in the world. If men followed the Holy Counsels and the Teachings of the Prophets, if Divine Light shone in all hearts and men were really religious, we should soon see peace on earth and the Kingdom of God among men.
– 'Abdu'l-Bahá, *Paris Talks*, pp. 107-108.

Why does humanity treat its prophets so harshly?

Whenever a prophet of God appears, we persecute, torture, exile or execute him.

History has proven that pattern [repeatedly.] The major prophets of God—Buddha, Krishna, Zoroaster, Moses, Christ, Muhammad, the Báb and now Bahá'u'lláh—all suffered tremendously when they tried to bring their message of love, peace and unity to the world.

They were persecuted by their own people, their neighbors, even the clergy of the faiths whose prophecies they came to fulfill.

Bahá'u'lláh's mission, as just the latest example, was prescribed and definite: to unify humanity and bring an end to war. Bahá'u'lláh suffered enormously as he worked toward that mission, as did his early followers and martyrs, as do the innocent Bahá'ís in Iranian prisons today for their religious beliefs.

Why? Bahá'u'lláh addressed that question this way:

We have accepted to be tried by ills and troubles, that ye may sanctify yourselves from all earthly defilements. Why, then, refuse ye to ponder Our purpose in your hearts?

By the righteousness of God! Whoso will reflect upon the tribulations We have suffered, his soul will assuredly melt away with sorrow. Thy Lord Himself beareth witness to the truth of My words. We have sustained the weight of all calamities to sanctify you from all earthly corruption, and ye are yet indifferent.
– *Gleanings from the Writings of Bahá'u'lláh*, p. 307.

Why do people cause such great suffering to the hearts and souls of these divine Gems of Holiness?

Bahá'u'lláh [states]:

Consider the past.

How many, both high and low, have, at all times, yearningly awaited the advent of the Manifestations of God in the sanctified persons of His chosen Ones.

How often have they expected His coming, how frequently have they prayed that the breeze of Divine mercy might blow, and the promised Beauty step forth from behind the veil of concealment, and be made manifest to all the world.

And whensoever the portals of grace did open, and the clouds of divine bounty did rain upon mankind, and the light of the Unseen did shine above the horizon of celestial might, they all denied Him, and turned away from His face — the face of God Himself....
– Bahá'u'lláh, *Gleanings from the Writings of Bahá'u'lláh*, p. 17.

And then [He] answers it this way:

Consequently, such behavior can be attributed to naught save the petty-mindedness of such souls as tread the valley of arrogance and pride, are lost in the wilds of remoteness, walk in the ways of their idle fancy, and follow the dictates of the leaders of their faith. Their chief concern is mere opposition; their sole desire is to ignore the truth.

Unto every discerning observer it is evident and manifest that had these people in the days of each of the Manifestations of the Sun of Truth sanctified their eyes, their ears, and their hearts from whatever they had seen, heard, and felt, they surely would not have been deprived of beholding the beauty of God, nor strayed far from the habitations of glory.

But having weighed the testimony of God by the standard of their own knowledge, gleaned from the teachings of the leaders of their faith, and found it at variance with their limited understanding, they arose to perpetrate such unseemly acts....
– Ibid., pp. 18-19.

#

How Hard Is It, Really, To Be Kind?

Teachings

How hard is it, really, to be kind?

This has been my wife's rhetorical question/advice to me since we married 44 years ago. Luckily, thanks to her kindness, our "niceness" has been imparted to both our children in spades.

My wife's emphasis on niceness and kindness to others reminds me that every human being has a story to tell. Sometimes they are stories of pain, injustice, deceit, or crime, but often, once we open our ears we hear stories very akin to our own happier experiences.

Every day has 24 hours. Many people use most of those hours for themselves, but one way to use time well is to show kindness to others. The truth is, many of us are torn between spending time only on our own selves, and service to others, such as our children and families, our jobs, and organizations. Using time efficiently and effectively is a balancing act, especially when you have six errands to run and only one hour to get them finished. So, we rush, rush, rush, barely pausing and rarely stopping for the brilliant rainbow after a rain or a kind word to a stranger.

Being kind takes practice, time, and discipline until it is ingrained, unless you are fortunate enough to be one of those naturally pleasant people, happy under all conditions. For myself, I [must] work at it. Being kind entails learning courtesy, niceness, thankfulness, appreciation, and faith; and then applying those qualities with everyone you meet.

From day one, new Bahá'ís learn that service to humanity brings joy and happiness.

To me, service involves asking, "How can I show kindness in this situation?" whether removing a blown trash can from the middle of the road, or opening a door for someone else, or giving a smile and greeting of "Hello! How ya doin' today?"

After a while, with practice, kindness becomes second nature.

Most, and I mean 99%, of all people I have ever met, have been kind. I've travelled extensively, and no matter where I go people have always extended themselves and been helpful when asked. Most of us are willing to help others, but true kindness means helping before being asked.

True kindness involves seeing our humanity in others automatically, rather than seeing fear or foreignness:

When a man turns his face to God he finds sunshine everywhere. All men are his brothers. Let not conventionality cause you to seem cold and unsympathetic when you meet strange people from other countries. Do not look at them as though you suspected them of being evil-doers, thieves and boors. You think it necessary to be very careful, not to expose yourselves to the risk of making acquaintance with such, possibly, undesirable people.

I ask you not to think only of yourselves. Be kind to the strangers, whether come they from Turkey, Japan, Persia, Russia, China or any other country in the world.

Help to make them feel at home; find out where they are staying, ask if you may render them any service; try to make their lives a little happier.

In this way, even if, sometimes, what you at first suspected should be true, still go out of your way to be kind to them — this kindness will help them to become better.

After all, why should any foreign people be treated as strangers?

Let those who meet you know, without your proclaiming the fact, that you are indeed a Bahá'í.
– 'Abdu'l-Bahá, *Paris Talks*, p. 15.

This sentiment is even more necessary today, when "getting to know someone" may only be a few scraps of conversation in the supermarket aisle or a quick interaction on the street. Even in those short encounters, kindness can improve everyone's day. Evincing kindness can help alleviate the pain of poverty, war, injustice, depression, economic woes, crime, and other ills. It can, as 'Abdu'l-Bahá suggests, make us all better people.

If you practice kindness, I promise you, you'll find that it's much easier, more fun, and [more] interesting to be nice than it is to be a hardcase.

What's your experience been?

#

Religion in Film: Making A Leap of Faith

Arts PART 1 IN SERIES: WATCHING MOVIES ABOUT GOD

All the Prophets are lights, they only differ in degree; they shine like brilliant heavenly bodies, each have their appointed place and time of ascension. Some are like lamps, some like the moon, some like distant stars, and a few are like the sun, shining from one end of the earth to the other. All have the same Light to give, yet they are different in degree.
– 'Abdu'l-Bahá, *'Abdu'l-Bahá in London*, pp. 62-63.

On this Earth, our life-giving lamp has always been the fixed star we call the Sun. Another Sun also appears in the midst of creation: The Sun of Truth, or the Prophet of God:

The spiritual cycles of the Sun of Truth, like the cycles of the physical sun: are in a state of perpetual motion and renewal. The Sun of Truth can be likened to the material sun, which rises from many different points.

One day it rises from the sign of Cancer and another day from the sign of Libra... Yet the sun is but one sun and one single reality.

The possessors of true knowledge are lovers of the sun and are not attached to its dawning points. Those who are endued with insight are seekers of the truth itself, not of its exponents and manifestations. Thus they bow in adoration before the sun, from whatever sign and above whatever horizon it may appear, and seek the truth from any sanctified soul who might reveal it...

Thus the Sun of Truth at one time shed its rays from the sign of Abraham; later it dawned above the sign of Moses and illumined the horizon; and later still it shone forth with the utmost power, heat and radiance from the sign of Christ.

Those who were searching after truth worshipped it wherever they saw it, but those who were attached to Abraham, when once that Sun cast its rays upon Sinai and illumined the reality of Moses, were deprived thereof. And those who clung to Moses, when once the Sun of Truth shed its heavenly splendour in the fullness of its radiance from the point of Christ, were likewise veiled, and so forth.
– 'Abdu'l-Bahá, *Some Answered Questions*, revised edition, pp. 86-87.

I'm on my way to our local movie theatre to see *The Young Messiah,* which some critics have panned as "dull." It's sharing billing with a more dramatic version of Christ's life: *Risen*, Kevin Reynolds' Resurrection-as-mystery flick. In all, there have been so many Christ-related movies since the first one in 1903, that I can't count them all.

The films about Christ that I've seen, [basically] the same story or variants about the Apostles and others, have pretty much stayed with me. For the life and behavior and words of Christ are spirit-thrilling and mysterious in the extreme. How could one personage have such a massive influence on the people of the world since his days as a messenger of God?

We associate Christ's life and death with A.D. 33, the year he was crucified so unjustly. In fact, A.D., Anno Domini, means the Year of Our Lord and is the basis for the calendar we use today as modified by Pope Gregory XIII, who introduced it in October of 1582. Even that calendar was a modification of the one instituted by the Romans, specifically by Julius Caesar, in 45 B.C.

Ah, but I digress. Back to religious movies. At the age of 11, I saw blue-eyed, long blond shiny-haired Jeffrey Hunter play Jesus on the big screen in Technicolor. Or was it widescreen Panavision? Either way it confirmed all I had [learned] as a Catholic boy growing up in Sacred Heart Church and Elementary School. Catechism and bible stories every day, in one form or another, were drilled into my young memory.

All sunk into my spirit, if not into my Christian behavior.

That "mysterious spirit" portrayed in the innumerable Christian movies and books I've seen and read, didn't reveal itself to me until I was 19 years old. As I listened to *Street Fighting Man* by the Rolling Stones rockin' in one ear, a young man I had just met, an artist and pure soul named Ted, mentioned the Bahá'í Faith to me for the first time. He answered my rush of questions in my other ear.

That moment kick-started the next phase of my spiritual journey. I began to see the next movie series of faith, so to speak, or the sun rising from a new point on the horizon. I recognized the same light I'd followed and worshipped in Christianity, dawning from a new place and time.

And I had just begun my giant leap.

What religious movies affected you, and what leaps of faith have you made?

Next: Looking for the Lord—at the Cinema
#

Looking for the Lord — at the Cinema

Arts PART 2 IN SERIES: WATCHING MOVIES ABOUT GOD

I love watching films about religion and spirituality.

When I went to see *The Young Messiah* recently, the theatre only held 12 adults out of its 120 seats, including myself and my movie buddy Richie. It was a far cry from the packed houses for action thrillers with car chases and shoot-em-ups, or the sci-fi flicks with the word "Star" in their titles. That's a pity, because films about religion and spirituality can really open your mind and heart to the reality of how humans initially treated the great founders of Faith. They can even deepen your own experience of the spiritual.

For example: *The Young Messiah* tells a bible-based but fictional account of the young Son of God, and the dangers Jesus and his family faced from the clergy, political leaders and Roman centurions. The trials and tribulations faced by all the prophets of God from time immemorial would have crushed mortal men:

God has sent all His messengers and Prophets to establish love amongst humanity.
All the Heavenly Books are written for the sake of Love.
All the prophets have borne trials and martyrdoms in order that Love may become established in the hearts of the children of God. The wise men and philosophers of every age have suffered and endured so that this Love might become reality.
–Attributed to "Abdu'l-Bahá, *Star of the West*, Vol 3, pp. 88-89.

Just so in this young Christ at the turn into the first millennium. Displays of his godly powers caused fear; fear that they were the devil's work. The film shows us an innocent young boy of six, hunted from birth by an order to kill from the maniacal King Herod, grappling with all the natural questions every child has about their being and purpose.

Even though we know Christ's ultimate purpose—personal salvation, exhibited through his later example, teachings, death and resurrection—this young actor was mesmerizing in his genuineness and that of his holy parents, as well.

The dialogue and scenes are all appropriate and impactful, moving this gripping story along to Jesus' discovery and imminent death at age seven in the courtyard of the Temple. Most importantly, the last scene where we hear the young prophet run and shout for life creates the perfect climax. If you think of yourself as spiritual in any way, you'll want to see this movie. If it's not showing near you, and you can't find it on Netflix or elsewhere, pick up a copy of Anne Rice's 2005 novel *Christ the Lord: Out of Egypt*, the basis for the film.

All this brings me to the major spate of religious films during these past few years. Did you experience 2014's *Exodus: Gods and Kings* starring the incomparable Christian Bale as Moses and the dynamic Joel Edgerton as the unforgettable Rameses II? This epic film—which shows us the Seven Plagues, the flight from Egypt by the Jews, and the parting of the Red Sea—presents a Moses few have ever experienced before. I rooted for his humanity throughout, and I came away understanding a little more about how badly humanity has treated the prophets of God.

Exodus: Gods and Kings tells the story of a prophet looking for peace, security and well-being—[first for himself, later for His people]--what we all wish for in a war-free world someday.

Exodus and many other films about God's messengers make it clear—just like the Bahá'í teachings do—that we won't get there without God in our lives and behaviors:

[Bahá'u'lláh wrote:] **The well-being of mankind, its peace and security, are unattainable unless and until its unity is firmly established.**

This unity can never be achieved so long as the counsels which the Pen of the Most High hath revealed are suffered to pass unheeded.
--*Gleanings*, p. 286.

My recommendations for spiritual films wouldn't be complete without including the serious, historical look at Muhammad titled *The Message,* starring Anthony Quinn as his defender Hamzah. That movie—originally titled *Muhammad: Messenger of God* (not to be confused with the new 2015 film)—transformed my view of Islam.

Someday I'll publish my book of religious movie reviews. But until then, the point I'm trying to make is that movies about the prophets of God can be wonderful, emotionally moving and convincing stories of religion in real life.

All in all, these kinds of films do one thing for me: help me [develop] my relationship to God, whatever be His name, and in whatever reality He shows Himself.

#

[**Author's update:** The list of icons, statues, paintings and films depicting the would-be Manifestation of God is long indeed. Incalculable. It is one measure of their impact on humanity. Nonetheless, accurate depictions of these holy personages appearances or features are impossible given the shadows of history and time. What is important is not Their looks, but Their stories.

Although the Bahá'ís possess a painting(s) and passport photograph of Bahá'u'lláh, their display is reserved for special circumstances only as a sign of respect, and then, only under special conditions.

To view them is currently a privilege reserved for Bahá'ís.]

#

How Does Wealth Get Us to Peace?

Culture

What does anyone really want, but to live in peace and security?

So how do we get there? The principled views of Bahá'ís, for their well-known solutions to solving the world's problems, rest on this fundamental answer: by recognizing the unity of humanity:

Two points bear emphasizing in all these issues [affecting the unification of mankind].

One is that the abolition of war is not simply a matter of signing treaties and protocols; it is a complex task requiring a new level of commitment to resolving issues not customarily associated with the pursuit of peace. Based on political agreements alone, the idea of collective security is a chimera.

The other point is that the primary challenge in dealing with issues of peace is to raise the context to the level of principle, as distinct from pure pragmatism. For, in essence, peace stems from an inner state supported by a spiritual or moral attitude, and it is chiefly in evoking this attitude that the possibility of enduring solutions can be found.

– The Universal House of Justice, *The Promise of World Peace*, p. 9.

The major path to peace—security brought about by the Rule of Law—starts with a moral code in the individual and extends outward. It also requires, oddly enough, a measure of wealth.

No sane person wants to put up with corruption, crime, terrorism and other evils if they ever hope to feel secure. So, on the surface it's easy to say that the vast majority of human beings want peace and security for themselves, their families, their cities and towns and their nations.

But in today's world, peace and security come with high price tags, and we can debate how much is enough and how much is too much.

Suffice it to say that we all want—and are generally willing to pay for—peace and security. Sadly, the wealthy typically have peace and security, while the poor often don't.

We all want peace and security, together with a solid work ethic, a good paying job, a suitable dwelling, food and drink, and healthcare. Those things all require wealth—not only personal wealth, but a reasonably wealthy and successful society, like most of the developed nations of the world.

"With wealth comes great responsibility," said Bill Gates. And of all the people to say it, he was the perfect choice. His Bill & Melinda Gates Foundation parses out enormous wealth for good causes to millions.

The Gates Foundation is the largest private foundation in the world

Of all the things I might personally wish for myself, and you, and every single person on Earth, it's wealth. We all need sufficient wealth to provide for our needs, and to keep our civilizations peaceful and secure. Our societies all need a modicum of wealth to operate fairly and equitably, to provide for the needs of their people, and to keep everyone safe and secure.

The Bahá'í teachings say:
Wealth is praiseworthy in the highest degree, if it is acquired by an individual's own efforts and the grace of God, in commerce, agriculture, art and industry, and if it be expended for philanthropic purposes.

Above all, if a judicious and resourceful individual should initiate measures which would universally enrich the masses of the people, there could be no undertaking greater than this, and it would rank in the sight of God as the supreme achievement, for such a benefactor would supply the needs and insure the comfort and well-being of a great multitude.

Wealth is most commendable, provided the entire population is wealthy.

If, however, a few have inordinate riches while the rest are impoverished, and no fruit or benefit accrues from that wealth, then it is only a liability to its possessor.

If, on the other hand, it is expended for the promotion of knowledge, the founding of elementary and other schools, the encouragement of art and industry, the training of orphans and the poor—in brief, if it is dedicated to the welfare of society—its possessor will stand out before God and man as the most excellent of all who live on earth and will be accounted as one of the **people of paradise.**
– 'Abdu'l-Bahá, *The Secret of Divine Civilization*, p. 24.

So earn some wealth and help create and deliver the welfare and well-being your society needs for its peace and security.

And, if you are able, please share it.

The Human Will and the Will of God

Spirituality

We human beings are exceedingly complex creatures.

Don't believe it? Just contemplate the automatic response systems of the body, for example. When hungry or thirsty we get the urge to eat or drink, and the body does the rest. Blinking is automatic, yet we can stare. Walking is automatic, yet we can stop. Even the brain's primitive limbic system, our primordial reflex to fight, freeze or flee, can be modified by the exercise of our will.

Humans have been gifted with intelligence, or what we sometimes call reason, and through the use of reason we have also been given the gift of choice. Most of us, using our reasoning abilities to override the body's automatic systems, call this the human mind. The Bahá'í teachings refer to mind as the rational soul:

The foremost degree of comprehension in the world of nature is that of the rational soul.

This power and comprehension is shared in common by all men, whether they be heedless or aware, wayward or faithful. In the creation of God, the rational soul of man encompasses and is distinguished above all other created things: It is by virtue of its nobility and distinction that it encompasses them all.

Through the power of the rational soul, man can discover the realities of things, comprehend their properties and penetrate the mysteries of existence. All the sciences, branches of learning, arts, invent-ions, institutions, undertakings, and discoveries have resulted from the comprehension of the rational soul. These were once impenetrable secrets, hidden mysteries, and unknown realities, and the rational soul gradually discovered them and brought them out of the invisible plane into the realm of the visible.

This is the greatest power of comprehension in the world of nature, and the uttermost limit of its flight is to comprehend the realities, signs, and properties of contingent things.

– 'Abdu'l-Bahá, *Some Answered Questions*, newly revised edition, pp. 250-251.

If the rational soul, emanating through the use of the mind, discovers the realities of things, then our human self will choose how to proceed further, because… we want to know.

Yet, here is an important distinction worth noting from 'Abdu'l-Bahá:

As to the second criterion—reason—this likewise is unreliable and not to be depended upon. This human world is an ocean of varying opinions.

If reason is the perfect standard and criterion of knowledge, why are opinions at variance and why do philosophers disagree so completely with each other? This is a clear proof that human reason is not to be relied upon as an infallible criterion.

For instance, great discoveries and announcements of former centuries are continually upset and discarded by the wise men of today. Mathematicians, astronomers, chemical scientists con- tinually disprove and reject the conclusions of the ancients; nothing is fixed, nothing final; everything continually changing because human reason is progressing along new roads of investigation and arriving at new conclusions every day.

In the future much that is announced and accepted as true now will be rejected and disproved. And so it will continue ad infinitum.
– *Foundations of World Unity*, p. 46.

However, whatever the "reason" we choose to believe anything, we must exercise our will in investigating further or taking action:

The attainment of any object is conditioned upon knowledge, volition and action.

Unless these three conditions are forthcoming there is no execution or accomplishment. In the erection of a house it is first necessary to know the ground and design the house suitable for it; second, to obtain the means or funds necessary for the construction; third, to actually build it.

Therefore a power is needed… – Ibid., p. 101.

That power is our volition, or will power. Because human beings have the gift of free will, [nearly] every endeavor requires it.

So, the question becomes, why do we choose to do the things we do? Why this, not that? Why inaction over action? Why silence over speaking out? Why loving now [versus] spurning kindness before?

Simply put, believers of every faith, including Bahá'ís, would say that understanding the Will of God is the greatest boon to choosing wisely in this world, in all our actions.

Do we wish to be wise or to be a sheep, following the masses right or wrong?

Choosing wisely means investigating the facts of a matter, testing them by finding evidence or confirmation, and acting on that knowledge by choosing to exercise our will. It also means measuring our own will with the standard of the Divine Will, by understanding the message of the prophets of God and endeavoring to align our actions with their eternal wisdom.

Bahá'ís call this the principle of the independent investigation of truth, and it is indispensable to the process of discovery.

Gambling: To Wager or Work?

Culture

"Hey, somebody's gotta win, right? Why not me?"

The billion-dollar Powerball lottery recently had odds of 292.2 million to one. But, somebody won, didn't they?

The thought, hope, fantasy, wish and desire to be independently wealthy can strike us all—as if one lucky, million-to-one occurrence will suddenly make our own and our family's lives instantly better.

That allure explains why gambling establishments, once the purview of only a few places, abound all over the world today. California currently has 191 casinos and Nevada 363, leading the way in the United States, and other states and countries now scramble to catch up.

Governments often rely on gambling revenue like they used to rely on taxation, counting on those common hopes and fantasies of sudden wealth, while relying on the fact that a few people win and millions of people lose.

Sure, we all hear the stories of the big winners. But life doesn't work like that very often, does it? No, most of everything we accomplish and acquire we achieve through our own efforts.

That's part of the reason why the Bahá'í teachings [prohibit] gambling. Asked whether the Bahá'í view of gambling applies to games of every description, 'Abdu'l-Bahá replied:

No, some games are innocent, and if pursued for pastime there is no harm. But there is danger that pastime may degenerate into waste of time.

Waste of time is not acceptable in the Cause of God. But recreation which may improve the bodily powers, as exercise, is desirable.
– A Heavenly Vista: The Pilgrimage of Louis G. Gregory, Bahá'í Library Online, p. 9.

If you've ever spent time in the world's gambling capitals—places like Las Vegas, Atlantic City, Monaco—you've seen the huge palaces that legalized gaming built. Of course, they built those palaces with the proceeds of millions of bets placed by hopeful gamblers—most of whom lost.

According to the 2006 Gross Annual Wager Report, "Americans lost nearly $91 billion on all forms of gambling combined." The National Gambling Impact Study Commission (NGISC) noted that <u>Americans spend more on gambling than on recorded music, theme parks, video games, spectator sports and movie tickets combined."</u> [Emphasis added]

That means, for many people, that a pastime has become an addiction. "Problem gambling" and gambling addiction treatment programs and centers have now proliferated. In the U.S. we have National Problem Gambling Helpline 1-800-522-4700, and many states have there own helplines, because our cultures give people the constant opportunity to risk—and lose—just about everything.

Precious societal resources are provided for help with legal addictions like gambling, drinking and smoking. Long before the term "gambling addiction" came into general usage, the Bahá'í teachings defined some forms of gambling as a disease:

Betting on horse racing is a pernicious disease. It hath been seen in Europe what distress this hath caused. Thousands have become afflicted and distraught. The friends of God must engage in work which is lawful and attracted blessings, so that God's aid and bounty may always surround them.
– 'Abdu'l-Bahá, from a tablet to an individual Bahá'í, Lights of Guidance, p. 357.

You rarely hear about the consequences of problem gambling—the loss of people's livelihoods, family unity, entire life savings. The media loves the excited, promotional stories profiling the few winners, but you'll never read or see stories about the millions of losers. That's because those fantasy-fulfillment stories keep gambling's lucrative profitability going.

So, instead of counting on random luck to make your life successful, the Bahá'í teachings encourage everyone to work. Opportunities to earn a decent living abound in life, for teens, men and women [but can be hard to find also depending on different factors]. [Regardless, we] all need productive work to help fulfill our untapped potential as human beings in this contingent world. [Opportunity and education have large parts to play in finding work.]

As the working person gradually earns wealth, so does the state and the nation. It's an effective, timeless model that ensures prosperity and self-esteem. From a Bahá'í perspective, work is more than an absolute necessity—it actually qualifies as worship:

It is enjoined upon every one of you to engage in some form of occupation, such as crafts, trades and the like.

We have graciously exalted your engagement in such work to the rank of worship unto God, the True One.

Ponder ye in your hearts the grace and the blessings of God and render thanks unto Him at eventide and at dawn. Waste not your time in idleness and sloth.

Occupy yourselves with that which profiteth yourselves and others. Thus hath it been decreed in this Tablet from whose horizon the day-star of wisdom and utterance shineth resplendent.

The most despised of men in the sight of God are those who sit idly and beg. Hold ye fast unto the cord of material means, placing your whole trust in God, the Provider of all means. When anyone occupieth himself in a craft or trade, such occupation itself is regarded in the estimation of God as an act of worship; and this is naught but a token of His infinite and all-pervasive bounty.

– Bahá'u'lláh, *Tablets of Bahá'u'lláh*, p. 26.

The next time you think about placing a wager or playing a game of chance, remember how hard you worked to obtain your livelihood, and count on the power of your own labor rather than Dame Fortune—she'll let you down just about every time.

#

The Law: Are You a Conformer, Reformer or Rationalizer?

Culture

When it comes to obeying the law, do you think of yourself as a conformer, reformer or rationalizer?

Not that any person is only one or the other, just like many people [who] are [not] solely introverted or extroverted. Human beings are complex enough to contain parts of most labels.

To answer the question, I have components of all three behaviors, depending on what the situation is at any given moment. But as a student of religion, I believe Bahá'u'lláh when he said:

Religion is the greatest of all means for the establishment of order in the world and for the peaceful contentment of all that dwell therein.
– *World Order of Bahá'u'lláh*, p. 186.

Referring to the eclipse or corruption of religion, he wrote:

Should the lamp of religion be obscured, chaos and confusion will ensue, and the lights of fairness, of justice, of tranquility and peace cease to shine.
– *Tablets of Bahá'u'lláh*, p. 125.

Believing that religion establishes order in the world means acting on my beliefs. I consciously try to reform myself, in other words. It goes with saying that reform means changing myself first. I accept that it's a process, like losing weight or quitting smoking.

All the prophets, saints and sages were reformers, from Confucius to Moses to Bahá'u'lláh, to Gandhi and Martin Luther King Jr. in modern times. They established and exemplified moral codes for humanity, showing us how to behave toward each other. They reformed existing laws and gave us new ones.

The ultimate laws—those codes of moral behavior brought to humanity by the prophets of God—gave us the basis for our sense of right and wrong, our morality, and ultimately our jurisprudence.

But I can't reform [unjust] laws all by myself. Democratic societies try to enforce the rule of law, and conformity is necessary to [them]. I am writing a book, in fact, on driving laws. They exist, are clear as day, yet most drivers—and I think most is 95% on some roads in many countries—do not strictly obey speed limit laws. How much more difficult to obey God's laws, those moral rules of personal conduct!

And of course, in that example, rationalization [for breaking laws] takes over. Many people feel that [exceeding] speed limit laws is acceptable, mainly "Because everybody else does it." Yet, famously, we are each aware of the rhetorical exposé of such falsities when we ask our teenage children, "If Johnny jumps off the Brooklyn Bridge, does that mean you have to?"

In the rule of law, fear of consequences, or conscience, is the greatest motivator. That's why we are exhorted to fear God, and to use that fear as a moral ruler.

But let me ask you, if not enough people actually fear the consequences of breaking the law, or one feels entitled, what's to stop illegal and hurtful behaviors?

That's why Bahá'u'lláh taught us another important attribute of humans when he said:

The fear of God hath ever been a sure defense and a safe stronghold for all the peoples of the world. It is the chief cause of the protection of mankind, and the supreme instrument for its preservation.

Indeed, there existeth in man a faculty which deterreth him from, and guardeth him against, whatever is unworthy and unseemly, and which is known as his sense of shame.

This, however, is confined to but a few; all have not possessed, and do not possess, it.

It is incumbent upon the kings and the spiritual leaders of the world to lay fast hold on religion, inasmuch as through it the fear of God is instilled...
– *Epistle to the Son of the Wolf*, p. 27.

I freely admit, when speeding past traffic while in the fast lane, I haven't felt a large sense of fear, or shame, for breaking the law. But there are consequences, especially when I've been pulled over by a trooper. When that happens, embarrassment takes over, and a sense of stupidity prevails. I think we've all experienced those emotions. [It's also a good motivator for obeying the law, period.]

Fear of consequences is a powerful motivator in humankind, probably as powerful as love itself. These two pillars of civilization—Love and Fear, or Reward and Punishment—mean there's something to be said for conforming to just laws. [For the record, Bahá'ís are to obey the laws.]

#

What If You Wore a Badge of Your Belief?
Religion

The much-vaunted American Dream, shared by billions around the world, promises that we can become something admired and successful from very humble beginnings, if we only work hard and achieve.

We tell our children, "You can become anything you want," and, based on hard work, attainments in education and [good fortune], networking and chance, [many] of them do indeed become successful.

This hope arises from a desire to "be better," "become wealthy," or simply, like the previous U.S. Army slogan, "Be all you can be." We learn our goals from [as a youngster], and, given our endeavors, personality, inclinations and tenacity, we sometimes become what we seek.

Every human spirit has the desire to become known. Based on all Holy Scriptures the world over, this desire to become known is shared with a deep desire to know. The goal of "to know" involves knowing our Creator.

But the real, eternal loving Creator has a different purpose:

The mission of the prophets, the revelation of the holy books, the manifestation of the heavenly teachers and the purpose of divine philosophy all center in the training of the human realities so that they may become clear and pure as mirrors and reflect the light and love of the Sun of Reality.

Therefore I hope that whether you be in the east or the west you will strive with heart and soul in order that day by day the world of humanity may become glorified, more spiritual, more sanctified; and that the splendor of the Sun of Reality may be revealed fully in human hearts as in a mirror.

This is worthy of the world of mankind. This is the true evolution and progress of humanity. This is the supreme bestowal.

Otherwise, by simple development along material lines man is not perfected. At most, the physical aspect of man, his natural or material conditions may become stabilized and improved but he will remain deprived of the spiritual or divine bestowal. He is then like a body

without a spirit, a lamp without the light, an eye without the power of vision, an ear that hears no sound, a mind incapable of perceiving, an intellect minus the power of reason.
– 'Abdu'l-Bahá, *The Promulgation of Universal Peace*, pp. 59-60.

Religion—its very heart and soul and meaning—opens our souls to our own reality and to the reality of God and His teachings.

But how do we do this? By [adhering to] one religious tradition to the exclusion of others? Do we exclude other Faiths, along with tolerance and acceptance of diversity of thought, practice, and opinion?

Young people today have become so disheartened by the outward trappings and hypocrisy they see in many religious traditions that they increasingly shun religious affiliation and communities. The Pew Forum on Religion and Public Life found more than a quarter of Americans aged 18-29 have no religious preference or affiliation—and fewer than one in five attend services regularly. Not just in the United States but throughout the Western world, we've raised the least religious generation ever.

Perhaps that has happened because we have failed to act on our religious beliefs. Is it so difficult for religious or spiritual people to demonstrate and act on their faith? So difficult that others cannot see their devotion to morals and ethics, or honesty and truth? For whatever reason, it does not appear that enough right-minded people, especially our political leaders, have an influence in today's world.

Bahá'ís believe that, [as stated above,] "The mission of the prophets, the revelation of the holy books, the manifestation of the heavenly teachers and the purpose of divine philosophy all center in the training of the human realities so that they may become clear and pure as mirrors and reflect the light and love of the Sun of Reality." The Sun of Reality is of course God and all His attributes and virtues, such as goodness, truthfulness, generosity, caring, love, consideration, and cooperation.

By the age of seven we human beings can usually tell the difference between right and wrong. We've learned it through observed behaviors of others, modeling by those we love or trust, like teachers, parents, and relatives, and by our experiences which include all we've seen, heard and felt.

So why is it so difficult to model good behavior? To be nice and kind rather than cruel and hurtful? To be selfless instead of selfish?

All it takes, from anyone who believes in the basic teachings of their Faith, is to act as if every child, teen-ager and adult on the planet knows their innermost convictions. Imagine, just for a minute, what the world would be like if we each wore a badge that identified our beliefs.

Whether they believe in the Buddhist, Christian, Muslim, Bahá'í or any other Faith, people don't often talk about it. We have come a long way since the beginnings of these faiths— but even those who accept them completely don't always show it. We know the blessed Buddha taught Right Speech and Right Thoughts, and what that looks like in action. We know that Christ's greatest law is to love our neighbor as we do ourselves, and that Bahá'ís teach the unity and cooperation of all humanity.

If we believed that every person on earth knew our innermost beliefs, it would become much harder to behave badly, wouldn't it?

#

Green Acre: Where Happiness and Peace Live

Spirituality

Some days ago, I returned from my seven-hour drive back from Green Acre Bahá'í School in Eliot, Maine, just a few miles from the still-quaint city of Portsmouth, New Hampshire.

Green Acre, as Bahá'ís lovingly refer to it, is in God's country. It offers beautiful forested glens, a sparkling river, fresh air unlike humid New Jersey where I live, and cool, invigorating, sun-filled breezes in spring and summer. Bahá'ís from all over the world visit the spot. Part of its charm is its remoteness in small-town America, nestled in towering pines and dappled fields of dewy grasses.

One of Green Acre's attractions is that the Master himself, the indefatigable 'Abdu'l-Bahá, visited and stayed at its 50-room inn in August 1912. [Far left in picture below]

The Inn, opened in 1890 by founder Sarah Farmer and a group of investors, intended as a retreat and center of interfaith discourse by the leaders and prominent personages of the day, was an oasis for relief from the crowded confines of city tenements. The Farmers were Transcendentalists who were associated with the Abolitionists and other progressive movements. Their home was a way station on the Underground Railroad. Sarah Farmer grew up knowing influential writers, inventors, and thinkers of her day, including John Greenleaf Whittier, Harriet Beecher Stowe, and Sojourner Truth.

In 1892, Sarah Farmer had a vision that the facility should offer conferences on progressive subjects like the sciences, arts and religion, universal in scope and open to all races and creeds. Over time, these conferences brought together leading writers, educators, philosophers, artists and activists.

In 1894, under a tent banked by fragrant pines, Sarah Farmer dedicated Green Acre to the ideals of peace and religious unity as she founded the "Green Acre Conferences." There she raised the world's first known peace flag, which measured 36 feet long.

In 1896 the Monsalvat School for the Comparative Study of Religion, a progressive development seen against conservative religious experience, was established as an institution hosted at Green Acre. Monsalvat was named after the sacred mountain in Wagner's *Parsifal*, where the Holy Grail was kept. In 1900, after visiting the 'Abdu'l-Bahá in Akka, Palestine, Farmer devoted herself to the Bahá'í Cause until her death in 1916, having turned over its operation to the Bahá'ís three years earlier.

Since those early days Green Acre has functioned as a school, a place of [visitation] and a nature-filled refuge for Bahá'ís and their families, friends, and spiritual seekers. Thousands have attended classes there, all promoting universal religious and humanitarian values within a Bahá'í context.

I first attended in 1972 with my wife and friends, to facilitate study of Shoghi Effendi's indispensable treatise on Bahá'í beliefs titled *The Dispensation of Bahá'u'lláh*. Green Acre drew us back almost every year—we would return to teach different subjects and visit almost every summer thereafter, and met, greeted, and listened to wonderful and knowledgeable Bahá'í teachers and scholars.

The great theme that runs through Green Acre's charms, and indeed, in my opinion its greatest assets, are learning, transformation, and service to the world of humanity. One cannot help but be happy and caring of others needs while at Green Acre, in keeping with what 'Abdu'l-Bahá said when he visited the United States:

But—praise be to God!—this banquet and this assemblage are for none other purpose than love, for the purpose of announcing the divine Kingdom, for the manifestation of the ineffable traces of God, for reflecting the effulgences of the Kingdom of God, for binding

hearts together, for service to the world of humanity, for the promulgation of humanitarian and altruistic realities, for the advancement and advocating of international peace, for the illumination of the whole world.
– *The Promulgation of Universal Peace*, p. 419.

As I said earlier, I have just returned from Green Acre, working, and serving in the dining room and kitchen during stays by various groups from a dozen to almost 80 people. Bonnie the Manager, Head Cook, meal planner and preparer; Tom, the general cook and assistant manager; Julie; Ann and I, together ran the operation for both permanent and temporary staff meals and those of guests. It was the hardest, most demanding physical labor I've ever performed—except for tarring roofs when I was 17. Green Acre operates with volunteers [so as] to keep costs reasonable for attendees of all ages. But besides the obvious advantages to just being on the property and staying at the Inn, I did get to have unlimited private sessions alone, on the porch under the many stars, alone in the pines, and alone in 'Abdu'l-Bahá's room; just talking to God, Bahá'u'lláh and 'Abdu'l-Bahá in my prayers.

Green Acre, you see, is not a place. It is a great throbbing heart of love, pouring its universal spirit into every soul, mind, body and spirit that steps into its environs. It is a holy place, not only because 'Abdu'l-Bahá stayed there in one of the rooms of the Inn, but because the spirit of happiness there is simply contagious and ever-present.

When he visited Green Acre, 'Abdu'l-Bahá said, **"May everyone point to you and ask, 'Why are these people so happy?' I want you to be happy in Green Acre, to laugh, smile and rejoice in order that others may be made happy by you."** – Ibid., p. 218.

There is no place like Green Acre because Green Acre is not a place: it is a condition. I encourage you to register for a session, volunteer, or just visit, before there's no room left at the inn.

Go to Greenacre.org for more details.

Are We Meant to Kill Each Other?

Culture

According to Genesis, humanity's symbolic first parents had two male children, Cain, and Abel:

And it came to pass that Cain, the eldest, was not favored by God when he did sacrifice to Him, yet his brother Abel's sacrifice was favored. And Cain was so wroth that he slew his brother and was cursed by God. Yet God placed a mark upon Cain's forehead that others might not slay him.
– Genesis 4:1-7.

Why, if the Bible is inspired, does this gruesome tale of murder become our unavoidable human destiny? What was the purpose of giving us this example if we weren't meant to take something important from it? Have we learned anything about man's inhumanity to his fellow human beings?

Here we can witness God's love and forgiveness. First creating man and woman, and second, even protecting their bad offspring, ensuring that Cain cannot be slain in turn after he kills his brother.

Not only did God condemn Cain's murder of his own flesh and blood, He also condemned, seven times seven, anyone that would slay Cain. In other words, God does not condone murder, whether in vengeance or in anger, or even as retribution.

Have we learned these lessons yet?

The Bahá'í teachings say that simple reason can teach us this vital truth:

...the divine philosophers hold that the excellence or baseness of things depends upon both reason and religious law.

Thus, the prohibitions on murder, theft, treachery, falsehood, hypocrisy and iniquity are based on reason: Every rational mind can grasp that these are all vile and reprehensible. For if you merely prick a man with a thorn he will cry out in pain: How well must he realize then that murder, according to reason, is vile and reprehensible.

And were he to commit such a crime, he would be held accountable for it whether the prophetic message had reached him or not, for reason itself grasps the reprehensible character of this deed. Thus, when such a person commits such base actions, he will assuredly be held to account.

– 'Abdu'l-Bahá, *Some Answered Questions*, newly revised edition, pp. 306-307.

Clearly, every person needs to take responsibility for the evil they commit. Society itself would not be able to exist without this great moral understanding of justice: we are responsible to others, to society, for our actions. In turn society is responsible to every person, youth, and child, to protect them from evil, to provide security and well-being and wealth, as in decent wages for a decent day's labor.

So human cultures and societies institute laws that rest on the pillars of reward and punishment, and judges and courts and juries adjudicate and punish transgressions of those laws.

Yet, given the example in Chapter 4 of Genesis, God can be merciful, as man should be. For He did not strike Cain down, nor allow others to do so—and neither should we.

No matter the reason, no one condones murder, and I believe, neither should the state. Perhaps because of this early lesson in the Bible, and because of subsequent religious laws given to humanity as society has advanced, we have begun to move away from the harsh punishments of old:

Moses dwelt in the desert. As there were no penitentiaries, no means of restitution in the desert and wilderness, the laws of God were an eye for an eye, a tooth for a tooth.

Could this be carried out now?

If a man destroys another man's eye, are you willing to destroy the eye of the offender? If a man's teeth are broken or his ear cut off, will you demand a corresponding mutilation of his assailant?

This would not be conformable to conditions of humanity at the present time. If a man steals, shall his hand be cut off? This punishment was just and right in the law of Moses, but it was applicable to the desert, where there were no prisons and reformatory institutions of later and higher forms of government.

Today you have government and organization, a police system, a judge and trial by jury. The punishment and penalty is now different. Therefore, the nonessentials which deal with details of community are changed according to the exigency of the time and conditions.

– 'Abdu'l-Bahá, *The Promulgation of Universal Peace*, p. 169.

As an example, take the United States. After 30+ years of tough sentencing laws, "Three strikes you're out" and so forth, we find that the U.S. has 25% of those incarcerated in the world, yet only 4% of the world's population, a major disconnect.

Criminal justice officials at many levels have begun to reexamine that hard-core stance, and some prison systems now provide actual rehabilitation, instead of strictly punitive, mind-numbing, and soul-killing days behind bars.

In other words, as times change, the balance between reward and punishment is mediated by mercy. Unless we keep every prisoner behind bars forever, most will eventually be released back into society. That means we need to [provide] meaningful training, socialization, and rehabilitation within our prisons.

Guess what? It's already been proven by countries like Germany that this rehabilitation-based approach cuts repeat offenders by more than half. By contrast, currently in the United States the recidivism rate is 76.6% within five years of release.

The Bahá'í teachings recommend a rehabilitative-based approach:

The body politic is engaged day and night in devising penal laws and in providing for ways and means of punishment.

It builds prisons, acquires chains and fetters, and ordains places of exile and banishment, of torment and hardship, seeking thereby to reform the criminal, whereas in reality this only brings about the degradation of morals and the subversion of character.

The body politic should instead strive night and day, bending every effort to ensure that souls are properly educated, that they progress day by day, that they advance in science and learning, that they acquire praiseworthy virtues and laudable manners, and that they forsake violent behaviour, so that crimes might never occur.
– 'Abdu'l-Bahá, *Some Answered Questions*, newly revised edition, pp. 312-313.

Just as God showed mercy to Cain, it's time the criminal justice system did more than execute or incarcerate criminals. Man's inhumanity to man should not be perpetuated in [the name of justice.]

#

Why Do We Blame God for Our Suffering?

Spirituality PART 1 IN SERIES: **SUFFERING AND ITS PURPOSE**

"Why me?" I asked the universe. "Why not you?" the universe replied.

It's easy to blame others or "things" for our problems, and not look at ourselves first. Avoiding personal responsibility for our actions—whether fired from a job, losing retirement savings in the Great Recession, or [acting like] an errant child—our first tendency is to look for external causes, and not finding a clear one, blame the mean boss, "the system," [the parent,] or even God.

I'm not saying we are the cause of all the problems that affect us, for at times we are not.

Often, we [are] caught up in events and circumstances beyond our control. But at times, depending on the problem or issue, especially when others take umbrage with us, we are the cause, directly or inadvertently. Unable to see ourselves as the source of the problem, we retreat into denial and the blame game.

Once we realize the limits of our actual control over life events, it can comfort us to know that we do not bring all horrors on ourselves. The sinking of the Titanic in the frigid Atlantic Ocean in 1912 was a tragedy, but was it caused by human error—or an iceberg? Daily tragedies beset us, like the recent devastating earthquake in Ecuador, or one a year ago in Nepal, or in Haiti in 2010. We naturally ask, "Why did this happen? Why must so many men, women and children suffer so? How could God let this happen?"

The corollary is, "If God is loving and kind, how could He allow this to happen?"

I'd like to suggest a simple answer: He didn't, and He doesn't, and He never will.

If God did wreak havoc and disaster and suffering on humanity, how could He be All-loving, All-Merciful, All-Forgiving? Can we even conceive of a God who is All-Evil, All-Vengeful, All-Diabolical?

No. He would cease being God, according to all religious traditions.

In the case of natural disasters, science and our own intelligence teaches us to neither blame God nor mindless and relentless nature. When we understand God as the initial impulse for all creation, we also understand God as the creator of our self-motivation, self-determination, self-awareness and free will. We know that God gave human beings those intelligent and creative attributes to overcome the myriad forces imposed or exacted by nature. We know that we can anticipate disasters, prepare for them and save lives as a result.

God is not responsible for our personal problems or deficiencies, whether individually or collectively, because we each and all are products of our environment—the natural order we find ourselves a part of, and nature's environment, beginning at birth. Is God responsible for the pain in my left shoulder caused by a fall? Or for the mentally deranged who hear voices and murder? Or those who incite others to violence as "religious" terrorists? Most would agree not.

The difference, of course, is motivation. Nature has a rigid motivating force–to grow, shift, change and adapt. Nature is not concerned with justice and fairness and the altruism we see in humanity. People all have an animal nature as well, which motivates us to do things from one extreme to the other, some extremely kind, others evil. But even though the animals live according to circumscribed natural tendencies, we can rise above our animal nature and control some of these decisions—we have the free will to act on our conscience and choose justice or injustice:

Certain matters are subject to the free will of man, such as acting with justice and fairness, or injustice and iniquity—
in other words, the choice of good or evil actions.
It is clear and evident that the will of man figures greatly in these actions.
But there are certain matters where man is forced and compelled, such as sleep, death, sickness, failing powers, misfortune and material loss: These are not subject to the will of man and he is not accountable for them, for he is compelled to endure them. But he is free in the choice of good and evil actions, and it is of his own accord that he performs them.
– 'Abdu'l-Bahá, *Some Answered Questions*, newly revised edition, p. 287.

So why, although I try to be good, does trouble still assail me? Tune in for the second part of this essay, when we'll try to answer that big question.

Next: Why Does God Still Pick on Me?

#

Why Does God Still Pick On Me?

Spirituality PART 2 IN SERIES: SUFFERING AND ITS PURPOSE

The Bahá'í teachings explain the central human paradox:

> ...all the doings of man are sustained by the power of divine assistance, but the choice of good or evil belongs to him alone.
>
> It is like when the king appoints an individual as governor of a city, grants him full authority, and shows him that which is just or unjust according to the law. Now, should the governor commit injustice, even though he acts by the power and authority of the king, yet the king would not condone his injustice. And should the governor act with justice, this too would be through the royal authority, and the king would be well pleased and satisfied with his justice.
>
> Our meaning is that the choice of good and evil belongs to man, but that under all circumstances he is dependent upon the life-sustaining assistance of Divine Providence.

– 'Abdu'l-Bahá, *Some Answered Questions*, newly revised edition, p. 289.

We have life, and living means suffering, even from good intentions. The simple honest answer is that God does not create suffering. [Yet] suffering according to the Buddha, Christ, and Bahá'u'lláh is man's condition in this material universe.

Let's take the "Four Noble Truths of Buddhism" as a format to compare and contrast suffering.

In brief form, they state:

> Suffering is our existence.
>
> Suffering is caused by craving, wanting or desirousness.
>
> Freedom from suffering can be secured.
>
> The way out of suffering is to follow the path.

This is obviously a mixed message when it comes to natural disasters we do not cause, yet it's common to all religious traditions. The hope contained here, as in religion, is that with God's help and by following a spiritual path, we can ameliorate our suffering and the suffering of others. We can stop blaming God for our suffering and asking "Why does God still pick on me?" in our lowest moments. We can begin to see beyond [our] immediate pain and begin to see its purpose.

So, what is the purpose of suffering? Here's an explanation from the Bahá'í teachings:

Physical pain is a necessary accompaniment of all human existence, and as such is unavoidable. As long as there will be life on earth, there will be also suffering, in various forms and degrees.

But suffering, although an inescapable reality, can nevertheless be utilised as a means for the attainment of happiness. This is the interpretation given to it by all the prophets and saints who, in the midst of severe tests and trials, felt happy and joyous and experienced what is best and holiest in life.

Suffering is both a reminder and a guide. It stimulates us better to adapt ourselves to our environmental conditions, and thus leads the way to self improvement. In every suffering one can find a meaning and a wisdom.

But it is not always easy to find the secret of that wisdom. It is sometimes only when all our suffering has passed that we become aware of its usefulness. What man considers to be evil turns often to be a cause of infinite blessings. And this is due to his desire to know more than he can.

God's wisdom is, indeed, inscrutable to us all, and it is no use pushing too far trying to discover that which shall always remain a mystery to our mind.

– Shoghi Effendi, *Unfolding Destiny*, p. 434.

Moore Oklahoma tornado disaster

It would be glib of me to suggest we embrace our suffering, yet it's obvious that many people get stronger from it, and indeed, overcome it. They serve as examples to all of us:

To the sincere ones, tests are as a gift from God, the Exalted, for a heroic person hasteneth, with the utmost joy and gladness, to the tests of a violent battlefield, but the coward is afraid and trembles and utters moaning and lamentation.

Likewise, an expert student prepareth and memorizeth his lessons and exercises with the utmost effort, and in the day of examination he appeareth with infinite joy before the master.

Likewise, the pure gold shineth radiantly in the fire of test.

Consequently, it is made clear that for holy souls, trials are as the gift of God, the Exalted; but for weak souls they are an unexpected calamity.

This test is just as thou hast written: it removeth the rust of egotism from the mirror of the heart until the Sun of Truth may shine therein.

For, no veil is greater than egotism and no matter how thin that covering may be, yet it will finally veil man entirely and prevent him from receiving a portion from the eternal bounty.
–Attributed to "Abdu'l-Bahá in *Bahá'í World Faith*, p. 371.

Finally, if you neither accept nor agree that "tests are a healing medicine," perhaps on your journey you may come to accept the following:

Verily the Will of God acts sometimes in a way for which mankind is unable to find out the reason. The causes and reasons shall appear.

Trust in God and confide in Him, and resign thyself to the Will of God.

Verily thy God is affectionate, compassionate and merciful... and will cause His Mercy to descend upon thee.
– 'Abdu'l-Bahá, *Bahá'u'lláh and the New Era*, p. 110.

#

Who Do We Talk to When We Talk to Ourselves?

Spirituality

Who do we talk to when we talk to ourselves? And don't say, "No one." And don't say, "Myself." Ah, unless you know your self, of course.

I don't completely know who I am yet, so when I talk aloud to myself I am discovering who I want to be.

Oh, and I only do it while alone of course, except for the occasional, "You've got to be kidding!" at some outrageous driver who cuts me off, only usually it's much worse than that. And it changes nothing.

My favorite places to converse alone are in my garage and my car, and not when they're in the same space. In my garage it's usually "Stupid, stupid cigarette!" on a cold freezing day. It took me years not to blame my smoking habit on cigarettes or the legality of selling them. "Oh, if they just didn't sell 'em I wouldn't buy 'em," I'd say. That's stupid too, of course.

In my car I'm free to observe aloud and comment on anything and everything, to muse and conjecture, plot and plan my next moves, and even pray. Oh, how many of the world's problems I've solved in my car!

(Stock photo of being in a car alone)

If only someone would listen, of course.

That means someone in authority with the power to effect change, but these days that usually takes many people from the clerks up to the highest leaders.

Certainly, musing aloud about it in the car or kibitzing with friends doesn't solve poverty, but at least others are also taking steps toward that laudable goal.

So, I am free to rave [or] rant, curse [or] praise, admire [or] detest, alone in the enclosed cockpit of my car. Luckily, it's changed over months and years as I've grown more observant, more able to listen, more tolerant and more open. It has been a process, as is everything, for I, like you, certainly do not know everything.

I've learned that adding my voice to choruses of others does have an effect—just not in the rapid time span I envisaged. It's still a matter of reaching the right people with the right message at the right time.

But by talking to myself first I work out the pros and cons of my ideas, the plusses and minuses, the works and won't works, and mainly, I've become one heck of a philosopher, or so I like to think.

But when I really think about it, the True Philosopher always has the real wisdom.

For example: the Bahá'í teachings ask us to overlook the faults of others and see their virtues. On the other hand, they ask us to find our own faults, and concentrate our efforts on addressing our own spiritual growth. Bahá'u'lláh says in the [following] *Hidden Words*:

O Son of Being! How couldst thou forget thine own faults and busy thyself with the faults of others? Whoso doeth this is accursed of Me.
–[Arabic, #26,] p. 10.

The tongue I have designed for the mention of Me, defile it not with detraction. If the fire of self overcome you, remember your own faults and not the faults of My creatures, inasmuch as every one of you knoweth his own self better than he knoweth others.
–[Persian, #66,] p. 45.

'Abdu'l-Bahá gave us the same basic advice:

Let your life be an emanation of the Kingdom of Christ. He came not to be ministered unto, but to minister.
... In the religion of Bahá'u'lláh all are servants and maidservants, brothers and sisters. As soon as one feels a little better than, a little superior to, the rest, he is in a dangerous position, and unless he casts away the seed

of such an evil thought, he is not a fit instrument for the service of the Kingdom.

Dissatisfaction with oneself is a sign of progress... If a person has a thousand good qualities he must not look at them; nay, rather he must strive to find out his own defects and imperfections.

...However much a man may progress, yet he is imperfect, because there is always a point ahead of him. No sooner does he look up towards that point than he becomes dissatisfied with his own condition, and aspires to attain to that. Praising one's own self is the sign of selfishness.
–Attributed to "Abdu'l-Bahá in *Star of the West*, Vol 4, pp. 179-180.

So, I talk to myself, whoever that may be [in] the moment, and test out my theories of life in the privacy of my chamber, confident that someone, or some part of me, is always listening—listening and learning from the world, the largest echo chamber known to Man.

#

Do You Believe in Miracles?

Spirituality

We all [have asked] ourselves this basic human question:
"How could an All-Loving, All-Merciful, All-Gracious God allow such terrible things to happen?"

But have you ever asked yourself this corollary: "Why do good things happen? Why do miracles happen?"

Certainly, the universe seems silent, neutral, indifferent and uncaring on those important questions.

Yet we ascribe many things to God, or more accurately, to God's intervention. We often say after a catastrophe or personal setback, "It could have been much worse," which is a kind of acknowledgement of receiving some grace in our poor human existence.

So why, every hour, do we read about or watch a miracle? If you really look, the world seems filled with miracles. I mean, Facebook alone contains thousands of unexpectedly miraculous outcomes, which show the silly things people do that look imminently fatal to when they stand up unharmed.

As rational beings, when there simply is no physical or outward explanation for such miraculous occurrences, it's easy to think out loud, "Boy, he was lucky!" We might attribute it to pure luck, but we know for a certainty that "luck" only means we've been the recipients of beneficial circumstances.

[Humanity] has grown up with miracle upon miracle from its infancy—from the "miracle" of controlling fire, to the "miracle" of flying 500 people across vast distances in the sky in a [jumbo] jet, to hundreds of accounts of miracles in the world's holy scriptures. We almost expect miracles now, because we're so bombarded with technological marvels every day—which would all be miracles to the people of the past.

Heck, to the people of last year.

Yet miracles cannot be relied upon because they are not universal, are fleeting, and can be reasoned away.

The Bahá'í teachings view miracles as no proof of anything:

But in the Sacred Scriptures a special terminology is used, and in the sight of the Manifestations of God these marvels and miracles are of no importance, so much so that They do not even wish them to be mentioned. For even if these miracles were considered the greatest of proofs, they would constitute a clear evidence only for

those who were present when they took place, not for those who were absent.
– 'Abdu'l-Bahá, *Some Answered Questions*, newly revised edition, p. 113.

Yet the concept of "miracles" has become part of our lexicon, to explain happy occurrences where no probable cause exists.

So, if a miracle happens, has God intervened? Has God taken a part, even a small one, to guide an outcome? I learned as a young boy in catechism class that, "God is everywhere, knows everything, and is the cause of all creation." Yet it seems more people cite miracles than the few who receive them.

It may help to think about miracles this way: as the physical symbols of the true miracle of spiritual transformation:

Our meaning is not that the Manifestations of God are unable to perform miracles, for this indeed lies within Their power. But that which is of import and consequence in Their eyes is inner sight, spiritual hearing, and eternal life. Thus, wherever it is recorded in the Sacred Scriptures that such a one was blind and was made to see, the meaning is that he was inwardly blind and gained spiritual sight.
– Ibid., pp. 115-116.

The holy prophets and manifestations of God, even the lesser prophets of Israel described in the Old Testament, all had the power to perform miracles or benefit from them, like Daniel in the lion's den. If we believe our scriptures, miracles do exist and can [come] into existence.

But I ask you, could it also be that the lions were particularly well-fed that day Daniel was thrown [in with] them?

So, the final question becomes: Do we beg God in prayer for a miracle, or do we exert effort ourselves and with others to cause that "miracle?" And what's wrong with hedging our bets and doing both simultaneously?

In other words, do we test God to prove he is God? Or do we, as His servants, thank Him for the natural good we see in our lives and in others and in the world?

Or, simply, do we believe what Christ trusted in almost 2,000 years ago: "Thy will be done on earth as it is in heaven."

It's always your choice.   **#**

Marriage for the 21ˢᵗ Century

Culture

"Rod, don't forget to call Richie about seeing a movie."
"Rod, don't forget we have a meeting tonight."
"Rod, don't forget to take an umbrella tomorrow, it's going to rain."

And simple me, five minutes later asking my loving she-mate, "Do you think it's going to rain tomorrow?"

"I just said that!"

Marriage is a wealth of learning and wisdom, isn't it? We are forgetful, of both little and big things, like how to listen and retain. So, God kindly reminds us, in myriad ways, of our duties and responsibilities, one to another:

Consider, moreover, how frequently doth man become forgetful of his own self, whilst God remaineth, through His all-encompassing know-ledge, aware of His creature, and continueth to shed upon him the manifest radiance of His glory.

It is evident, therefore, that, in such circum- stances, He is closer to him than his own self. He will, indeed, so remain forever, for, whereas the one true God knoweth all things, perceiveth all things, and comprehendeth all things, mortal man is prone to err, and is ignorant of the mysteries that lie enfolded within him....

– Bahá'u'lláh, *Gleanings from the Writings of Bahá'u'lláh*, p. 188.

I'm convinced that the institution of marriage [is] to remind us of ourselves and our relations to others. Ah, marriage, that grouping of two souls and two bodies and two minds [nearly] into one spirit that will [commune] together for eternity.

"Rod, don't forget to call the dentist and change your appointment, we're visiting our son that day, remember?"

The perfect training for my person, from my helpmate and consort, who repeatedly has said, "I'm not your secretary." Yet she lets me, an adult, figure it out. Like training children, God sends us helpers and loving counterparts to train us.

'Abdu'l-Bahá, that master educator said:

Bahá'í marriage is union and cordial affection between the two parties. They must, however, exercise the utmost care and become acquainted with each other's character.

This eternal bond should be made secure by a firm covenant, and the intention should be to foster harmony, fellowship and unity and to attain everlasting life. ...

In a true Bahá'í marriage the two parties must become fully united both spiritually and physically, so that they may attain eternal union throughout all the worlds of God, and improve the spiritual life of each other. This is Bahá'í matrimony.
– quoted by J.E. Esslemont in *Bahá'u'lláh and the New Era*, p. 177.

Thankfully, gratefully, not used to reminders at all as a young man, carefree, unattached, and unalloyed, I came to realize my wife Janet was a gift from God to my side – the side where my rib was. Oh, not just for reminders, or critical observations leading to my well-being, but so, so much more.

For marriage between two parties, as 'Abdu'l-Bahá says, is "...fully united...." In other words, true marriage creates symbiosis, an interdependent relationship, an "eternal union."

Ideally—in a relationship initially based on infatuation, then love, then true love when full trust [exists] and not blind love—a couple can help each other become more than either one of them could become individually.

Certainly, we learn from birth that old maxim, "No man is an island," coined by the English poet John Donne almost 400 years ago:

No man is an island,
Entire of itself,
Every man is a piece of the continent,
A part of the main.
If a clod be washed away by the sea,
Europe is the less.
As well as if a promontory were.
As well as if a manor of thy friend's
Or of thine own were:
Any man's death diminishes me,
Because I am involved in mankind,
And therefore never send to know for whom the bell tolls;
It tolls for thee.

Simply put, a morally and ethically grounded relationship is the cherry on top of the whipped cream, on top of the hot fudge sundae, my favorite. Yours may be a banana split or an ice cream cone.

Either way, any way, what works is what counts, and each of us have wants and needs that our mate understands, usually better than any parent, especially after decades together.

So, let's not write marriage off just yet, please.

What's your experience with marriage?

#

Earth: The Original Magic Kingdom

Spirituality

Where can you find the happiest place on Earth, or the most magical place on Earth? If you guessed a Disney theme park, you know their marketing slogans.

Magic Kingdom Park, the first-built of the four theme parks near Orlando, Florida, opened on October 1, 1971. Its layout and attractions mimic the original Disneyland—"the happiest place on Earth"—in Anaheim, California, which opened in 1955. In 2014, Florida's Magic Kingdom Park—"the most magical place on Earth"—hosted 19.3 million visitors from around the globe, making it the world's most visited theme park for the sixth consecutive year.

Cinderella Castle

The Park's most iconic structure—Cinderella Castle, inspired by the fairy tale castle seen in the 1950 Disney animated film—has become known worldwide as a symbol of the Magic Kingdom [and Disney].

I saw a smaller version—the original Sleeping Beauty's Castle—at age 15, when a high school buddy with a driver's license and an open-air Jeep drove us three friends to Disneyland [in Anaheim, California], purportedly to meet girls. We danced the Watusi and the Twist on the stage together under a large open-air canopy, then rode under Space Mountain and reveled in the excited faces of adults, youth and especially children.

The price of admission was $4.00 each, much more than the twenty-five cents a gallon to drive the thirty miles there and back. Today, plan on paying about $100 per person per day to feel happy or magical.

As glorious and thrilling as Disneyland seemed to my 15-year-old self, its ersatz colors, costumes, attractions, and stands of every kind from food to souvenirs pale before the real thing.

The diversity of humanity and of nature itself, and then of man's creations and myriad wonders, all outstrip any mere amusement park's imitations. Even our creature comforts, from running water and toilets and the systems that support them, to appliances run by gas and electricity in hundreds of millions of homes and facilities, to solar-powered rooftops and vehicles—they all exceed any fantasy reality we've managed to create.

So, while millions of people have enough good fortune to afford tickets to the Theme Park of the Good Life, billions of people [can't enter.]

In truth, the greatest Magic Kingdom ever created is the Earth we co-inhabit with nature and its unnumbered creatures. Are we cherishing its beauties and benefits as much as we cherish our man-made creations?

In this age of transition toward a world society, protection of the environment and conservation of the earth's resources represent an enormously complex challenge.

The rapid progress in science and technology that has united the world physically has also greatly accelerated destruction of the biological diversity and rich natural heritage with which the planet has been endowed.

Material civilization, driven by the dogmas of consumerism and aggressive individualism and disoriented by the weakening of moral standards and spiritual values, has been carried to excess.

Only a comprehensive vision of a global society, supported by universal values and principles, can inspire individuals to take responsibility for the long-term care and protection of the natural environment. Bahá'ís find such a world-embracing vision and system of values in the teachings of Bahá'u'lláh – teachings which herald an era of planetary justice, prosperity and unity.

– Statement from the Bahá'í International Community on Conservation and Sustainable Development, 1995

Bahá'ís believe that humanity is up to this challenge.

I won't iterate the consequences if we fail, since [many] enlightened societies are familiar with them. Under-developed and developing nations, caught between using up their natural resources for bare survival and economic realities, are [understanding this] as well. The Kyoto Protocol established in 2005, [and other efforts,] represent a good basis toward finding amenable, worldwide solutions.

It's a simple matter of stewardship for this trust mankind has been given, our very planet itself.

Many countries, [the U.S.] included, have established Environmental Commissions at the local and regional levels to meet this challenge. Where I live in New Jersey, we have over 350 such local and regional commissions. These commissions review developers' plans to build homes, businesses, and commercial facilities.

You may be unfamiliar with such grassroots organizations in your community, but they all have been established to provide balance between construction and development and open spaces, forests, streams, and wetlands.

The balance they strive for, the Bahá'í teachings say, aims to curb the excesses that threaten to permanently harm our environment:

The civilization so often vaunted by the learned exponents of arts and sciences will, if allowed to overleap the bounds of moderation, bring great evil upon men... If carried to excess, civilization will prove as prolific a source of evil as it had been of goodness when kept within the restraints of moderation...
– Bahá'u'lláh, *Gleanings from the Writings of Bahá'u'lláh*, pp. 342-343.

It's time we all held a ticket to the magic kingdom, to the happiest place on Earth: life and peace, fresh water and clean air, sunshine and moon fall, justice and fairness, pay [equity] and work for all, the abolishment of slavery and domination by the elite. The time has come for that blessed day when we trust each other to do the right thing and do the thing right.

Are there things you are doing in your home or local community to steward the resources you [have?]

#

What Will Make Me Happy?

Culture

If you're searching for happiness in your life, and haven't found it yet, you might want to read this.

From time immemorial, Bahá'ís believe, God has always desired happiness for humanity, and has provided the wisdom and guidance of the prophets from age to age to make sure we find it.

Now a new prophet has come—Bahá'u'lláh, the founder of the Bahá'í Faith—and given us a recipe for happiness, prosperity and fulfillment:

...man should know his own self and recognize that which leadeth unto loftiness or lowliness, glory or abasement, wealth or poverty.

Having attained the stage of fulfilment and reached his maturity, man standeth in need of wealth, and such wealth as he acquireth through crafts or professions is commendable and praiseworthy in the estimation of men of wisdom, and especially in the eyes of servants who dedicate themselves to the education of the world and to the edification of its peoples. They are, in truth, cup-bearers of the life-giving water of knowledge and guides unto the ideal way.

They direct the peoples of the world to the straight path and acquaint them with that which is conducive to human upliftment and exaltation.

The straight path is the one which guideth man to the dayspring of perception and to the dawning-place of true understanding and leadeth him to that which will redound to glory, honour and greatness.
– Bahá'u'lláh, *Tablets of Bahá'u'lláh*, p. 35.

Basically, you can summarize what Bahá'u'lláh recommends with these three steps:

- Know yourself and recognize what will truly benefit you.
- As you mature, develop a profession, a craft or a trade, and focus on what will edify the world's peoples.
- Direct your path toward the "dawning-place of true understanding."

Knowing oneself doesn't come easy, but it does come with persistent effort – the effort to understand our inner self, to improve, to be better, to do our best. That's why we experience "tests" of all kinds, from a bout with disease, to finding ourselves in a bad relationship, to losing our job through no fault of our own. All require that we "rise to the occasion," pick ourselves up, and move on.

Bahá'u'lláh recommends having a profession that produces prosperity, as a major contributor to a sense of self-worth and purpose in our lives. In fact, in this day, work is not only commendable and enjoined, but when performed in a spirit of service to our fellow humans, the Bahá'í teachings elevate it to an act of worship.

Besides the spiritual and self-esteem benefits of working, work provides the wealth we need to survive in a world where each of us is called upon to contribute to society. Part of our work income, simply put, not only helps ourselves, but also helps those less fortunate or in need of social services.

Home office worker

The tremendous sense of self-worth brought on by being self-sufficient and capable in whatever arena we choose— that's a good starting-point for a definition of happiness.

Construction workers

But any job, important as it may be, is still only part of the happiness equation. Some look for happiness from others, and some think they've found it. Others do not and become disillusioned and depressed. But as Bahá'u'lláh's quotation above makes clear, happiness does not come from others, no matter how saintly, loving or kind. Instead, it comes from our own inner and outer self, the self only we can develop and nurture. It comes from turning to the straight path of spiritual search and discovering our own souls:

Bahá'u'lláh taught that hearts must receive the Bounty of the Holy Spirit, so that Spiritual civilization may be established. For material civilization is not adequate for the needs of mankind and cannot be the cause of its happiness. Material civilization is like the body and spiritual civilization is like the soul. Body without soul cannot live.
– 'Abdu'l-Bahá, *'Abdu'l-Bahá in London*, p. 30.

In the final analysis, it's up to humans to solve problems caused by humans.

Meaningful employment, fair wages and an ever-increasing understanding of the spiritual "day-spring of perception" can accomplish that lifelong goal and lead us toward lasting happiness.

The tremendous sense of self-worth brought on by being self-sufficient and capable in whatever arena we choose— that's a good starting-point for a definition of happiness.

#

Giving in to Temptation

Culture

Me in NYC with a 1957 Chevy Bel Air, once my first car

I love to drive. I am a driving fanatic, since I'm in my car every day for one or more trips on local roads or highways. Driving, of course, means sharing the road with other drivers, and that means sometimes having close calls. I've found that they're mostly unnecessary, if the other driver either wasn't in such a hurry or didn't feel compelled to "jump the gun" by pulling out directly in front of my speeding automobile.

You'd think I'd be used to it after 50 years on the roads, but in some past moments my ire took control and I was tempted to do something stupid, like follow the person too closely, or curse them out, or heaven forbid, accost them for their apparent stupidity and lack of caution.

It's taken me years to develop the patience and reserve to do none of those things—because I make mistakes too.

So, I've had to ask myself: what tempts us to take risks that jeopardize our own or other's lives, at least potentially, in a two-ton moving hunk of steel and plastic?

For all people, the temptation to slide into uncontrolled, impulsive and selfish ways is a constant battle with the self. We all face it.

The temptation to not do a thing, by procrastinating; or to do something perhaps out of the ordinary, against the grain or illegal, like surpassing highway speed limits by large margins; is part of human nature.

Oscar Wilde famously said, "I can resist anything except temptation." Mae West said, "I generally avoid temptation unless I can't resist it."

Everyone is tempted by one thing or another. We're constantly tempted, especially in today's world where the right amount of money will procure anything on earth, to give in to those inner emotions, whether spontaneous or well thought out, whether good or evil, in between or innocuous.

But does giving in to temptation always cause harm? Hmmm, that's like asking Jean Valjean if stealing a loaf of bread to feed his sister's seven starving children was worth nineteen years in prison. The motivation and intention of an act may be innocent or even altruistic, but society at the time may think otherwise. Often, it's what others would think that prevents us from acting illegally, or at least without caution.

Sometimes temptations present themselves to us, and other times we generate a need within ourselves. Regardless, when we act, whether for good or ill, we all have a sense from childhood on that every action not only has a reaction, but also has a reward or a punishment:

Justice, which consisteth in rendering each his due, dependeth upon and is conditioned by two words: reward and punishment.

From the standpoint of justice, every soul should receive the reward of his actions, inasmuch as the peace and prosperity of the world depend thereon, even as He saith, exalted be His glory:

"The structure of world stability and order hath been reared upon, and will continue to be sustained by, the twin pillars of reward and punishment."

In brief, every circumstance requireth a different utterance and every occasion calleth for a different course of action. Blessed are they that have arisen to serve God, who speak forth wholly for His sake, and who return unto Him.

– Bahá'u'lláh, *The Tabernacle of Unity*, p. 40.

Every action, even non-action in the face of a call to action, has a consequence. The temptation to do a thing has always been presented as negative, as if temptation itself is evil.

But temptation can also serve the urge to do good, such as stopping on a busy highway to help a stranded motorist.

Those who want to serve their fellow man and woman will pause in their rush to an appointment to make that stop and see it through. That stranded motorist will be grateful for any help offered, in an age when hundreds of drivers will speed past with no thought of stopping.

So, when the temptation to do a good thing enters your mind or heart, please feel free to give in.

As the Bahá'í teachings promise, you will be blessed.

What Cause Should I Join?

Culture

Strive ye with all your hearts, raise up your voices and shout, until this dark world be filled with light, and this narrow place of shadows be widened out, and this dust heap of a fleeting moment be changed into a mirror for the eternal gardens of heaven, and this globe of earth receive its portion of celestial grace.
– 'Abdu'l-Bahá, *Selections from the Writings of 'Abdu'l-Bahá*, p. 36.

Animal Rights. Civil Rights. Human Rights. Black Lives Matter. Brexit. Save the Whales. Climate Change. The list goes on and on. In today's world, a huge host of causes clamors for our membership, urges our commitment and participation, and generally duns us for donations.

These three elements exist in most movements where larger and larger numbers of members and supporters act on the part of leaders and those in power to affect the "demands, desires or wishes" of the stated goals of the movement.

Let's take a simple, noncommittal example: Facebook. Maybe it's called Facebook because it faces all of us with multiple levels of appeals, from a simple "Like," to "Type Yes" to "Share," to even "Type Amen." Millions of people of all ages do at least one of these, every hour. They call for little commitment from the responder, other than a click or a few words or emojis to show their approval (or disapproval). Soon we may even have an "Unlike" button.

The committed Facebook response on the other hand usually means clicking a button that says "Join," or "Subscribe," or even "Donate." However, the full implications of such clicks are not described in detail, unless a "Learn More" button happens to be included.

As a matter of due diligence, I rarely would join, subscribe, or donate unless I understood much more about the cause, group, or organization. After all, the obvious Facebook goal is to [evoke] a spur of the moment reaction on the part of the viewer to click, and therefore build up the momentum of their "Cause" rapidly. During this election cycle, almost every political pushout has a "Donate" button.

What's so remarkable about Facebook is its diversity, which leads to its addictiveness. It really has something for everyone, from statements and pictures of injustice, to new scientific developments, to the beauty of nature, to sickness, healthy foods, wounded warriors, newlyweds, birthdays and old age. I especially like the jokes and funny memes.

The overall goal of all of these great and interesting and sometimes astounding pictures, statements and videos still remains the number of Likes or Shares garnered, yet the sentiments they express mostly go unharnessed. There's the rub.

Running through my allotted time scanning FB every morning has shown me how similar we all feel and think: sad at sickness and hoping for health, mad at injustice and wanting things fixed, pleased with tips on loving and living better, and amazed at what others can do and speak and demonstrate, inspiring us.

So, with all [these] Facebook invitations flying at us, how do we choose from among millions of causes worth joining, sharing, and donating either our time, energy or money to?

No question—we have thousands of worthy causes. The number of individual charities, and churches that do likewise, number in the hundreds of thousands. Causes such as nuclear disarmament, equal treatment by police, feeding the poor and hungry, fairness in elections, curbing pollution, reasonable gun control and on and on, all vie for our attention. The vast array of these causes presents us with a host of problems to be solved, diseases eradicated, behaviors changed, and resources used most effectively.

So where should I put my limited time and efforts?

How can I be most effective improving my life and the lives of others? Is there a sure way of curing humanity of the ills that beset us?

For Bahá'ís, the answer begins inside our minds, hearts and souls:

Thou hast inquired regarding the teachings and instructions of Bahá'u'lláh!
Thou must instruct the people of the world
in the Love of God,
that they may eradicate the foundation of warfare and strife,
be attracted by the Glad- tidings of the kingdom…,
lay the basis of love and amity,
raise the melody of affinity, and the oneness of the Kingdom of humanity;
transmute tyranny and persecution into love and faithfulness,
efface the traces of bloodshed and carnage; construct the edifice of reconciliation,
dispel the darkness of estrangement, diffuse the light of unity;
change the poison of animosity into the honey of sympathetic affection;
destroy the religious, national and social prejudices from the individuals of humanity;
live and act, with and toward each other as though they were from one race, one country, one religion, and one kind.
– 'Abdu'l-Bahá, *Star of the West*, Volume 2, p. 5.

Every cause starts within.

Our commitment to love and justice begins with the acquisition and refinement of our human virtues—developing behaviors such as equity and fairness, honesty and trustworthiness, kindness, and generosity, sacrifice and sharing, love and caring, responsibility and citizenship, education, and universal suffrage and many more.

These human qualities only need a pure heart and active goodwill to effectuate change—perhaps the cheapest yet most effective means of changing the world.

#

Beating Swords into Words

Spirituality PART 1 IN SERIES: | THE POWER OF THE WORD

And He shall judge among the nations, and shall rebuke many people: and they shall beat their swords into plowshares, and their spears into pruning hooks: nation shall not lift up sword against nation, neither shall they learn war any more.
– Isaiah 2:3–4

When you move the letter "s" in "sword," you get "words."

We've all spoken or heard words that hurt or ease, incite or calm, elucidate or obfuscate, inspire or depress, confirm or deny, and have the power to engender love or hate. Our words can be swords or plowshares—either weapons or creative tools that benefit humanity.

In these times we utter trillions of words every day. Without a doubt, words, in any language, can inflame or bring peace to millions of us.

Before writing there was speech, before speech there was language, before language there were grunts and hand motions. Communication of any kind, from body motions to neurolinguistics to the art of persuasion, have all been part of the human experience for tens of thousands of years.

Today we see a veritable flood of words on television, in videos and in films. We hear them in conversation and speeches, on radio talk shows and in music lyrics. We read, read, read—in books, essays, reports, blogs, magazines; in myriad ways. The types of human communication can't be counted nor limited.

The power of words has become much more obvious over past decades.

From advertisements, to simple directions that elucidate or muddle, to the spiritual effects of Rumi's poetry on the heart and mind, words are much more powerful today than swords were previously. Today words, once used to create war and subjugation, can now end them. The growing spheres of civil discourse, mediation, arbitration, and diplomacy all lead to peace between peoples and nations. Written binding treaties now create new relationships, particularly economic, that never existed in past ages.

Millions of people of all backgrounds, regardless of their thought processes, education levels, and viewpoints share words of wisdom and tolerance publicly. They even share secrets. Take Daniel Ellsberg's release of the Pentagon Papers in 1971, Edward Snowden's turnover of thousands of classified NSA documents in 2013, and this year, the new bombshell, the Panama Papers—all expose the previously unknown, behind-the-scenes words and actions that have effects on tens of millions of peoples and billions of dollars.

Sometimes it seems as if we have no more secrets.

Now an enormous number of "how-to" books exist, describing once-secret or little-known processes. Have you ever looked at a few of the thousands of short explanatory videos on the Internet? The "Dummy" series of books has taken the mystery out of hundreds of processes. We're increasingly ensconced in the age of transparency and openness, beating our swords into words.

That's not surprising, nor should it be. Why? Bahá'ís believe this explosion of words and the knowledge they represent are caused by the advent of a new revelation from God. Inaugurated in 1844 by the Báb, and fulfilled in 1863 by Bahá'u'lláh. These prophetic words announced the revelation's enormous impact on the sum total of human learning:

Knowledge is twenty and seven letters. All that the prophets have revealed are two letters thereof. No man thus far hath known more than these two letters. But when the Qa'im [the new prophet] shall arise, He will cause the remaining twenty and five letters to be made manifest.
– The Báb, quoted by Shoghi Effendi in *The World Order of Bahá'u'lláh*, p. 125.

Words have power, from Rumi and Hafiz on our hearts, to the wise sound bites of presidents and popes on our views and beliefs. No words, though, have more potency than those of the prophets and messengers, those perfect beings who appear in every age and lead humanity to new religious awakenings. The prophet of God reveals the essence and meaning of all words when he releases the regenerative power of the word of God contained in the new teachings and scriptures of a great, world Faith.

The Bahá'í teachings say that has happened again.

Next: The Power of the Prophet's Words

#

The Power of the Prophet's Words

Religion PART 2 IN SERIES: THE POWER OF THE WORD

It is clear and evident to thee that all the Prophets are the Temples of the Cause of God, Who have appeared clothed in diverse attire. If thou wilt observe with discriminating eyes, thou wilt behold them all abiding in the same tabernacle, soaring in the same heaven, seated upon the same throne, uttering the same speech, and proclaiming the same Faith.
– Bahá'u'lláh, *The Book of Certitude*, pp. 153-154.

With these words, the founder of the Bahá'í Faith announced the unity of all religions. The prophets of God, he wrote, "soar in the same heaven, utter the same speech and proclaim the same Faith."

That's the nexus of Bahá'í belief—that no religion trumps any other; that religion is progressive by nature; and that all religions are one:

To contend that any particular religion is final, that **"all Revelation is ended, that the portals of Divine mercy are closed, that from the daysprings of eternal holiness no sun shall rise again, that the ocean of everlasting bounty is forever stilled, and that out of the Tabernacle of ancient glory the Messengers of God have ceased to be made manifest"** would indeed be nothing less than sheer blasphemy.

"They differ, explains Bahá'u'lláh in that same epistle, "only in the intensity of their revelation and the comparative potency of their light." And this, not by reason of any inherent incapacity of any one of them to reveal in a fuller measure the glory of the Message with which He has been entrusted, but rather because of the immaturity and unpreparedness of the age He lived in to apprehend and absorb the full potentialities latent in that Faith.
– Shoghi Effendi, *The World Order of Bahá'u'lláh*, p 58 (portions enclosed in quotations from Bahá'u'lláh, *The Book of Certitude*.)

These excerpts from the Bahá'í teachings show the power of the word of God on our minds to introduce earth-shaking and unifying new concepts.

Like turning swords into ploughshares—that is, into healing words—the utterances of the prophets contain power and truth. That power and truth inevitably result in change. The change begins in the human heart, affects us deeply, and then translates itself into action. The Bahá'í teachings, in the context of today's misconception and abominable belief that religion must be promoted through the use of the "sword," or modern weapons and bombs, exalts the power of words and utterance:

We have decreed that war shall be waged in the path of God with the armies of wisdom and utterance, and of a goodly character and praiseworthy deeds. Thus hath it been decided by Him Who is the All-Powerful, the Almighty.
There is no glory for him that committeth disorder on the earth after it hath been made so good...
Beware lest ye shed the blood of any one. Unsheathe the sword of your tongue from the scabbard of utterance, for therewith ye can conquer the citadels of men's hearts.
We have abolished the law to wage holy war against each other. God's mercy hath, verily, encompassed all created things, if ye do but understand.
– Bahá'u'lláh, *Epistle to the Son of the Wolf*, pp. 24-25.

My convictions regarding the power of words—which I've seen amply demonstrated in my own 20-year experience as a dispute mediator in my local court system—centers on Bahá'u'lláh's peaceful approach to the influence of moderation, tact and wisdom in choosing what we say:

Human utterance is an essence which aspireth to exert its influence and needeth moderation.
As to its influence, this is conditional upon refinement, which in turn is dependent upon hearts which are detached and pure. As to its moderation, this hath to be combined with tact and wisdom as prescribed in the Holy Scriptures and Tablets.
– Bahá'u'lláh, *Tablets of Bahá'u'lláh*, p. 143.

Just as a mother does not feed steak to her newborn, the milk of loving-kindness and patience is the nourishment required.

If you've ever been involved, even as an onlooker, in a disagreement between people, you will know that calmness, control, and keen listening brings insight into the principles of truth contained in their spoken words. This can often best come from the perspective of a neutral observer, learned in the skills of mediation, diplomacy, and arbitration, so universally used in today's world to solve human problems.

Active listening, emphasized in schools for decades now, is more than just hearing someone's words. It means truly attempting to understand the thoughts, motivations, and feelings behind the words. We can best respond to those thoughts, motivations, and feelings, the Bahá'í teachings say, when we allow our own words to aspire to purity and moderation:

Utterance must needs possess penetrating power. For if bereft of this quality it would fail to exert influence. And this penetrating influence dependeth on the spirit being pure and the heart stainless.

Likewise it needeth moderation, without which the hearer would be unable to bear it, rather he would manifest opposition from the very outset. And moderation will be obtained by blending utterance with the tokens of divine wisdom which are recorded in the sacred Books and Tablets.

Thus when the essence of one's utterance is endowed with these two requisites it will prove highly effective and will be the prime factor in transforming the souls of men.
– Ibid., pp. 198-199.

Next: Scripture, Facebook, and the Impact of the Written Word

#

Scripture, Facebook, and the Impact of the Written Word

Teachings PART 3 IN SERIES: THE POWER OF THE WORD

The difference between the right word and the almost right word is the difference between lightning and the lightning bug.
– Mark Twain, October 1888 letter

What Mark Twain said holds much meaning for the spoken word, but even more so for Facebook.

My wife Janet has said to me, "Don't post that – it's not public," or asked, "Rod, how could you write that?" when one of my (I thought), innocuous Facebook comments caused umbrage from an FB friend. Finally, I asked Janet how to edit (or delete) my poor or insensitive wording—and I think I'm always careful!

The written word can have an enormous impact.

Granted, you can't please everyone. You can't know where others have been or come from, or how they'll feel about a subject unless perhaps you know them. But as human beings, we have an innate desire to express ourselves, and we will. Hence over 17 million books now available on Amazon, a drop in the bucket of the 129 million ever published.

Spoken words have an immediate effect, but can be forgotten, overlooked, or forgiven. We've all had experience with that, with our own or other's words.

But the written word is permanent; it can leave a stain on one's character that cannot be removed by the most heartfelt protestations. The written word lasts ages and centuries and is timeless. Rereading the written word invokes its power endlessly, for good or ill, inspiration or degradation, upliftment or cruelty.

As a writer I am keenly aware of this.

Listening to others' stories in multiple writing groups and seeing their words on paper always has immediate and sometimes long-lasting impact on my emotions, as well as in my thoughts and beliefs.

That permanence makes the goal of every balanced writer to "write with authority"—so different than those blog rants these days, which may be true but offer no solution to any problem. Balanced writing calls for understanding both sides of the issue.

Of course, you can find the longest-lasting and most influential writing in the scriptures.

The scriptures of all great Faiths depart from the writings of us mere mortals. They contain more than balance and truth as we perceive it, for their words give us life's true balance. They create entire civilizations, influence history forever, and change the lives of billions of people. Granted, it's difficult to accept the veracity of some of those words, written hundreds of years in some cases after the prophet's death.

Nonetheless the power of universal truth they contain is unmistakable.

The founders of those great Faiths, each and every one, are the original sources of true authority, the authority inherent as the mouthpiece of the unknowable essence God. Their role: to converse with God's creatures and guide them to peace and security, despite their lower natures, concerned with ego and self.

Whole books have been written on this theme, from St. Paul to Freud, but the point I wish to make is that the words, "the speech," and writings of the Prophets change, in one master stroke, the concepts and fortunes of all of humankind's social as well as religious relationships.

Explaining this, 'Abdu'l-Bahá wrote:

... when difference and variety of thoughts, forms, opinions, characters and morals of the world of mankind come under the control of one Supreme Power and the influence of the Word of the One True God, they will appear and be displayed in the most perfect glory, beauty, exaltation and perfection.

Today nothing but the power of the Word of God which encompasses the realities of things can bring the thoughts, the minds, the hearts and the spirits under the shade of one Tree. He is the potent in all things, the vivifier of souls, the preserver and the controller of the world of mankind.

Praise be to God, in this day the light of the Word of God has shone forth upon all regions, and from all sects, communities, nations, tribes, peoples, religions and denominations, souls have gathered under the shadow of the Word of Oneness and have in the most intimate fellowship, united and harmonized!
– *Tablet to The Hague*, p. 13.

History has proven the power of the written word of God to create whole civilizations, encompassing most of humanity.

Bahá'ís believe the word of God has now appeared again— that the future holds, in this unsurpassed cycle of unending knowledge and abilities, great promise for the stability and peace of humankind's ordered life on this planet.

In this age, as in none gone before, we have access to hundreds of books and written tablets from the newest founder of a great world Faith. In his hand, Bahá'u'lláh wrote down this new revelation, confirming the spiritual teachings of those gone before him and bringing a new cycle of divine guidance to the world.

The Mystical, Mythic Name of 'Abdu'l-Bahá

History

> **You who are the servants of God fight against oppression, hate and discord, so that wars may cease and God's laws of peace and love may be established among men.**
> – 'Abdu'l-Bahá, *Paris Talks*, p. 98.

To millions of Bahá'ís around the world, the name 'Abdu'l-Bahá has a unique and profound meaning.

'Abdu'l-Bahá

As a reader of BahaiTeachings.org, you've no doubt seen numerous quotes from 'Abdu'l-Bahá's words and many examples from his life. A remarkable figure, unique in all religious history, 'Abdu'l-Bahá's name means "servant of Baha," or "servant of the glory." 'Abdu'l-Bahá's unprecedented role—as the Exemplar of the Bahá'í teachings—makes him the role model for all Bahá'ís.

In many ways, the Bahá'í Faith today, one hundred seventy-two years after its beginnings, could not be fully understandable without the spoken and written words, and the examples set, by 'Abdu'l-Bahá.

Born in Tehran, Persia on the auspicious date of May 23, 1844—the same day the Bábi Faith began—his illustrious father Bahá'u'lláh named his firstborn child Abbas. Eight years later Abbas would visit his father in the prison called the Black Pit, where Bahá'u'lláh received the revelation that confirmed his mission as the prophet and founder of the Bahá'í Faith. Abbas, the first to recognize Bahá'u'lláh's station, served his father and his father's Faith for his entire life. Even as a child 'Abdu'l-Bahá mastered the Bahá'í teachings, so Bahá'u'lláh singled out the title "Master" for his son while still a youth. Up until his own death Bahá'u'lláh gave his eldest son other names and titles such as "the Exemplar" and "the Mystery of God."

[The Master] was truly a mystery, because he was not a prophet of God—but rather a perfect Bahá'í, the living example of the spiritual teachings of Bahá'u'lláh, "the remembrance of God amongst you and His trust within you…" wrote Bahá'u'lláh in his Tablet of the Branch.

If you study 'Abdu'l-Bahá's life of love and sacrifice, you'll see that he spent more than half of it [as a prisoner] with Bahá'u'lláh, and only obtained his release in 1908, sixteen years after Bahá'u'lláh named 'Abdu'l-Bahá as his successor. After Bahá'u'lláh's passing, [the Master] was designated in his father's written will as the Center of Bahá'u'lláh's covenant, the person every Bahá'í should turn to for guidance and inspiration.

In the history of religion, this has never happened before—a living prophet naming a successor.

The Master had long been a firm believer and trusted confidante. He served his father, family and the believers with distinction and devotion throughout Bahá'u'lláh's life, after his passing, and during the early 20th Century establishment of Bahá'í communities throughout the world. According to his grandson Shoghi Effendi, the Heroic, Apostolic Age of the Bahá'í Faith ended with 'Abdu'l-Bahá's death in 1921.

'Abdu'l-Bahá said this about his name and his unique spiritual station:

My name is 'Abdu'l-Bahá. My qualification is 'Abdu'l-Bahá. My reality is 'Abdu'l-Bahá. My praise is 'Abdu'l-Bahá. Thralldom to the Blessed Perfection [Bahá'u'lláh]

is my glorious and refulgent diadem, and servitude to all the human race my perpetual religion …

No name, no title, no mention, no commendation have I, nor will ever have, except 'Abdu'l-Bahá.

This is my longing.
This is my greatest yearning.
This is my eternal life.
This is my everlasting glory.
– 'Abdu'l-Bahá, quoted by Shoghi Effendi, *The World Order of Bahá'u'lláh*, p. 139.

Because the title 'Abdu'l-Bahá literally means "servant of the glory," or "servant of Bahá'u'lláh," you can see the double meaning here in 'Abdu'l-Bahá's words. He firmly establishes his station as one of humble servitude, not only to the Bahá'í teachings but to the Bahá'ís themselves, and to all the world. 'Abdu'l-Bahá exemplified that servitude in his life and words.

To Bahá'ís, 'Abdu'l-Bahá, designated one of the three Central Figures of the Bahá'í Faith, showed the world his true station through his innumerable acts of kindness and charity to others; through his global campaign for unity and peace; and through his powerful spiritual counsel to the entire planet.

One of 'Abdu'l-Bahá's missions, given to him by Bahá'u'lláh, was to spread the Bahá'í teachings among the world's people. In his travels across the Middle East, Europe, and North America, the Master proclaimed openly the teachings of this new worldwide religion, with the pivot the unification of the entire human race. In hundreds of [written down] talks and in innumerable settings, 'Abdu'l-Bahá left a legacy of tens of thousands of documents for posterity, relied upon by the Bahá'ís as explanations of the import and breadth of the Bahá'í teachings on the future of society and the spiritual destiny of humankind.

The Master, as amply illustrated by his many talks and letters, always encouraged and never disparaged. His words and actions always uplifted and never depressed, always stayed positive and never turned negative. To all Bahá'ís, 'Abdu'l-Bahá's words hold binding and authoritative meaning, guiding a global community in their conduct and outlook.

For Bahá'í writers, the entire body of believers, and the entire world, the words and life of 'Abdu'l-Bahá not only serve as sources of wisdom and guidance, but act as the practical example and encouragement needed to "change this darksome world to light."

#

Who Really Raises Our Children?
Culture

I'd like to believe God helps us.

Certainly, I've had some help from above, looking back on my 66 years and comparing where I was at low times to my circumstances now. My wife and I live comfortably in New Jersey's suburbia, and that doesn't come easily for a middle-class bloke like me. I meditate and give thanks every morning and during the day for my good fortune.

At some point we all realize our material condition relative to others, most pointedly when we see extreme want and think or say aloud, "There but for the grace of God go I." Like so many other fathers and mothers, I really give thanks when it comes to our children, especially when they grow up to become independent, upstanding citizens.

Was it by chance they became thoughtful, productive members of society? Or did God guide our path, and theirs?

The better question might be, looking back, "Did God guide our actions in raising them?" Was it coincidence that they themselves had the strength of inner character as well? Or did the fact that my wife was a teacher and knew the stages of moral development so well, to effect how we trained them accordingly? Were there difficulties? Sure. Obstacles? Definitely. Disappointments? Of course. But just as in our own lives, when perseverance and patience won out, desirable outcomes appeared in theirs.

If thy daily living becomes difficult, soon thy Lord will bestow upon thee that which shall satisfy thee. Be patient in the time of affliction and trial, endure every difficulty and hardship with dilated heart, attracted spirit and eloquent tongue in remembrance of the Merciful.

Verily this is the life of satisfaction, the spiritual existence, heavenly repose, divine benediction and the celestial table! Soon thy Lord will extenuate thy straightened circumstances even in this world.
– 'Abdu'l-Bahá, [*Tablets of 'Abdu'l-Bahá Abbas*, vol. 1, p 98]

My dear wife and I believed our kids were spiritual beings as well as material, and life's cycle of ups and downs, side paths and straightaways, disasters and crowning achievements tested that theory. Was God there to help?

It depends of course, on whether one believes in divine assistance or solely in one's own abilities and no others. Certainly, in raising our two children, consistency and stability greatly aided the results—and faith played a major role.

Faith sustains us, or should, in times of trials and setbacks. We have faith that things will turn out for the best, that a divine purpose illumines humankind's mutual life on this planet, and by extension, that each of us has a role to play in making our children's lives better. We have faith that God wants the best for us:

In the spiritual world the divine bestowals are infinite, for in that realm there is neither separation nor disintegration, which characterize the world of material existence. Spiritual existence is absolute immortality, completeness and unchangeable being.

Therefore, we must thank God that He has created for us both material blessings and spiritual bestowals. He has given us material gifts and spiritual graces, outer sight to view the lights of the sun and inner vision by which we may perceive the glory of God. He has designed the outer ear to enjoy the melodies of sound and the inner hearing wherewith we may hear the voice of our Creator.

We must strive with energies of heart, soul and mind to develop and manifest the perfections and virtues latent within the realities of the phenomenal world, for the human reality may be compared to a seed. If we sow the seed, a mighty tree appears from it.

– 'Abdu'l-Bahá, *The Promulgation of Universal Peace*, p. 90.

If we believe hope is gone, that all hope has deserted us, then our lives turn truly bleak. But if we believe that sowing a seed can create a mighty tree, we have faith and hope.

Physically and spiritually our union created children, as blessings to our beings. From those seeds mighty trees sprouted and have spread their branches. From the fruit of those branches a granddaughter has been born and brought even more joy, more purpose to our lives. God has given us the joy of knowing that life continues, and that these young ones will fulfill their purpose, the happiness and betterment of all humanity.

Do you think God has had a role to play in your upbringing, or that of your children?   **#**

Does God Really Help (Me)?

Spirituality

Does God really help us?

Surely, He did after I heard these words in April of 1979: "Rod, you're fired."

I worked then for the State of New Jersey, first and second shifts in the Treasury Department Computer Room, with an unblemished record. But I blew it one night in a three-minute act of disloyalty, earning my supervisor's immediate distrust.

I felt completely distraught. My two-year-old son and young wife at home, all of us, relied on my income. Now it was over, kaput, nine hard years down the toilet through an unforgiveable error of judgment.

But was it unforgiveable? I heard those dreaded words on Friday, and on Saturday I went to my supervisor's home and begged forgiveness. He listened, but I had no real hope for a reprieve. Back home I prayed, I moaned, I went through scenarios of doom. Only my wife Janet had positive words of comfort.

But Monday I received a call, "Rod, come in." Immediately transferred to a new section of the Bureau and a new boss, I began afresh what would be another 30 years in the Treasury Department. "Oh thank you Lord!" I said that night, many times over.

I've always asked myself since, "What made them change their minds?" Was it my sincere pleading? Or was it God's intervention?

O ye beloved of the Lord!

Beware, beware lest ye hesitate and waver. Let not fear fall upon you, neither be troubled nor dismayed.

Take ye good heed lest this calamitous day slacken the flames of your ardor, and quench your tender hopes. Today is the day for steadfastness and constancy.

Blessed are they that stand firm and immovable as the rock, and brave the storm and stress of this tempestuous hour.

They, verily, shall be the recipients of God's grace, verily shall receive His divine assistance, and shall be the truly victorious.

– 'Abdu'l-Bahá, *Selections from the Writings of 'Abdu'l-Bahá*, pp. 17-18.

'Abdu'l-Bahá addressed these words to the Bahá'ís, urging them to remain steadfast. I took comfort [and strength] from them.

Steadfast. Like my wife Janet at the time of my firing and subsequent depression, who said, "Surely Rod, you have skills. You'll find another job."

How many times have I called upon God's unknowable essence to protect me, or us, or our children and others, to help and assist! How many times have I looked within myself for some trace of the traceless Friend, the Supreme Being who helps us all:

Upon the reality of man ... He hath focused the radiance of all of His names and attributes, and made it a mirror of His own Self....

These energies ... lie, however, latent within him, even as the flame is hidden within the candle and the rays of light are potentially present in the lamp.... Neither the candle nor the lamp can be lighted through their own unaided efforts, nor can it ever be possible for the mirror to free itself from its dross.

-- Bahá'u'lláh, *Gleanings from the Writings of Bahá'u'lláh*, pp. 65-66.

As in this personal example, where did my supervisor's mercy come from, and his boss', and their bosses? It seems to me that mercy, an attribute of God also possessed by humans, "latent," was at work in my case.

So it is in life. We do not live unaided. By or through God's will, or by or through His will discovered and opened in others' minds and hearts, we manage and thrive.

Have you had an experience you attribute to God's assistance?

#

Brexit, Nationalism and World Unity

Culture

By now you've heard plenty on the news about Brexit. Hundreds of articles, news reports and opinions have covered the referendum question: "Should the United Kingdom remain a member of the European Union?"

So now that most of the shouting has died down, let's review. The United Kingdom has four national entities—England, Scotland, Wales and Northern Ireland.

Here's how they voted:
  England   53.2% to 46.8%   **Leave**
  Scotland 62%   to 38%   **Remain**
  Wales   51.7% to 48.3%   **Leave**
  N. Ireland 55.7% to 44.3% **Remain**

Essentially, England and Wales decided to go it alone, to retain full sovereignty over their nations, while Scotland and Northern Ireland chose to retain the benefits of full EU membership by ceding part of their own rulemaking authority.

Without ceding some sovereignty rights to a world authority, or in this case, a limited federalized political body [in the interim], humankind will remain in the throes of disunity and self-destruction.

That's not to say that every union, whether 50 states in the U.S. or other political unities [like the European Union], began perfectly or operates seamlessly. We here in the States still try to form "a more perfect union" every day.

When European countries started to cooperate economically in 1951, only Belgium, Germany, France, Italy, Luxembourg and the Netherlands participated. Now there will be 26, not 28 European Union member states, and loud voices, especially in the Netherlands and France, urge those nations to do what the United Kingdom has just done.

Now we will see how history views their decision, and what effects will occur. Already the British Pound has suffered significant value loss in the markets, and the United Kingdom itself is questioning the wisdom of pulling out of the EU permanently.

The Bahá'ís and others have known for some time that diplomatic unification of peoples and nations has become a necessary, critical process toward permanent world security and peace. As early as 1941 the Guardian of the Bahá'í Faith, Shoghi Effendi, wrote about the dangers of exalting nationalism above international peace and unity:

The theories and policies, so unsound, so pernicious, which deify the state and exalt the nation above mankind, which seek to subordinate the sister races of the world to one single race, which discriminate between the black and the white, and which tolerate the dominance of one privileged class over all others — these are the dark, the false, and crooked doctrines for which any man or people who believes in them, or acts upon them, must, sooner or later, incur the wrath and chastisement of God.
– *The Promised Day is Come*, pp. 113-114.

A return to isolationism, or a backward march toward "the good ole days" of pure nationalism is a chimera. It cannot be done in a globalized world. Every under-standing person knows the old, obsolescent doctrine of pure national sovereignty will [not] succeed [long] in a shrinking world governed by constant change. In the 21st century, a century of light, globalization is the road to life, as so evidenced by economic realities and banded unities such as the World Trade Organization.

The Bahá'í teachings equate [unbridled] nationalism with war, and advocate an ongoing process of global unification to counter the chaos of pure national sovereignty:

Contrasting with, and irreconcilably opposed to, these war-engendering, world-convulsing doctrines are the healing, the saving, the pregnant truths proclaimed by

Bahá'u'lláh, the Divine Organizer and Savior of the whole human race — truths which should be regarded as the animating force and the hallmark of His Revelatiocitizens."

"Let not a man glory in that he loves his country; let him rather glory in this, that he loves his kind."

And again: "Ye are the fruits of one tree, and the leaves of one branch."

"Bend your minds and wills to the education of the peoples and kindreds of the earth, that haply ... all mankind may become the upholders of one order, and the inhabitants of one city.... Ye dwell in one world, and have been created through the operation of one Will."

"Beware lest the desires of the flesh and of a corrupt inclination provoke divisions among you. Be ye as the fingers of one hand, the members of one body."

And yet again: "All the saplings of the world have appeared from one Tree, and all the drops from one Ocean, and all beings owe their existence to one Being."

And furthermore: "That one indeed is a man who today dedicateth himself to the service of the entire human race."
— Ibid., p. 114.

"Loves his kind" has been interpreted by over 17 million [voters] in the case of Brexit, to mean only one's countrymen—[perhaps only those who agree]--at the expense and [possible] detriment of others.

I for one hope that the native England of my wife's war-bride mother will survive and thrive, somehow, and regain its senses [and remain unified]. Perhaps we will see a Referendum such as: "Can we regain our position as one unified nation among a group of unified nations?"

Yes, there may have been "good ole days" for some; but certainly not for all Americans or British or any other people. I for one, and many others, look forward to and work hard for better tomorrows, not a return to a mythical yesterday.

[**Author's update:** The Bahá'í Faith does not take a position on Brexit, the European Union or politics. But the Faith has much to say about achieving unity and reasons preventing it.

These are my own impressions and opinions as in all the articles herein.]

#

How to Delve Deeper into Your Soul

Spirituality PART 1 IN SERIES: **WORDS OF WISDOM**

When I read sacred scriptures or even the "Words of Wisdom" in every Time magazine issue, I am always moved to thoughtfully consider the import of those words—to try to delve a little deeper.

First, I take personal meaning from them. I usually ask myself, "How does this effect my life? My outlook on life? My relationships with others? With God?"

If you do that, too, you're "deepening" your knowledge—and your self-knowledge. You're delving deeper into what you know and what you don't know, with the hope of increasing your understanding and becoming a deeper person.

For decades, I've studied the Bahá'í writings this way. Bahá'ís often call that kind of study "deepening," and many Bahá'ís have regular deepening classes to study together. Essentially, that sort of serious study involves delving into the depth of the meaning of the words, what they signify, what they symbolize, and what actions they call forth in personal transformation.

Every religion has spent ages delving, interpreting, organizing, spreading and acting upon the holy words of their founders, and the Bahá'í Faith follows that pattern, too, with one exception: Bahá'ís have no clergy. That means every individual becomes responsible for their own level of knowledge and understanding.

So, if you'd like a better, more penetrating knowledge of the Bahá'í teachings, you can start deepening by yourself. Bahá'u'lláh, the prophet and founder of the Bahá'í Faith, encouraged everyone to do exactly that:

Immerse yourselves in the ocean of My words, that ye may unravel its secrets, and discover all the pearls of wisdom that lie hid in its depths.
– *The Most Holy Book*, p. 85.

The Guardian of the Bahá'í Faith, Shoghi Effendi, expounded on Bahá'u'lláh's advice:

Indeed if an avowed follower of Bahá'u'lláh were to immerse himself in, and fathom the depths of, the ocean of these heavenly teachings, and with utmost care and attention deduce from each of them the subtle mysteries

and consummate wisdom that lie enshrined therein, such a person's life, materially, intellectually and spiritually, will be safe from toil and trouble, and unaffected by setbacks and perils, or any sadness or despondency.
– Attributed to "Abdu'l-Bahá in a letter to the Bahá'ís of Adhirbayjan, January 1923.

That's quite a promise! Who wouldn't want to be freed from toil and trouble?

That kind of freedom comes from fully absorbing the hopeful, happy message of the Bahá'í teachings, and then beginning to live that message. While deepening relates to knowing oneself and freeing that self, it can also involve questioning one's own motives and actions. To deepen means to read the Bahá'í writings with intention, searching out one's spirit, mind and body on the most personal level, through meditation and introspection.

As an example of deepening, let's examine this passage from Bahá'u'lláh:

Were man to appreciate the greatness of his station and the loftiness of his destiny he would manifest naught save goodly character, pure deeds, and a seemly and praiseworthy conduct.
– *Tablets of Bahá'u'lláh*, p. 172.

These words seem apparent: man has a nobler station than he himself realizes, and if he could share that nobility with others, soon the whole earth would be unified. We see this exemplified all the time on the news by actions of heroes and heroines, ordinary people performing selfless acts by providing aid to others.

Bahá'u'lláh's quote continues:

If the learned and wise men of goodwill were to impart guidance unto the people, the whole earth would be regarded as one country. Verily this is the undoubted truth. This servant appealeth to every diligent and enterprising soul to exert his utmost endeavor and arise to rehabilitate the conditions in all regions and to quicken the dead with the living waters of wisdom and utterance, by virtue of the love he cherisheth for God, the One, the Peerless, the Almighty, the Beneficent.
– Ibid.

These words of wisdom, when they become the subject of true deepening, don't simply reside in the mind. They take root in the soul and cause us to want to fulfill their visionary spiritual advice.

They ask us to aspire to a nobler, higher reality.

They call upon our souls to exert our "utmost endeavor" and "arise to rehabilitate the conditions in all regions." These words inspire us to serve others, the true calling of all real religion.

The Bahá'í teachings call for selfless action. If we truly want to succeed at uplifting the plight of hundreds of millions from poverty or injustice, from destitution, or genocide and oppression, we'll respond to that call, because of the love of God—which brings with it the love for every human soul and by extension, the hope, desire and wish for everybody's well-being, not just our own.

Next: How to Consult about Reality–Lovingly

#

How to Consult About Reality – Lovingly

Teachings PART 2 IN SERIES: WORDS OF WISDOM

The heaven of divine wisdom is illumined with the two luminaries of consultation and compassion. Take ye counsel together in all matters, inasmuch as consultation is the lamp of guidance which leadeth the way, and is the bestower of understanding.
– Bahá'u'lláh, *Tablets of Bahá'u'lláh*, p. 168.

In the previous essay we delved into the meaning of deepening in the Bahá'í writings, on one level an act of personal introspection and individual discovery of the truth. Now we'll examine the benefit of consultation—of sharing and discussing those writings with others.

All of us begin deepening our knowledge of faith and spirituality by ourselves—a necessary and natural process. When we encounter a new source of wisdom, we automatically want to learn more, to question ourselves and the world around us. We explore that new knowledge by reading, deepening, meditating and reflecting.

But how do we do make sense of it all? How do we know what is right, and truth? How do we share it with others?

It's really a question of investigating reality:

The first teaching is that man should investigate reality, for reality is contrary to dogmatic interpretations and imitations of ancestral forms of belief to which all nations and peoples adhere so tenaciously.

These blind imitations are contrary to the fundamental basis of the divine religions, for the divine religions in their central and essential teaching are based upon unity,

love and peace, whereas these variations and imitations have ever been productive of warfare, sedition and strife.

Therefore, all souls should consider it incumbent upon them to investigate reality. Reality is one and when found, it will unify all mankind.
Reality is the love of God.
Reality is the knowledge of God.
Reality is justice.
Reality is the oneness or solidarity of mankind.
Reality is international peace.
Reality is the knowledge of verities.
Reality unifies humanity.
– 'Abdu'l-Bahá, *The Promulgation of Universal Peace*, p. 372.

We cannot make it, do it, understand it, or survive it, alone. If we really want to deepen our knowledge and ourselves, we have to share it with others, discuss it with others, and refine our understanding with others. Even the great basketball star Michael Jordan had to be fed the ball by teammates.

In consultative deepening, Bahá'ís and their friends simply share a passage from the Bahá'í teachings and discuss it openly and honestly. You're familiar with the concept if you've ever participated in just about any meeting:

A topic is brought up, discussion follows, consensus arises, and action of some kind results. Bahá'í consultation follows that basic pattern—but focuses on finding the truth:

In this Cause consultation is of vital importance, but spiritual conference and not the mere voicing of personal views is intended. In France I was present at a session of the senate, but the experience was not impressive. Parliamentary procedure should have for its object the attainment of the light of truth upon questions presented and not furnish a battleground for opposition and self-opinion. Antagonism and contradiction are unfortunate and always destructive to truth.

In the parliamentary meeting mentioned, altercation and useless quibbling were frequent; the result, mostly confusion and turmoil; even in one instance a physical encounter took place between two members. It was not consultation but comedy.

The purpose is to emphasize the statement that consultation must have for its object the investigation of truth.
– Ibid., p. 72.

'Abdu'l-Bahá defines Bahá'í consultation as "spiritual conference in the attitude and atmosphere of love:

"Consultation is to deepening as breathing is to living. Bahá'ís find deep pleasure in discussing any topic, and sharing it amongst others for their honest reactions and feedback. That consultative process produces thoughtful interchange, considered opinion and the openness necessary to change everyone's thinking.

Even a majority opinion or consensus may be incorrect. A thousand people may hold to one view and be mistaken, whereas one sagacious person may be right.

Therefore, true consultation is spiritual conference in the attitude and atmosphere of love. Members must love each other in the spirit of fellowship in order that good results may be forthcoming. Love and fellowship are the foundation.
— Ibid., pp. 72-73.

These two essentially spiritual processes—deepening and consultation—form the basis for the thoughtful study of the Bahá'í teachings.

What words of wisdom guide you?

#

National Sovereignty: A Blight on Humanity
Culture

For thousands of years, men have battled and killed each other over territory, fighting for their tombs.

For the past few hundred years, those battles have increased in severity, as nations began to fight with other nations over their "sovereign" lands.

The Bahá'í teachings call for an end to this blight on the name of humanity:

That all nations should become one in faith and all men as brothers; that the bonds of affection and unity between the sons of men should be strengthened; that diversity of religion should cease, and differences of race be annulled—what harm is there in this?
... Yet so it shall be; these fruitless strifes, these ruinous wars shall pass away, and the 'Most Great Peace' shall come. ...
Do not you in Europe need this also? Is not this that which Christ foretold?
...Yet do we see your kings and rulers lavishing their treasures more freely on means for the destruction of the human race than on that which would conduce to the happiness of mankind.
...These strifes and this bloodshed and discord must cease, and all men be as one kindred and one family. ...
Let not a man glory in this, that he loves his country; let him rather glory in this, that he loves his kind.
– Bahá'u'lláh, quoted by J. E. Esslemont in *Bahá'u'lláh and the New Era*, pp. 39-40.

Bahá'u'lláh spoke these words to British orientalist Professor Edward Granville Brown in 1890, 24 years before World War I, and 51 years before World War II. Both wars were fought over land [aquisition, for] the domination of peoples and resources—all because rulers wanted to expand or guard their national sovereignty.

For the past 71 years, shooting wars over national sovereignty have largely diminished. Instead, we now fight "trade wars" for economic domination. Sovereign nations battle economically, rather than with bombs and guns. Of course, these non-violent wars, primarily fought through the setting of tariffs and restrictions, have also gone on for thousands of years.

The primary transnational organization actively working to balance competing economic desires and demands today is the World Trade Organization (WTO). It officially commenced on 1 January 1995 under the Marrakesh Agreement, signed by 123 nations. The WTO deals with regulation of trade between participating countries by providing a framework for negotiating trade agreements, and a dispute resolution process aimed at enforcing participants' adherence to WTO agreements, all signed by representatives of member governments and ratified by their parliaments.

The WTO in session

The WTO is a premier example of how peoples and nations can work out their differences through diplomacy, consultation and open discussion, a model increasingly applied to end [armed] conflicts when at all possible.

Although no man-made organization will ever be perfect, words are always better than guns.

Despite its unresolved problems—some of the WTO's policies have demonstrably widened the economic gap between the world's wealthy and poor nations, for example—its focus on trade across the entire globe has likely prevented some wars.

But this trend toward globalization threatens some people. Brexit showed the world one example of a return to national sovereignty in the face of a feeling of a loss of control of a nation's [social and] economic well-being. Because hard-won tax revenues are increasingly more difficult to generate, Brexit is an example of a return to isolation, and hence, a false feeling of 100% control over a population's own destiny. Of course, this kind of nationalist thinking in the age of globalization, where borders matter less and less, [may end up being] self-defeating at best.

Whether a physical armed conflict, a conflict of religious or other ideologies and "isms," or a conflict of trade dominance—whether we want to admit it or temporarily ignore it—we are moving to a single world order and world government as the only means of reconciling competing interests on national scales. Bahá'u'lláh's own words proclaimed it more than a century ago:

"**Soon will the present day Order be rolled up, and a new one spread out in its stead.**"
– *Gleanings from the Writings of Bahá'u'lláh*, p. 7.

The Guardian of the Bahá'í Faith, Shoghi Effendi, described the inevitable trend this way:

The Revelation of Bahá'u'lláh, whose supreme mission is none other but the achievement of this organic and spiritual unity of the whole body of nations, should, if we be faithful to its implications, be regarded as signalizing through its advent the coming of age of the entire human race.

It should be viewed not merely as yet another spiritual revival in the ever-changing fortunes of mankind, not only as a further stage in a chain of progressive Revelations, nor even as the culmination of one of a series of recurrent prophetic cycles, but rather as marking the last and highest stage in the stupendous evolution of man's collective life on this planet.

The emergence of a world community, the consciousness of world citizenship, the founding of a world civilization and culture... should, by their very nature, be regarded, as far as this planetary life is concerned, as the furthermost limits in the organization of human society, though man, as an individual, will, nay must indeed as a result of such a consummation, continue indefinitely to progress and develop.
– *The World Order of Bahá'u'lláh*, p. 163.

The prescient phrase "the furthermost limits in the organization of human society" describes a unified global community that has progressed far past the old wars of the past, whether fought with bullets or tariffs.

Given sufficient time and effort, humankind may achieve it sooner rather than later.

#

How Do Words Become Holy?

Culture

Wise men speak because they have something to say; Fools because they have to say something. – Plato

The single biggest problem in communication is the illusion that it has taken place. – George Bernard Shaw

Don't tell me the moon is shining; show me the glint of light on broken glass. – Anton Chekhov

Each of us has our own language, vocabulary, creed and background, with varying educational levels and experiences—but we all use the same basic words to express ourselves.

I admit, it's tough not just writing a poem or such and leaving it to readers to interpret those words any way they wish. But the base principle behind all words, spoken or written, is communication.

And boy are words tricky! Talking about a grill-fired backyard barbecue is one thing. But shouting "Fire!" in a crowded movie theater when there is none has legal ramifications for the shouter. The polar opposites "I love you!" and "I hate you!" cause untold joy or pain.

Words have histories, context, and hidden meanings. They can put you in a state of joy or a state of utter depression. There is no end to understanding the meanings of words; how they are spoken and used, how they can be dissected when written, how they can affect our behavior, our perceptions, even our entire lives.

The holy words of the prophets have affected billions of lives.

We recognize that holy words have special powers and meanings other than just concrete forms, because they are directed at our own soul, not just our physical needs, head or heart.

The words of the prophets are meant for every human being. No words have as much impact. The Bible, [for example, has] been translated into 531 languages, and 2,883 languages have at least some portion of [it in them.]

The positive, uplifting, and yes, challenging or condemning words of the prophets, all of them, are indeed world-encompassing in their import, which is why there are over six billion adherents in Christianity, Islam, Hinduism, Chinese folk religions, and Buddhism alone. The majority of the world's people see the words of their prophet as sacred and filled with deep meaning.

Just about everyone has heard and seen the words of God in some form, whether orally or reading them with their own eyes. Just about everyone endeavors to understand them. When you make the effort to understand the words of God, you begin to grasp the nature and extent of religion's power in mankind's affairs, and the myriad interpretations and thousands of sects that have evolved.

But which words will unify us?

Are we doomed to squabble and fight to the death over the meaning of a few words, holy or not? Do we fight over those words because some leaders have given them special meaning they feel everyone should obey?

If we go directly to the words of the founders of the world's great Faith, we can find a never-failing remedy for the ills we suffer. That is not a generalization. If we believe in some form or name of a Supreme Being, even if He [is] called "Nameless," we have the holy texts to lead us aright – right now:

Consider the flowers of a garden: though differing in kind, colour, form and shape, yet, inasmuch as they are refreshed by the waters of one spring, revived by the breath of one wind, invigorated by the rays of one sun, this diversity increaseth their charm, and addeth unto their beauty.

Thus when that unifying force, the penetrating influence of the Word of God, taketh effect, the difference of customs, manners, habits, ideas, opinions and dispositions embellisheth the world of humanity.

– 'Abdu'l-Bahá, *Selections from the Writings of 'Abdu'l-Bahá*, p. 291.

I invite you to peruse the writings of the Bahá'í Faith, and savor the penetrating influence of the Word of God.

#

Love Songs: All About God?

Spirituality

Sing for joy in the Lord, O you righteous ones; Praise is becoming to the upright. Give thanks to the Lord with the lyre; Sing praises to Him with a harp of ten strings. Sing to Him a new song; Play skillfully with a shout of joy.
– Psalm 33:1-3.

Music is regarded as a praiseworthy science at the Threshold of the Almighty...
By virtue of this, consider how much the art of music is admired and praised. Try, if thou canst, to use spiritual melodies, songs and tunes, and to bring the earthly music into harmony with the celestial melody. Then thou wilt notice what a great influence music hath and what heavenly joy and life it conferreth.
Strike up such a melody and tune as to cause the nightingales of divine mysteries to be filled with joy and ecstasy.
–Attributed to "Abdu'l-Bahá in a tablet to an individual Bahá'í.

Gospel music is alive.

Whether it's singing the song *We Are Soldiers In God's Army*, or shakin' my feet watching the dynamic and funny 1992 movie *Sister Act* starring undercover choirmaster Whoopi Goldberg, gospel music lives. Participating in Sunday services at Trenton, New Jersey's Shiloh Baptist Church confirmed it for me, although I was put on the spot and asked to hold out the donations basket while folks stood and walked over to me to contribute, a far cry from just passing the anonymous basket around the pews.

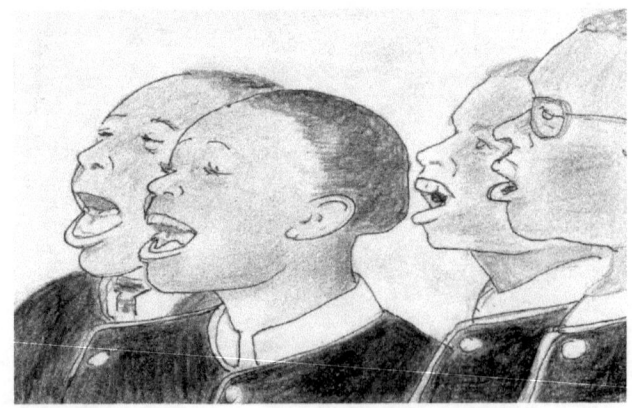

We lose our souls, our minds, our feelings, our hearts, especially our fingers, toes and feet, to the sounds and words of music. All musical genres—gospel, rock, hip-hop, country, pop, Latino, world music, New Age, R&B, EDM/Dance, Party, and much more—don't just entertain and delight or sadden, but cause human wakefulness and mindfulness.

As a writer, before setting down the first word I listen to my daily inspirational dose of music in the background—or many times, in the foreground. I pick the genre that fits my mood at 4 a.m., and away I go, floating within the space of sounds and syllables. For Bahá'ís like me, music sings the praise of God:

...that the essence of all beings may sing Thy praise before the vision of Thy grandeur. Reveal then Thyself, O Lord, by Thy merciful utterance and the mystery of Thy divine being, that the holy ecstasy of prayer may fill our souls—a prayer that shall rise above words and letters and transcend the murmur of syllables and sounds—that all things may be merged into nothingness before the revelation of Thy splendor.
– 'Abdu'l-Bahá, *Bahá'í Prayers*, p. 71.

These days, I especially [appreciate] love songs.

Love songs have been popular, even if sung only to one's beloved, since antiquity. The great Sufi mystical poet Rumi sang his love song like this:

I want to see you. Know your voice.
Recognize you when you first come 'round the corner. Sense your scent when I come into a room you've just left.
Know the lift of your heel, the glide of your foot.
Become familiar with the way you purse your lips then let them part, just the slightest bit, when I lean in to your space and kiss you.
I want to know the joy of how you whisper "more."

Any student of Rumi knows his true love was not himself, nor a woman, man nor child—but Allah, God, the One Beloved.

My challenge to you, as I challenge myself when listening to music, is to imagine God, the One Beloved, as the object of the singer's desires. Try it with the next love song you hear, and you'll see how perfectly the analogy fits. Love songs, at their core, are all about God, and our love for that divine spiritual essence we see in others.

I didn't think of this myself, of course. Years ago a close friend said, "I think God is the object of every love song."

After listening to all genres of music at home and in my car with that deep observation in mind, I began to agree with my friend. Now I believe that all songs and all music are about the Unknowable one. The more I try to "test" music lyrics, the more I realize how true my friend's comments are. The pounding beats and notes reinforce this feeling, and almost every song I listen to now transports me to that Rumi-like place of love.

That, I've concluded, is the essence of "Soul" music, "Heart" music, and gospel music, maybe the oldest forms of all songs about love and life.

The Bahá'í teachings reinforce that feeling, especially when they encourage music as "spiritual food for the soul and heart:"

In this new and wondrous dispensation the veils of superstition have been torn asunder and the prejudices of eastern peoples stand condemned

Among certain nations of the East, music was considered reprehensible, but in this new age the Manifest Light hath, in His holy Tablets, specifically proclaimed that music, sung or played, is spiritual food for soul and heart.

The musician's art is among those arts worthy of the highest praise, and it moveth the hearts of all... play and sing out the holy words of God with wondrous tones in the gatherings of the friends, that the listener may be freed from chains of care and sorrow, and his soul may leap for joy and humble itself in prayer to the realm of Glory.

– 'Abdu'l-Bahá, *Selections from the Writings of 'Abdu'l-Bahá*, p. 112.

#

Do You Believe in Fate or Destiny?
Spirituality

I've always held a negative impression of fate, and a more positive one of destiny.

What's the distinction, you ask? If both fate and destiny mean that things happen through no control of our own, how do they differ? Let's look at the dictionary definitions:

Fate: the development of events beyond a person's control, regarded as determined by a supernatural power.

Destiny: the events that will necessarily happen to a particular person or thing in the future.

With fate, things happen beyond our control—but with destiny, we exert at least some conditional control over our future.

Do you see why I always liked destiny better? I feel much more comfortable knowing that my own actions influence what will happen to me, rather than only broad external forces.

Of course, that's specious thinking because none of us have control over outside events at all—we only have control over ourselves. Fate is fait accompli, events we're powerless to stop; and destiny is the ability, however slight, to conditionally mold the future through character and actions.

Do you believe in fate or in destiny?

It seems to me that by these definitions we need to accept both into our lives, with open arms and no fears.

The Bahá'í teachings define it this way:

Fate is of two kinds: One is irrevocable and the other is conditional, or, as it is said, impending. Irrevocable fate is that which cannot be changed or altered, while conditional fate is that which may or may not occur.

Thus, the irrevocable fate for this lamp is that its oil will be burnt and consumed. Its eventual extinction is therefore certain, and it is impossible to change or alter this outcome, for such is its irrevocable fate...

But conditional fate may be likened to this: While some oil yet remains, a strong wind blows and extinguishes the lamp. This fate is conditional. It is expedient to avoid this fate, to guard oneself against it, and to be cautious and prudent.

– 'Abdu'l-Bahá, *Some Answered Questions*, newly revised edition, p. 283.

To follow this analogy, the lamp itself can do nothing other than fulfill its created purpose: to burn oil and keep the flame lit. The oil represents the capacity we are given in this life, not the time we have on Earth.

So—what's the purpose of a human being on this planet, in this life? Are we here just to burn our oil?

As the purpose of the oil is to enkindle the lamp, so the purpose of our soul is to enkindle our spirit. Just as the lamp gives light to a home, so our lives give light to the world, transcending "the world of material existence:"

Man is intelligent, instinctively and consciously intelligent; nature is not. Man is fortified with memory; nature does not possess it. Man is the discoverer of the mysteries of nature; nature is not conscious of those mysteries herself.

It is evident, therefore, that man is dual in aspect: as an animal he is subject to nature, but in his spiritual or conscious being he transcends the world of material existence. His spiritual powers, being nobler and higher, possess virtues of which nature intrinsically has no evidence; therefore, they triumph over natural conditions.

These ideal virtues or powers in man surpass or surround nature, comprehend natural laws and phenomena, penetrate the mysteries of the unknown and invisible and bring them forth into the realm of the known and visible. All the existing arts and sciences were once hidden secrets of nature.

By his command and control of nature man took them out of the plane of the invisible and revealed them in the plane of visibility, whereas according to the exigencies of nature these secrets should have remained latent and concealed.

According to the exigencies of nature electricity should be a hidden, mysterious power; but the penetrating intellect of man has discovered it, taken it out of the realm of mystery and made it an obedient human servant. In his physical body and its functions man is a captive of nature; for instance, he cannot continue his existence without sleep, an exigency of nature; he must partake of food and drink, which nature demands and requires.

But in his spiritual being and intelligence man dominates and controls nature, the ruler of his physical being.
– 'Abdu'l-Bahá, *The Promulgation of Universal Peace*, p. 81.

Human beings have souls. That spirit animates our bodies and sparks the intelligence that radiates from our minds. Therefore, although our ultimate fate may be decreed, we do have some abilities to challenge it and make a new destiny for ourselves, given the right conditions of awareness and susceptibility.

#

Building True Global Security

Culture PART 1 IN SERIES: TRUE PEACE COMES FROM TRUST

Experiencing an earthquake, monsoon, typhoon, or hurricane, and living to tell the tale, is easier than living through the chaos and death created by warring and distrustful groups of peoples, unstable governments and disunified nations. If you don't believe me, just ask the Syrians.

The fear, uncertainty and doubt caused by bad actors on the world stage bring continued upheavals and instability into world affairs.

In early October, voters in Colombia rejected a landmark peace deal with FARC rebels in a shocking referendum result, with 50.2% voting against it, missing passage by a mere 60,000 votes over 13 million cast. Most of those who voted "no" said they thought the peace agreement was letting the rebels "get away with murder." A tiny majority of voters said the agreement was too lenient.

Under the agreement, special courts would have been created to try crimes committed during the conflict. Those who confessed to their crimes would have been given more lenient sentences and would have avoided serving any time in conventional prisons. This, for many Colombians, was one step too far.

They also balked at their government's plan to pay demobilized FARC rebels a monthly stipend and to offer those wanting to start a business financial help. "No" voters said. This, some felt, amounted to a reward for criminal behavior, while honest citizens were left to struggle financially. Many also said that they simply did not trust the rebels to keep their promise to lay down arms for good. – BBC News

Whether it's a distrustful Colombian population or a devastating civil war in the Middle East or a toothless nuclear disarmament treaty, the list goes on and on. Protests have become a global phenomenon. Yet have tremendous strides toward peace been made?

A resounding "Yes" must follow.

Will they be enough to save humankind from greater terrors?

That's a scary question right now with more than 10,000 active nuclear warheads spread amongst nine nations—and projected to increase to 25 nuclear nations in the next 30 years.

Sketch of a Colombian opposition march to protest against President Juan Manuel Santos' plans

The real problem? Although we have dozens of worldwide, national, and regional consultative bodies who all work toward finding and establishing peaceful solutions to humanity's problems, they are not 100% effective. They seem only able to put forth stopgap half-measures.

Although these supranational bodies possess ideals and goals, because very few nations totally trust each other to abide by the solutions called for in their white papers, treaties, agreements and so on, they remain at each other's throats with unrealistic demands and bristling military hardware.

As a result, people die.

Too many governments appear lacking in reasonable, intelligent, and fair leaders, versus gut-based, strictly reactionary and protectionist leaders.

Witness the acts demonstrated by those individuals and factions throwing [punches,] or shoes, [or] verbal daggers at legislators in South Korea, Taiwan, Latin America, India, Ukraine and even the venerable House of Commons in Britain. [This is a sign of] derisive and divisive politics in their chambers and assemblies at home, which then sends mixed messages [to their citizens and] abroad. [Such acts, and others reported in the news, show that man-made political systems are lacking unity.] It's a wonder sometimes how we've made the progress we have to date!

Bahá'ís believe the core problem comes from disunity:

Disunity is a danger that the nations and peoples of the earth can no longer endure; the consequences are too terrible to contemplate, too obvious to require any demonstration.

"The well-being of mankind," Bahá'u'lláh wrote more than a century ago, "its peace and security, are unattainable unless and until its unity is firmly established."

In observing that "mankind is groaning, is dying to be led to unity, and to terminate its age-long martyrdom", Shoghi Effendi further commented that: "Unification of the whole of mankind is the hall-mark of the stage which human society is now approaching.

Unity of family, of the tribe, of the city-state, and nation have been successively attempted and fully established. World unity is the goal towards which a harassed humanity is striving. Nation-building has come to an end.

The anarchy inherent in state sovereignty is moving towards a climax. The world, growing to maturity, must abandon this fetish, recognize the oneness and wholeness of human relationships, and establish once for all the machinery that can best incarnate this fundamental principle of its life.
– The Universal House of Justice, *The Promise of World Peace,* October 1985, p. 13.

Nation-building has ended on paper perhaps, but as Russia's recent "annexation" of the Crimean Peninsula showed—with no global response to repel the invaders by force when diplomacy failed—some nations still consider it their prerogative to force other territories to submit to their will. Actions like this never engender trust, but only reinforce the real fears nations have of being overrun by a larger power. No excuse for such an action can be justified, when Ukraine itself was a sovereign nation with boundaries set on world maps.

What will be the next incursion? North Korea into South? India into Pakistan? Will the Falkland Islands become re-contested? Will someone use nuclear weapons?

That's the point. We are still so unstable, national actions still so uncertain, that no world body can guarantee any of these events won't happen.

When will we tire of this mistrust, distrust and fear that holds us back from living peacefully together as one human race? If we ever achieve true organic unity, the same unity that is our birthright, we must put aside these differences, identify the maladies, prescribe the remedies, and apply them fairly and equally to the entire human race.

Bahá'ís believe that only when humanity lets the spirit of God's immutable laws and healing powers wash through us, and sweep away these defunct and defective manmade systems, will we be fulfilled as the glorious and star-gazing race that we truly are.

Next: How to Build a Strong Nation with Consultation

#

How to Build a Strong Nation with Consultation

Culture PART 2 IN SERIES: TRUE PEACE COMES FROM TRUST

The shining spark of truth cometh forth only after the clash of differing opinions.
– 'Abdu'l-Bahá, *Selections from the Writings of 'Abdu'l-Bahá*, p. 87.

The world's internecine strife does have a positive side—it shows a deep caring and concern for the future of our countries and peoples. People have passionate ideas and opinions because they care. That means, of course, that opinions will inevitably clash. As you can see from the quotation above, though, the Bahá'í teachings don't shy away from that clash of divergent opinions—they encourage it.

In fact, Bahá'ís call respectful, careful, considered [discussion] and discourse *Consultation*. In Bahá'í consultation, everyone seeks the truth in an atmosphere of love and trust:

…consultation must have for its object the investigation of truth. He who expresses an opinion should not voice it as correct and right but set it forth as a contribution to the consensus of opinion, for the light of reality becomes apparent when two opinions coincide.

A spark is produced when flint and steel come together. Man should weigh his opinions with the utmost serenity, calmness and composure. Before expressing his own views he should carefully consider the views already advanced by others.

If he finds that a previously expressed opinion is more true and worthy, he should accept it immediately and not willfully hold to an opinion of his own. By this excellent method he endeavors to arrive at unity and truth.

Opposition and division are deplorable... Therefore, true consultation is spiritual conference in the attitude and atmosphere of love. Members must love each other in the spirit of fellowship in order that good results may be forthcoming. Love and fellowship are the foundation.
– 'Abdu'l-Bahá, *The Promulgation of Universal Peace*, p. 72.

The Bahá'í teachings say the sole means of solving the world's problems will come through using the tools of considered discourse and consultation—not global warfare or nuclear weapons or colonizing incursions into other nation's territories. That means our leaders need to adhere to beliefs and convictions that unite groups of people rather than separate us from each other.

Only through proper and civilized discourse based on evidence and facts, can we even hope to identify the maladies afflicting humankind, prescribe the remedies, and then, through our combined unity of will and purpose administer the proper medicines in doses that will heal the ailing body of humankind.

'Abdu'l-Bahá proclaimed this principle:

Not everything that a man knoweth can be disclosed, nor can everything that he can disclose be regarded as timely, nor can every timely utterance be considered as suited to the capacity of those who hear it." Such is the consummate wisdom to be observed in thy pursuits. Be not oblivious thereof, if thou wishest to be a man of action under all conditions.

First diagnose the disease and identify the malady, then prescribe the remedy, for such is the perfect method of the skillful physician.
– *Selections from the Writings of 'Abdu'l-Bahá*, pp. 268-269.

The Bahá'í teachings say that the Divine Physician has appeared once more—a Persian nobleman imprisoned for his social and religious beliefs titled Bahá'u'lláh, the Glory of God.

He asked us many times and in many ways: How long will humanity persist in ignoring his diagnosis and prescriptions for peace, unity and security?

He repeatedly stated that these prescriptions were not from himself, but rather from God. Bahá'u'lláh asks the central question of our era: how long will we persist in our old, outdated, useless ways, and how long do we have before those old ways destroy us?

As long as man waxes proud in his own deficient belief systems, in his own greed and love for power, in his wayward and unjust ways, that is how long it will take for the true unity of the human race to be restored. We need to unite to live, or persist in our separation and perish.

About five miles from my home a metal truss bridge over the Delaware River, originally built in 1835, separates New Jersey from Pennsylvania. A hundred years later the girded letters forming TRENTON MAKES, THE WORLD TAKES were added to the bridge, due to the astounding successes of Trenton's pottery works and the establishment of John A. Roebling's factories for turning out the thick cables that built the Brooklyn Bridge and other great spans.

Those thick coiled cables, one strand wound amidst others, remind me of unified consultation and discourse. Sometimes the outer, thinner wires must be peeled back to arrive at the core of truth—and yet, all the wires make up the whole truth, and one wire by itself won't support the structure. Once the main wire encircled with support wires is set in place correctly, as part of a firm foundation, the bridge will continue to stand indefinitely.

[For example, the New York City Brooklyn Bridge was made of Roebling's coiled wires and cables]

Those coiled wires symbolize the strong aspects of sincere consultation: of honest and forthright discussion, of unrestrained but respectful sharing of ideas and viewpoints, and uncovering the factual evidence that backs up those viewpoints. All the wires bundled together maintain the strength of the core truth. They support the facts of the matter at hand, so [participants] [can identify the malady] and apply the [remedies] of the Divine Physician.

#

Where Is God When We Need Him?

Spirituality

The majority of the world's people believe in one God.

Christians, Jews, Muslims, many Hindus and Buddhists, and even those without any formal religion all see a single Supreme Being as the sole King of Creation. Every one of these belief systems say that from time immemorial, only one Creator, one Great Spirit, has ever existed.

Those who don't accept the existence of a sole Creator generally believe only in the evidence provided by the senses:

...By materialists, whose belief with regard to Divinity hath been explained, is not meant philosophers in general, but rather that group of materialists of narrow vision that worship that which is sensed, that depend upon the five senses only, and whose criterion of knowledge is limited to that which can be perceived by the senses. All that can be sensed is to them real, whilst whatever falleth not under the power of the senses is either unreal or doubtful. The existence of the Deity they regard as wholly doubtful.
– 'Abdu'l-Bahá, [Tablet to Dr. Auguste Forel]

Yet even Albert Einstein, the great scientist and renowned expert on the physical world, said:

"The religion of the future will be a cosmic religion. It should transcend personal God and avoid dogma and theology. Covering both the natural and the spiritual, it should be based on a religious sense arising from the experience of all things natural and spiritual as a meaningful unity."

The Bahá'í teachings agree that religion provides transcendence and order and is indeed "cosmic" in that it permeates all creation.

The natural world contains the signs, metaphors and symbols of a supernatural Being's hand in everything. For a painting of the Mona Lisa to exist, for example, a Leonardo da Vinci must first exist.

Bahá'ís also believe that the natural and the spiritual can come together, as Einstein suggests, in a meaningful unity.

As to a personal God, just as da Vinci painted tiny strokes in a multitude of colors [for the Mona Lisa], God is a very personal God. As He does His work, though, it usually takes a miracle, or at least a higher level of spiritual awareness, for us to recognize those tiny strokes in our own lives. It's easy for us humans to get caught up in a "me" thing to the exclusion of reality, which consists of "me" and everything around "me" only.

For Bahá'ís, the spiritual reality of Buddhism and Christianity, Islam, Judaism, and all other great Faiths describe the same ethereal essence. They recognize that God does take part in human and natural affairs all the time, despite that we neither see it nor always acknowledge it.

How does that happen? Bahá'ís believe that the messengers and prophets who founded those great religions serve as the intermediaries between the Creator and His creation.

Bahá'ís believe that those messengers and prophets all form one continuous religion, exactly in the "cosmic" sense of "meaningful unity" Einstein predicted. In this passage from Bahá'u'lláh, the prophet and founder of the Bahá'í Faith, and the latest in that long series of divine messengers, he refers to all those prophets as the mirrors of God's being:

Know thou that God – exalted and glorified be He – doth in no wise manifest His inmost Essence and Reality. From time immemorial He hath been veiled in the eternity of His Essence and concealed in the infinitude of His own Being.

And when He purposed to manifest His beauty in the kingdom of names and to reveal His glory in the realm of attributes, He brought forth His Prophets from the invisible plane to the visible, that His name "the Manifest" might be distinguished from "the Hidden" and His name "the Last" might be discerned from "the First", and that there may be fulfilled the words: "He is the First and the Last; the Seen and the Hidden; and He knoweth all things!"

Thus hath He revealed these most excellent names and most exalted words in the Manifestations of His Self and the Mirrors of His Being.
– Bahá'u'lláh, *Gems of Divine Mysteries*, p. 26.

If you've ever wondered about God, and where God is when you need Him, look to those "Manifestations of His Self and the Mirrors of His Being" for guidance, assistance and connection to the Creator:

As to the Holy Manifestations of God, They are the focal points where the signs, tokens and perfections of that sacred, pre-existent Reality appear in all their splendour.

They are an eternal grace, a heavenly glory, and on Them dependeth the everlasting life of humankind.

To illustrate: the Sun of Truth dwelleth in a sky to which no soul hath any access, and which no mind can reach, and He is far beyond the comprehension of all creatures. Yet the Holy Manifestations of God are even as a looking-glass, burnished and without stain, which gathereth streams of light out of that Sun, and then scattereth the glory over the rest of creation. In that polished surface, the Sun with all Its majesty standeth clearly revealed.

– 'Abdu'l-Bahá, *Selections from the Writings of 'Abdu'l-Bahá*, p. 50.

\#

Power, Authority and Systems – Balancing "The Man"

Culture

The Man. Oh, you don't know the Man. He's everywhere. In the White House, down the hall... Ms. Mullins [the school principal], she's the Man. And the Man ruined the ozone, and he's burning down the Amazon, and he kidnapped Shamu and put her in a chlorine tank! Okay? And there used to be a way to stick it to the Man, it was called rock 'n roll. But guess what? Oh no. The Man ruined that, too, with a little thing called MTV! So don't waste your time trying to make anything cool, or pure, or awesome, 'cause the Man is just gonna call you a fat washed up loser and crush your soul.
– Dewey Finn (played by Jack Black), the lead character in the film *School of Rock*.

You know who "the Man" is, right? In street slang, the Man refers to anyone in a position of power, authority, or oppression. The Man could be an elected official, a police officer, a corporate CEO, a tax collector, or your boss at work. The Man means domination, control, and supremacy. The Man controls our lives, because the Man runs everything.

Today "the Man" continues in his wayward thinking and acting. For all of us, the Man's "subjects," whether king, dictator or democratic assembly, life is either grand and comfortable or pure hell. We usually submit, willingly or unwillingly, to the human authority the Man symbolizes—but we all know that human authority has not succeeded in creating fair and just systems that lead everyone to prosperity, happiness, and freedom.

In fact, the systems people create—and yes, they've usually been created by men—have proven themselves lamentably defective. Actually, the Bahá'í teachings use those exact words to describe "the prevailing order:

How long will humanity persist in its waywardness? How long will injustice continue? How long is chaos and confusion to reign amongst men? How long will discord agitate the face of society?...

The winds of despair are, alas, blowing from every direction, and the strife that divideth and afflicteth the human race is daily increasing.

The signs of impending convulsions and chaos can now be discerned, inasmuch as the prevailing order appeareth to be lamentably defective.

I beseech God, exalted be His glory, that He may graciously awaken the peoples of the earth, may grant that the end of their conduct may be profitable unto them, and aid them to accomplish that which beseemeth their station.
– Bahá'u'lláh, *Gleanings from the Writings of Bahá'u'lláh*, pp. 216-217.

We live today in a veritable Garden of Eden, made even better with ordered life and civilization in many places. But we have woefully forgotten that we are all stewards of this great planet we share, and the chief-stewards are woefully inadequate because of man-made politics and ill-adapted political systems. Those systems have failed to bring peace, security and prosperity to all the world's peoples and cultures. Those systems have built and sustained a severe disparity between extremes of wealth and poverty around the world. We have inherited a beautiful Earth, but the great natural diversity we cherish, instead of being treasured, is being torn apart. [It is] disrupted by internecine strife, self-aggrandizement and visions of personal wealth and power out of touch with modicums of fairness and justice at too many levels of society.

The earth will not continue to offer its harvest, except with faithful stewardship. We cannot say we love the land and then take steps to destroy it for use by future generations. – Pope John Paul II

Do you not know that God entrusted you with that money (all above what buys necessities for your families) to feed the hungry, to clothe the naked, to help the stranger, the widow, the fatherless; and, indeed, as far as it will go, to relieve the wants of all mankind? How can you, how dare you, defraud the Lord, by applying it to any other purpose? – John Wesley

For by him all things were created, in heaven and on earth, visible and invisible, whether thrones or dominions or rulers or authorities—all things were created through him and for him. – Colossians 1:16-17

So how can we fight "the Man?" How, given the lamentably defective prevailing order, can we change it? A major part of the solution, according to the Bahá'í teachings, is women. When women gain full equality, the Bahá'í teachings promise, the world will change.

Today, we're on the way to that lofty goal. The world is witnessing a remarkable period in human history. We might call it the Era of the Ascendancy of Women, as clearly evidenced by more women in positions of leadership, in obtaining college diplomas, in becoming scientists, doctors and lawyers, and above all in becoming statespersons.

Perhaps now the influence of the Man will finally be toned down, male aggressiveness and warlike behavior ameliorated, and manly self-centeredness and selfishness decreased by the moderating effects of intelligent, bright, caring, and productive women seeking unity, peace, and harmony:

In this Revelation of Bahá'u'lláh, the women go neck and neck with the men.

In no movement will they be left behind. Their rights with men are equal in degree. They will enter all the administrative branches of politics.

They will attain in all such a degree as will be considered the very highest station of the world of humanity and will take part in all affairs.

Rest ye assured. Do ye not look upon the present conditions; in the not far distant future the world of women will become all-refulgent and all-glorious, *For His Holiness Bahá'u'lláh Hath Willed It so*!

At the time of elections the right to vote is the inalienable right of women, and the entrance of women into all human departments is an irrefutable and incontrovertible question.
– 'Abdu'l-Bahá, *Paris Talks*, pp. 182-183.

The world of humanity has two wings—one is women and the other men. Not until both wings are equally developed can the bird fly. Should one wing remain weak, flight is impossible.
– 'Abdu'l-Bahá, *Selections from the Writings of Bahá'u'lláh*, p. 301.

Therefore, strive to show in the human world that women are most capable and efficient, that their hearts are more tender and susceptible than the hearts of men, that they are more philanthropic and responsive toward the needy and suffering, that they are inflexibly opposed to war and are lovers of peace.

Strive that the ideal of international peace may become realized through the efforts of womankind, for man is more inclined to war than woman, and a real evidence of woman's superiority will be her service and efficiency in the establishment of universal peace.

– 'Abdu'l-Bahá, *The Promulgation of Universal Peace*, p. 283.

Who Is God Anyway?

Spirituality

As a kid attending Catholic grammar school for eight impressionable years, kneeling, sitting, and standing in hard cold pews through mass on weekdays and Sunday mornings, and even during a short stint as an altar boy sneaking sips of wine in the sacristy, God seemed easy to picture.

To my childhood eyes God looked like an old, old white man, with a white beard bushier than Santa Claus's, wearing white robes and no jewelry, half hidden behind the billowing white cumulus clouds of heaven. No sweat, no problem – that was "God." He was a human, only much older and better and bigger than any human who ever existed or would ever exist.

God held a tall gold scepter in his right hand to represent his reign in heaven, and gold keys to unlock the Gates of Hell for the sinners. In many depictions the red devil Satan with a black goatee and black pitchfork stood as millions of these sinners filed past to go to their doom.

When I picture God now, no matter how hard I try not to, that first picture still jumps into my mind.

I mean, how else can I imagine what I now know as an Unknowable Essence, divine and omnipotent, who made the universe and understands everything in it. I mean, seriously?

No wonder atheists and agnostics doubt the existence of God.

I mean who could believe that such a being exists, when all we know is a physical reality composed of touchable and tangle items like trees and houses, [clothing and food,] and something called a "spirit" or "soul" (whatever that is!), within us?

Essentially that's what most of us have been taught no matter what our religious tradition, in some form or another. The point of it all is to believe and trust that God exists and is just as real as that tree or building or mountain we admire.

Not only that, religious scripture exhorts us to "know and worship Him," even though, and despite the amazing fact, that we are told over and again that we can never truly know God!

No wonder we've become skeptical and disbelieving. So, I ask, who is God, anyway?

To Bahá'ís it's as clear as the noonday sun: the Bahá'í teachings describe God as 'that "innermost Spirit of Spirits" and "Eternal Essence of Essences," an invisible yet rational God Who, however much we extol the divinity of His prophets on earth, in no wise incarnates His infinite, His unknowable, His incorruptible and all-embracing Reality in the concrete and limited frame of a mortal being:

To every discerning and illumined heart it is evident that God, the unknowable Essence, the Divine Being, is immensely exalted beyond every human attribute such as corporeal existence, ascent and descent, egress and regress... He is, and hath ever been, veiled in the ancient eternity of His Essence, and will remain in His Reality everlastingly hidden from the sight of men...
– Bahá'u'lláh, *Gleanings from the Writings of Bahá'u'lláh*, p. 46.

He standeth exalted beyond and above all separation and union, all proximity and remoteness ... 'God was alone; there was none else beside Him,' is a sure testimony of this truth.
– Bahá'u'lláh, *The Book of Certitude*, pp. 98-99.

A few important words stand out here.

Essence is defined as "the basic, real, and invariable nature of a thing or its significant individual feature or features."

In philosophical terms, essence is "the inward nature, true substance, or constitution of anything, as opposed to what is accidental, phenomenal, illusory, etc."

In other words, the essence of a thing in this case is the Reality of that thing, no matter what title we give it.

Of course, we all know what reality means: things we can touch, taste, smell and experience through all our other senses as well, such as temperature and balance.

But here, when speaking of God, we refer to a spiritual Reality above the ken and keen of mortal mind and understanding.

This spiritual Reality is a very real, very experiential, even emotional, and yes, physical reality, such as what we feel when we pray and meditate with absolute sincerity. If you've ever experienced any level of higher consciousness, any awareness of a reality beyond this physical world, you know what I mean.

Is there a God? Yes, I would unequivocally answer, and He ain't wearing any whiteface, white beard and white robe like I learned He did. He's not even a He—instead, any human concept of God falls far short of that ultimate Reality.

When we talk about this Unknowable Essence and Reality we named God along the way, it helps to know that He is love personified. Frankly, without that love we wouldn't exist. That same love maintains order in the universe, causes the supreme magnetic forces to hold suns and planets in their places and in their orbits, and especially touches our hearts whenever a child is born.

How do you conceive of this entity many called "God?"

#

How to Maintain a "Bright and Friendly Face"
Spirituality

We've all heard the platitudes about being friendly, kind, considerate and even happy—but maintaining these qualities in the face of severe tests presented by the myriad temptations in our modern world is a challenge.

Unless we are aware of them, we find ourselves enmeshed in trials and tests of our own or others making sooner than we can shout "Oh No!" We often become lost and perhaps succumb to the worst in the animal side of our nature unless we have strength of character and the inner resolve to do our best despite the test. The Bahá'í teachings clearly tell us that the material world will test our resolve:

O Son of Being! Busy not thyself with this world, for with fire We test the gold, and with gold We test Our servants.
– Bahá'u'lláh, The Hidden Words, p. 16.

"Busy not thyself with this world," to me, means being enmeshed in material, physical realities, to the exclusion of God-given and inner realities of the spirit, that we do not see a clear path to avoid tests or a way out once embroiled in them.

The way I see it, we are the cold iron rod thrust into the fire, while God, the Supreme Blacksmith like the Roman god Vulcan, hammers us on the anvil [over and over], shaping us and turning us in that crucible of red-hot coals until we are molded by His unerring guidance into the perfect instrument to carry out His will and purpose in this life.

Advice from all the world's scriptures adjure us to put our full faith and confidence in God's almighty abilities and powers, to carry us through our difficulties with assurance after assurance given that these trials are heaven-sent. They not only protect us from the worst that can happen, but usually save us from our own deficient understanding of how God's healing power will, in fact and in deed, make us stronger.

The Bahá'í writings state very clearly that our individual capacity to overcome tests, and to grow strong and tall under their onslaught, is a function of how we were each created. Our souls have a set capacity, each of us capable of education and training in the ways of existence and of God.

However, the size of our individual capacity is immaterial. No matter the size, we feel fulfilled when we reach the limits of that capacity. This is the apex of human achievement and accomplishment, enabling us to accomplish even more incredible, almost miraculous feats while endeavoring to fill our own potential.

So tests—once we understand that their purpose is to grow and develop our powers, not deflect them—become a Godsend to seekers of the truth, life, and love for all humankind.

O Thou Whose tests are a healing medicine to such as are nigh unto Thee, Whose sword is the ardent desire of all them that love Thee, Whose dart is the dearest wish of those hearts that yearn after Thee, Whose decree is the sole hope of them that have recognized Thy truth!

I implore Thee, by Thy divine sweetness and by the splendors of the glory of Thy face, to send down upon us from Thy retreats on high that which will enable us to draw nigh unto Thee.

– Bahá'u'lláh, Prayers and Meditations of Bahá'u'lláh, pp. 220-221.

This is the heart of [it]: Seeing the glory of God's face in every human being will most definitely ease our tests and difficulties. For God created everyone and everything to help us fulfill our capacities.

Simplicity, patience, compassion.
These three are your greatest treasures.

Simple in actions and thoughts, you return to the
  source of being.
Patient with both friends and enemies,
  you accord with the way things are.
Compassionate toward yourself,
  you reconcile all beings in the world.
— Lao Tzu, Tao Te Ching

In the same way, the Bahá'í teachings exhort everyone to:

  Be generous in prosperity, and thankful in adversity.
  Be worthy of the trust of thy neighbor, and look upon him with a bright and friendly face.
  Be a treasure to the poor, an admonisher to the rich, an answerer of the cry of the needy, a preserver of the sanctity of thy pledge.
  Be fair in thy judgment, and guarded in thy speech.
  Be unjust to no man, and show all meekness to all men. Be as a lamp unto them that walk in darkness, a joy to the sorrowful, a sea for the thirsty, a haven for the distressed, an upholder and defender of the victim of oppression...
  – Bahá'u'lláh, Gleanings from the Writings of Bahá'u'lláh, p. 285.

This prescription, the divine individual remedy concocted for each one of us by an unerring Physician, asks us to overcome our tests by loving our neighbors, parents, children, siblings, co-workers, and strangers, all the world over.

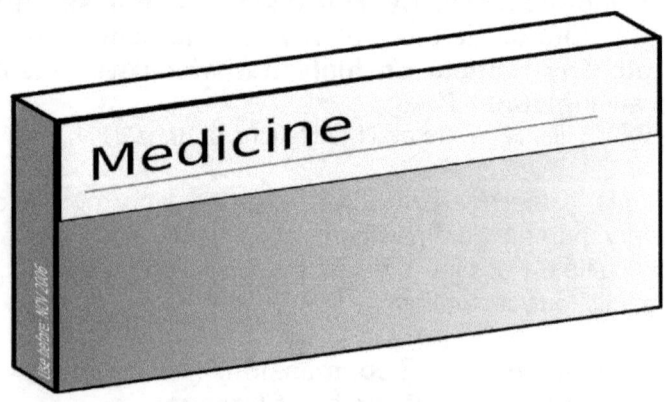

#

Why this Myth of White, Red, Black, Yellow Persists

Culture

I am not "white" until you see me in swim trunks, and then yes, you can call me white.

But with clothes on and my olive semi-Italian-heritage skin [showing], you'd have to call me "olive-complected," or maybe even brown. Tell me truly, are you so dark I can call you "black?" Yes, some folks are, and also [dark] brown, [or] tan, [or] albino and just about every tone in between. But these are not "races," as so many people think of them. Instead, they are at best only classifications by skin color and not by personality, background, skills, education, talents, or abilities.

This division by color, calling ourselves the white race, black race, red race, and yellow race must stop. Obviously, science has now proven we are one race and not four:

Despite notions to the contrary, there is only one human race. Our single race is independent of geographic origin, ethnicity, culture, color of skin or shape of eyes — we all share a single phenotype, the same or similar observable anatomical features and behavior.

Science highlights these similarities in our embryonic development, physiology (our organ-based systems), biochemistry (our metabolites and reactions), and more recently, genomics (our genetic makeup). As a molecular biologist, this last one is indeed the most important to me — data show that the DNA of any two human beings is 99.9 percent identical, and we all share the same set of genes, scientifically validating the existence of a single biological human race and one origin for all human beings. In short, we are all brothers and sisters.

Genetically speaking, studies have shown that there is much greater genetic variation *within* a given human population (e.g., Africans, Caucasians, or Asians) than *between* populations (Africans vs. Caucasions), indicating that human variation cannot be subdivided into discrete races.

— Michael Hadjiargyrou, chair of the Department of Life Sciences at the New York Institute of Technology, Live Science, August 29, 2014.

With that in mind, let's look at the history of racial classifications, and see if we can learn how they came about.

Carl Linnaeus [orig] 1775 oil on canvas Alexander Roslin

The 1735 classification scheme dreamed up by the early biologist Carl Linnaeus, inventor of zoological taxonomy, divided the human species *Homo sapiens* into four continental varieties: *europaeus*, *asiaticus*, *americanus*, and *afer*; or in more contemporary terms; European, Asian, American, and African.

Linnaeus also associated each of his four "races" with a different "humour:" sanguine, melancholic, choleric and phlegmatic. He called *europaeus*—the "white" race—"active, acute, and adventurous." He called *afer*—the "black race"—"crafty, lazy and careless."

So—does anyone think it's a good idea to continue using Mr. Linnaeus' classification scheme? Unfortunately, even though science now sees Linnaeus' ideas about race as a ridiculous, many people still think the way he did. Of course, we now know his classifications, both by skin color and character, were wildly unscientific and prejudicial.

Forty years after Linnaeus first proposed his treatise, another scientist named Johann Friedrich Blumenbach wrote his own paper on racial classifications, *The Natural Varieties of Mankind*. In it, he proposed five major racial divisions: the Caucasoid race, the Mongoloid race, the Ethiopian race (later termed Negroid), the American Indian race, and the Malayan race.

Blumenbach, at least, did not propose any value-laden or judgmental character-related hierarchy among the races. He also observed a graded transition in appearance from one group to other groups and suggested that "one variety of mankind does so sensibly pass into the other, that you cannot mark out the limits between them." Most scientific observers, however, paid little attention to Blumenbach, and continued to accept the Linnaeus classification scheme.

These attempts at classifying people by skin color eventually produced an ideology of race. That ideology, which has stuck around for several centuries now, insists that racial divisions are natural, distinct, and enduring; and that skin color has a direct relationship to character. In America, that ideology is particularly pronounced, not only because of the U.S. history of slavery but also because of the racial theories of Thomas Jefferson, which had a significant and lasting influence on public opinion. Jefferson suspected that Africans were naturally inferior to whites, especially [regarding] their intellects:

I advance it therefore as a suspicion only, that the blacks, whether originally a distinct race, or made distinct by time and circumstances, are inferior to the whites in the endowments both of body and mind. – Thomas Jefferson

As you can see, Linnaeus and Jefferson, and many others, set the tone for the initial mistaken concept of racial separation into skin color-determined categories. Predictably, that categorization scheme, conceptualized by Europeans, declared Europeans superior. It set public opinion in stone for the centuries that would follow and has lasted up until modern times.

Now, of course, these racial and skin color-related myths have been eruditely and clearly exposed for the fallacious and specious thinking they contain. No credible scientist accepts them today; because the science of genetics has proven, without any doubt, that all racial and skin color-based divisions of humanity are completely artificial. They have absolutely no basis in fact. We are one, not four or five.

The Bahá'í teachings promote the unification of one humanity, ask us to discard the "fancies and imaginations" of race, and encourage the elimination of every category that separates us as people:

Strive with heart and soul in order to bring about union and harmony among the white and the black and prove thereby the unity of the Bahá'í world wherein distinction of colour findeth no place, but where hearts only are considered. Praise be to God, the hearts of the friends are united and linked together, whether they be from the east or the west, from north or from south, whether they be German, French, Japanese, American, and whether they pertain to the white, the black, the red, the yellow or the brown race.
Variations of colour, of land and of race are of no importance in the Bahá'í Faith; on the contrary, Bahá'í unity overcometh them all and doeth away with all these fancies and imaginations.
– 'Abdu'l-Bahá, *Selections from the Writings of 'Abdu'l-Bahá*, pp. 112-113.

The world desperately needs good examples of unity and harmony, of loving and learning and living together.
Millions of Bahá'ís around the globe work hard to institute these qualities in their lives and the lives of their communities, and to practice unity in their work, play, families, meetings, and interactions with all peoples of all hues and shades.

Someday, sooner I hope rather than later, it shall become reality.

#

Gandhi and King: Nonviolence and Change

History

Mahatma Gandhi, the Indian seer, mystic, leader and philosopher, started what many call the modern Non-violence Movement.

Gandhi's movement and tactics, further studied, copied, and expanded by Reverend Martin Luther King Jr. in America, have influenced multiple generations all over the world. Gandhi and King both developed their peaceful movements by the dynamic force of their examples, and by calling on their followers to adhere to nonviolent, humanitarian principles. The results: the overthrow of entrenched British colonial power in India and freedom for the Indian people, and the demise of an equally entrenched "separate but equal" racial segregation policy in the United States.

Both these nonviolent men invoked what they knew of the soul, the scriptures, and the human spirit to translate their belief in God into modern contexts applied to the eras in which they lived. Their voices resonated with millions of people, and their movements changed the world. Both died from assassins' bullets, even while they continued to teach nonviolent resistance to oppression. They never lost faith in the essential goodness of humanity.

In fact, King would certainly agree with this statement by the Mahatma:

You must not lose faith in humanity. Humanity is an ocean; if a few drops of the ocean are dirty, the ocean does not become dirty.

Gandhi would certainly agree with this statement by Dr. King:

I believe that unarmed truth and unconditional love will have the final word in reality.

Both the Mahatma and the Reverend knew full well that the generality of humankind was composed of decent, hardworking, common folk, longing for equality and peace no matter where they lived. Both the Mahatma and the Reverend gave their lives for their shared belief in the essential goodness and unity of humanity:

[In speaking of enlightened, selfless souls, "Abdu'l-Bahá wrote:]

These souls have reached the highest station of self-sacrifice. Should the occasion arise, all that they possess would be freely given in order to unfurl the banner of the solidarity of the human race over the religions of the east and the west, so that all differences might be annulled and all peoples from one end of the earth to the other might sing in accord the song of life and peace, that it might be borne on the wings of light to the throne of the Father, there to be blended with the symphonies of the heavenly angels and thus heaven and earth become harmonized with the golden strains of the music of unity.
– 'Abdu'l-Bahá, *Divine Philosophy*, pp. 181-182.

Sketch of Mahatma Gandhi

These two great personages and their magnetic words and personalities did not happen by chance, but only developed through periods of personal and community suffering. Both were frustrated by their "masters" inability to give their followers (and all people), the rights they were entitled to– rights every human being is entitled to. They both fought for the right to be freed from slavery of any kind, the right to be respected and accepted, and the right to a safe and healthy life for all of God's creatures.

Gandhi said, **"Nonviolence is the first article of my faith. It is also the last article of my creed."**

King also preached nonviolence and peace, restraining his followers from taking up arms and fighting the extreme prejudice people [of color] faced up [before and] through the 1950s and 1960s. Dr. King's unspeakable assassination in 1968 removed that cap on pent-up righteous anger, and directly resulted in riots and violent actions all over the United States.

Sketch of Dr. Martin Luther King Jr.

Both King and Gandhi asked us all this question: when the justice system is stacked against the impoverished and the inadequately educated according to all statistics, who is to blame? The government? The system? The schools? Parents? Students themselves? All are important cogs in the wheel of civilization, yet both these men refused to blame others for society's troubles—instead, they focused on the content of our characters and the ability of the common people to fix the problems they inherited.

King and Gandhi derived the source of their power and truth from their own experiences and unique souls, yes; from their environments and need to raise their voices loud, yes; from their own personal God and religion, yes; and from the people themselves burdened by chains and misery, no matter how "civilized" the outward laws seemed at the time.

We still live in turbulent times.

Despite the sacrifices of leaders like King and Gandhi, [turbulent times] are not stopping and will not stop. Bahá'ís believe they won't stop until all people on earth recognize and love the oneness and wholeness of God; His one divine, continuing religion; and the oneness and wholeness of all humanity:

Wherever you find the attributes of God love that person, whether he be of your family or of another.

Shed the light of a boundless love on every human being whom you meet, whether of your country, your race, your political party, or of any other nation, colour or shade of political opinion.

Heaven will support you while you work in this in-gathering of the scattered peoples of the world beneath the shadow of the almighty tent of unity.

– 'Abdu'l-Bahá, *Paris Talks*, p. 39.

#

Are There Any Accidents in This World?

Science

Try this sometime: watch the news and see if you can separate what's accidental from what isn't.

A truckload of oranges overturns on an onramp, closing highway access for three hours; a drunk driver kills a family of four in a head-on collision; a piano falls on an unsuspecting and unlucky person below. A child shoots a sibling when a handgun goes off; a roof blows off a school in a hurricane; a pedestrian's foot is crushed by the tires of a passing truck; a schoolgirl is shot in a drive-by shooting. Are these all accidents?

Some would say yes, some no. Let's see if we can figure out the difference. Here's a dictionary definition:

ac·ci·dent *n.* 1. an unfortunate incident that happens unexpectedly and unintentionally, typically resulting in damage or injury. 2. an event that happens by chance or that is without apparent or deliberate cause.

We may agree that the examples in the first paragraph were "unfortunate incidents" that all resulted in "damage or injury"—but were all of them "unexpected and unintentional" without "apparent or deliberate cause?"

We usually reserve that determination for the courts or the insurance company. That's because, in most cases, we want someone or something to blame for causing the unfortunate event, even if it is an "Act of God," as if God would cause misery and death willy-nilly.

In this contingent physical reality we call the world, every effect has a cause, whether we can see it or not. When the wind blows the chimes and makes beautiful music, the effect is attached to and coincident with or subsequent to, the cause. The long-established rule of cause and effect, or causality, forms the basis of every scientific discovery and theory.

The Bahá'í teachings agree, saying **"unto every effect there must be a cause."**
– 'Abdu'l-Bahá, *Tablet to August Forel*, p. 16.

So is every accident really an accident? Should we blame the worn-out brakes on the SUV that crashed into a house, even though the driver was drunk or stoned?

It seems we need a new word for "accident," to separate truly accidental or unidentifiable causes from identifiable, blameworthy causes. That's why we have legal distinctions between premeditated murder, murder, justifiable homicide, and manslaughter. We need to own up to the fact that too many "accidents" are caused by the carelessness and unthinking ways of common and uncommon folk (such as criminals in many cases), rather than truly accidental causes like the snapping ropes binding that high-flying piano.

But even in that case, we can ask, why weren't stronger ropes used to raise the piano? Why didn't the truck driver with crates of oranges take the turn slower? Why was the handgun accessible to children playing alone at home?

I would have been shocked if my insurance rates had shot up after a recent driver on my neighborhood street plowed into my parked car.

Of course, no one can stop a hurricane or an earthquake—those kinds of natural events truly meet the definition of accidental. But few true accidents happen when it comes to adult human interaction—we all have responsibility for what we do, and the Bahá'í teachings say we will each face up to that responsibility either here in this world or in the next:

Know ye that the world and its vanities and its embellishments shall pass away. Nothing will endure except God's Kingdom which pertaineth to none but Him, the Sovereign Lord of all, the Help in Peril, the All-Glorious, the Almighty.

The days of your life shall roll away, and all the things with which ye are occupied and of which ye boast yourselves shall perish, and ye shall, most certainly, be summoned by a company of His angels to appear at the spot where the limbs of the entire creation shall be made to tremble, and the flesh of every oppressor to creep.

Ye shall be asked of the things your hands have wrought in this, your vain life, and shall be repaid for your doings. This is the day that shall inevitably come upon you, the hour that none can put back. To this the Tongue of Him that speaketh the truth and is the Knower of all things hath testified.

– Bahá'u'lláh, *Gleanings from the Writings of Bahá'u'lláh*, p. 125.

As mature beings, our job in life involves accepting and fulfilling our responsibility for the things our "hands have wrought." That deeply spiritual responsibility means we should endeavor to be no cause of grief to any other human being.

Before you pull out of the driveway, test your brakes. Don't drive if you're impaired. If you own a weapon, keep it in a locked case with the key on your person. But more than all that, spend some time each day contemplating whether you've caused anyone any grief or sadness, and resolve, before the end of that day, to do what you can to rectify and repair your actions.

#

Investigating Reality: The First Principle of Life and Love

Spirituality

If you find me not within you, you will never find me. For I have been with you, from the beginning of me. – Rumi

We each may perceive reality differently, yet true reality brooks no duplicity. Reality, by its very nature, is one.

We each have our own life experiences, good, bad or indifferent, forgettable or unforgettable. We each have grown up in certain environments of nature and nurture. We each may have good or poor health, wealth or poverty, a life full of achievements or hopes for achievements. No matter what our circumstances, our primary task in life involves determining what is real and what isn't—and making that determination independently.

Yet reality brooks no duplicity. The Bahá'í teachings say reality is one:

Reality is one; and when found, it will unify all mankind. Reality is the love of God. Reality is the knowledge of God. Reality is justice. Reality is the oneness or solidarity of mankind. Reality is international peace. Reality is the knowledge of verities. Reality unifies humanity.
–"Abdu'l-Bahá, *The Promulgation of Universal Peace*, p. 372.

"Reality is the love of God," 'Abdu'l-Bahá said, and as in life, love is between the lover and his or her beloved.

Love begins for us in the cradle with the love of our parents and grows and grows until that happy day, when we find a soulmate who loves us for who we are, without regard to limitations. That day is happy indeed when we open our own hearts and let their love pour in, which in turn sustains our love for them.

"Reality is the love of God," also works both ways, for we realize that He also loves us with unconditional love. Thousands of love songs from time immemorial have expressed this undying, unconditional love.

All love, again like life, begins when you truly and independently investigate reality, the first principle of the Bahá'í teachings:

Nearly 60 years ago when the horizon of the Orient was in a state of the utmost gloom, warfare existed and there was enmity between the various creeds; darkness brooded over the children of men and foul clouds of ignorance hid the sky—at such a time His Highness Bahá'u'lláh arose from the horizon of Persia like unto a shining sun. He boldly proclaimed peace, writing to the kings of the earth and calling upon them to arise and assist in the hoisting of this banner. In order to bring peace out of the chaos, He established certain precepts or principles.

The first principle Bahá'u'lláh urged was the independent investigation of truth.

"Each individual," He said, "is following the faith of his ancestors who themselves are lost in the maze of tradition. Reality is steeped in dogmas and doctrines.

If each investigate for himself, he will find that Reality is one; does not admit of multiplicity; is not divisible. All will find the same foundation and all ill be at peace.
–Attributed to "Abdu'l-Bahá in *Star of the West*, Vol 3, p. 5.

Is reality the food we eat or the love we make? Is reality the vicissitudes we bear or their overcoming? Is reality a comfortable chair, or a place in the grass? Is reality what our imagination holds, or what it releases?

We each have talents and faculties, abilities, and capabilities—all [so ewe can] investigate reality. We test it, try it on, discard it, wear another, and continue the process until we find the perfect garment for each of us:

What does it mean to investigate reality? It means that man must forget all hearsay and examine truth himself, for he does not know whether statements he hears are in accordance with reality or not. Wherever he finds truth or reality, he must hold to it, forsaking, discarding all else; for outside of reality there is naught but superstition and imagination.
–"Abdu'l-Bahá, *The Promulgation of Universal Peace*, p. 62.

Turn thou unto the Kingdom of Oneness and chant thou the verses of Singleness. Be thou invested with a robe, the embroidery of which is purity and sanctity and the woof and warp of which is the spirituality of the Mighty Lord, so that thou mayest inhale the fragrance of the

divine rose-garden from the garment of the real Joseph and so divest thyself of the mantle of bodily things that angelhood and ideal spirituality become realized (in thee).
–"Abdu'l-Bahá, *Tablets of Abdul-Baha*, Volume I, p. 124.

The robe picked out for us by the Beloved shall never grow old, shall never wear thin, shall never fade, shall never tarnish. That robe of reality is worth striving for, if we choose to do so, and the good Lord in His mercy and grace has given each of us free will to try it on for ourselves.

#

5 Fatal Thinking Errors, and How to Fix Them

Teachings PART 1 IN SERIES: HOW NOT TO THINK

Our mind is the heart of our heart as well as the seat of our mental abilities and power. With our minds, we construct reality and determine our future.

Because the way we think governs the way we act and believe, both within ourselves and with others, critically examining our thinking patterns becomes a necessity. In an age where one's deeds speak louder than one's words, thoughts that may lead us astray take on more significance. That's why conducting a careful examination of the way we think can help us enormously.

What are the most common thinking errors people tend to make?

The science of cognitive behavioral therapy—geared to changing our thought patterns with positive changes in behavior—has identified nine common errors in thinking. In this essay, we'll look at the first five and how to avoid them; and in the next essay, we'll explore the final four common errors.

1. Binocular Vision

Cognitive therapists call the first common thinking error "binocular vision." Imagine looking through a pair of binoculars—they can help you see further, but they restrict your entire field of vision by not allowing you to see everything. You can identify binocular vision by asking yourself these two questions: do I look at negative things in a way that makes them seem bigger than they really are? Do I look at good things in a way that makes them seem smaller than they really are?

If you answered yes to either of those questions, you may need to work on widening the focus of your thinking, balancing your positive and negative thoughts more realistically. The **Bahá'í** teachings recommend widening that focus by enlarging your field of vision to embrace the entire world:

… led by the light of the name of the All-Seeing God, make your escape from the darkness that surroundeth you. Let your vision be world-embracing, rather than confined to your own self.
– Bahá'u'lláh, *Gleanings from the Writings of Bahá'u'lláh*, p. 94.

2. Black-and-White Thinking

Ask yourself: do I think about things only in extreme or opposite ways? For example, do I categorize actions or events or people as good or bad, all or none, black or white? This kind of thought pattern, which makes no allowance for the grey areas that exist in between black-and-white thinking, can trap us in our own mental prison. By definition, black-and-white thinking makes only binary choices possible, and severely limits our options in the world.

The Bahá'í teachings recommend adopting a more moderate, nuanced approach to our thinking, through the use of reason and knowledge:

A good character is in the sight of God and His chosen ones and the possessors of insight, the most excellent and praiseworthy of all things, but always on condition that its center of emanation should be reason and knowledge and its base should be true moderation.

– 'Abdu'l-Bahá, *The Secret of Divine Civilization*, p. 59.

3. Wearing Dark or Rose-Colored Glasses

Do I think only of the bad side of things? Or do I see things in a rosy or naïve way? Sometimes we can filter our thinking through an unrealistic lens, mistaking our negative or overly positive impressions for the truth. We can take off those dark or rose-colored glasses, the Bahá'í teachings suggest, by acknowledging the reality that human beings are essentially spiritual in their nature:

As for the spiritual perfections they are man's birthright and belong to him alone of all creation. Man is, in reality, a spiritual being, and only when he lives in the spirit is he truly happy. This spiritual longing and perception belongs to all men alike ...
– 'Abdu'l-Bahá, *Paris Talks*, p. 24.

4. Fortune-Telling

Do I make negative predictions about what will happen in the future, without enough information? Am I a pessimist? Psychologists also call this kind of thinking "catastrophizing," and it can lead to a very dim view of the world and our place in it.

Regardless of what might happen, no one can predict the future. Only an optimistic, hopeful view of future events can sustain our enthusiasm for what may come.

The Bahá'í teachings advise us to:

Lift up your hearts above the present and look with eyes of faith into the future! Today the seed is sown, the grain falls upon the earth, but behold the day will come when it shall rise a glorious tree and the branches thereof shall be laden with fruit.

Rejoice and be glad that this day has dawned, try to realize its power, for it is indeed wonderful!
– Ibid., p. 22.

5. Making It Personal

Do I make things my responsibility when I don't need to? Do I blame myself for things I can't control? Sometimes, we blame ourselves for things beyond our scope or ability to direct. As individuals, we're powerless to control many of the forces that impact our lives and recognizing that powerlessness can have a very freeing effect.

The Bahá'í teachings ask us to admit that we're powerless over many of life's vicissitudes, and to accept them as the natural boundaries of our human existence:

Were any one to soar, on whatever wings, as long as Thine own Being endureth, throughout the immensity of Thy knowledge, he would still be powerless to transgress the bounds which the contingent world hath set for him.

– Bahá'u'lláh, *Prayers and Meditations by Bahá'u'lláh*, p. 133.

#

Fixing 4 More Fatal Thinking Errors

Teachings PART 2 IN SERIES: **HOW NOT TO THINK**

Cognitive behavioral therapy recognizes nine common and self-defeating errors in our thinking patterns.

Do you make any of them?

In the first essay in this series, we examined five of those common errors in our patterns of thinking: binocular vision; black-and-white thinking; wearing dark or rose-colored glasses; fortune telling [catastrophizing]; and "making it personal." Of course, all of us think in these restricted ways sometimes—that's an inevitable part of being human—but the problem becomes a critical one when we sink into these modes of thinking most of the time. When that happens, our own minds and the way they process information can become our worst enemies.

So how do we combat these thinking errors? The first step involves simply recognizing them. If we can identify and name a certain kind of self-defeating thinking, then we can begin to move past it.

With that in mind, here are the final four thinking errors we're all prone to:

1. Overgeneralizing

Ask yourself: do I make general conclusions based only on one specific action or event? If I see someone being unkind, for example, do I conclude that they're a fundamentally unkind person? Overgeneralizing defeats us because it draws conclusions based on insufficient evidence. It also reminds us that we never have enough information to know or understand the whole story. The Bahá'í teachings advise us to independently investigate the truth, and reach our conclusions based only a fair-minded assessment:

…Examine then and judge aright that which We shall reveal unto thee, that haply thou mayest be account-ed in the sight of God amongst those who are fair-minded in these matters.
– Bahá'u'lláh, *Gems of Divine Mysteries*, p. 74.

Discover for yourselves the reality of things, and strive to assimilate the methods by which noble-mindedness and glory are attained among the nations and people of the world. No man should follow blindly his ancestors and

forefathers. Nay, each must see with his own eyes, hear with his own ears and investigate independently in order that he may find the truth.
–Attributed to "Abdu'l-Bahá in *Divine Philosophy*, p. 24.

2. Labeling

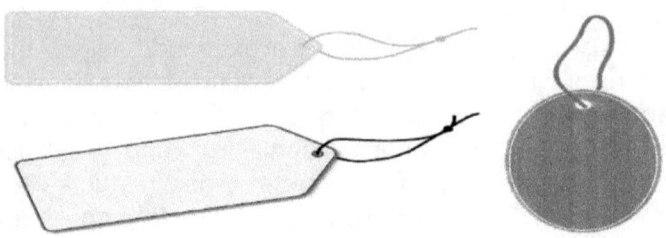

Do I put simple, unfair, and negative labels on people or things that are more complicated than the label suggests? Labeling, like stereotyping, divides people. When we label others, we put them into a category that rarely fits. Instead, the Bahá'í teachings recommend, we should refrain from labeling or judging others, and even from labeling ourselves:

We must look upon our enemies with a sin-covering eye and act with justice when confronted with any injustice whatsoever, forgive all, consider the whole of humanity as our own family, the whole earth as our own country, be sympathetic with all suffering, nurse the sick, offer a shelter to the exiled, help the poor and those in need, dress all wounds and share the happiness of each one.

Be compassionate, so that your actions will shine like unto the light streaming forth from the lamp ...

If we see a man acting after this manner we can say of him: "Verily, he is a reflector of servitude!" We cannot conceive of a star without light, a tree without seed. If we claim to be followers of light we must diffuse the light through our actions. To label ourselves will not be sufficient.
–Attributed to "Abdu'l-Bahá in *Divine Philosophy*, pp. 41-42.

3. Discounting the Positive

Do I discount positive things or thoughts by telling myself they don't really matter? Can I accept a compliment from another person without thinking it isn't so? Do I twist good situations into things that are bad? Since our thoughts determine our reality, the Bahá'í writings say, we should do everything we can to see the positive in others and in ourselves:

If you desire with all your heart, friendship with every race on earth, your thought, spiritual and positive, will spread; it will become the desire of others, growing stronger and stronger, until it reaches the minds of all men.
–"Abdu'l-Bahá, *Paris Talks*, p. 7.

4. Beating Up on Myself or Others

Do I insist or demand that things should or even must be done in a certain way? Am I unkind to myself, discounting my own good motives and beating up on myself when I fail? The Bahá'í teachings remind us that our positive, flexible thinking can carry us to great heights—but that beating up on ourselves or others can sink us into clinical depression and other maladies. With practice, though, negative neural pathways can atrophy from disuse, and new ones—healthier, more realistic and more positive—can take over:

I charge you all that each one of you concentrate all the thoughts of your heart on love and unity. When a thought of war comes, oppose it by a stronger thought of peace. A thought of hatred must be destroyed by a more powerful thought of love.

Thoughts of war bring destruction to all harmony, well-being, restfulness and content.

Thoughts of love are constructive of brotherhood, peace, friendship, and happiness.
– Ibid., p. 7.

From all the points above, it's clear that just like a song we can't get out of our head, negative or destructive types of thinking can become ingrained. Yet conscious efforts to implant, grow, and reinforce positive thoughts can cause negative, limited thoughts to diminish and gradually lose their power over our thinking.

[In all cases, it is critical to identify negative thinking when it occurs and to take corrective action.]

#

Aesop's Fables:
More Than Just Stories

History

Why do you think the ancient Greek storyteller Aesop's tales hold universal appeal, longevity and meaning? Why do we still read them today?

When Aesop died in 564 BC, his memorable stories with moral endings, which usually featured anthropomorphic creatures and elements of nature, must have seemed fairly normal to his limited audience. But for some reason they've now transcended time and the collapse of many civilizations and have lasted through the millennia.

Bust of Aesop

When large-scale printing became possible, collections of Aesop's fables were among the earliest books printed in a variety of languages. Through the means of later collections, and translations or adaptations of them, Aesop's reputation as a fabulist was transmitted throughout the world. You can find more than six hundred of his fables at **www.Aesopfables.com**.

Initially, Aesop addressed his fables, which covered religious, social, and political themes in Greek society, to adults. They were also [used] as ethical guides, and from the Renaissance onwards found wide usage in the education of children. We still use them today because of their charm and their simplicity, and because the unifying message of all fables comes from the usually unspoken, hidden meaning or intent behind the story. Some are more obvious than others, but all contain a life lesson for the reader or listener.

As a young boy my family had a book of Aesop's Fables, and they were read aloud to me as I took in the pictures. As I thumb through a more recent version illustrated by Arthur Rackham, it brings back those early memories and learnings instantly.

I'll never forget "The Goose that Laid the Golden Eggs" where the king in his greed sliced open the goose in his impatience for more, and thus lost all future golden eggs.

Or "The Lion and the Mouse," where the mouse begs the lion to let him go in return for some future favor. The lion laughs at such a thought, a mouse helping a lion, but lets him go. Soon the lion, caught in a net, roars his frustration and the mouse, coming upon him, gnaws the ropes freeing lion in return for his earlier generosity.

Another lion lying in a cave whining and moaning from a huge splinter in his paw is [discovered] by a man slave who carefully extracts the piece and heals the lion's wound, earning the lion's gratitude. When, later, the escaped slave is caught and thrown into an animal den to be eaten alive, the same lion fawns at his feet, earning both their freedom.

Surely, you've heard "Slow and steady wins the race" from the story of the "Hare and the Tortoise," the race being lost by the hare's overconfidence and overlong nap.

Finally, I'd like to mention the "Ants and the Grasshopper" story, one well-remembered from my young days.

At the end of summer, the Grasshopper approaches the Ants looking for food. The Ants ask why he hadn't been storing food for winter himself.

"I've been too busy singing," he replies.

"Then you can spend the winter dancing since you didn't make the time," the Ants respond, and all turn back to their work.

Rather than have you think this taught me to be hard and cruel towards the needy (which it did not), I learned it as a very good lesson in work ethics and earning a living. Thanks to these wonderful fables, I learned this and other moral lessons long before attending school or going out into the workforce.

From Aesop's simple stories I learned simple but profound life truths at an early age: Don't kill a good thing; Be kind and generous toward all; Persevere and show patience; Use your head at all times; Demonstrate a good work ethic, and more. Perhaps that's the reason Aesop's fables have lasted so long and had such a profound influence: they teach universal moral truths.

For impressionable young me, these stories and their representations seemed real, even though I knew animals and trees and other things didn't talk and move like humans. What we share and show, read and give and teach our children is all too real to them. That's our primary duty as parents—to train our children to grow into moral human beings:

Your fathers and mothers must educate you with greatest tenderness, and teach you the highest morals and ideals, so that in the utmost perfection you may be imbued with the virtues of the world of humanity.
–Attributed to "Abdu'l-Bahá in *Star of the West*, Volume 9, p. 115.

The Bahá'í teachings commend and exalt this early moral education:

O ye loving mothers, know ye that in God's sight, the best of all ways to worship Him is to educate the children

and train them in all the perfections of humankind; and no nobler deed than this can be imagined.

–"Abdu'l-Bahá, *Selections from the Writings of 'Abdu'l-Bahá*, p. 114.

All cultures, beginning with their oral traditions, have taught morality. We teach morals through fables, through family stories, and through the powerful spiritual principles of religion:

Each of the divine religions embodies two kinds of ordinances. The first is those which concern spiritual susceptibilities, the development of moral principles and the quickening of the conscience of man. These are essential or fundamental, one and the same in all religions, changeless and eternal—reality not subject to transformation.
–"Abdu'l-Bahá, *The Promulgation of Universal Peace*, p. 44.

Who knows? Maybe Aesop was a prophet in his own right, and his stories not fables at all.

#

So What? It's Just Another Day

Culture

After 66 years of life, I'll freely admit, some days I wake up and just go through the motions.

I think, another Tuesday, get copies for class, visit Mom and play Skip-Bo, off to writing class, then nap at home, dinner, and TV or a miscellaneous event for the evening. Boring. A few of my other heavily-scheduled days often seem repetitive, like the movie Groundhog Day.

No day is the same. Each day fills itself with somewhat similar but always different interactions, with people of varied backgrounds and tastes, with fresh experiences. Meeting new people never gets old, and even the familiar ones usually have something different to say, unlike the movie.

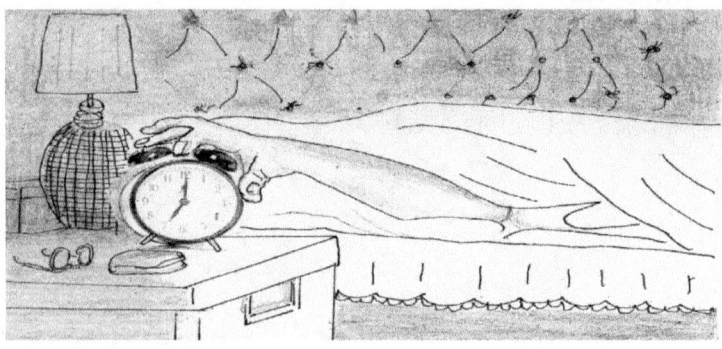

I ask myself: What do I want from this next day of my life that I've been given? Oh, sure, it would be great to have my words broadcast to the masses, changing hearts and minds with their sheer power and luminosity, as if I were a Gandhi or Martin Luther King Jr. Yet, I remember, they suffered terribly for their very public lives.

Which brings me to a universal question: during all my adult time on this earth, I've wondered, What is my purpose here? To be a good person, a nice person, an ensign of right-living, those seem to be the things that carry me. I don't aspire to fame or fortune—instead, I'd just like to do good and bring happiness to others.

Hundreds of scriptures and self-help books brim with ways to achieve lofty goals, and they all say we must forgive ourselves for not being perfect. Striving for perfection without getting hung up on its negative side, they tell us, will make all the difference.

The Bahá'í teachings have some powerful advice in that regard:

> You belong to the world of purity, and are not content to live the life of the animal, spending your days in eating, drinking, and sleeping. You are indeed men!
> Your thoughts and ambitions are set to acquire human perfection. You live to do good and to bring happiness to others. Your greatest longing is to comfort those who mourn, to strengthen the weak, and to be the cause of hope to the despairing soul.
> Day and night your thoughts are turned to the Kingdom, and your hearts are full of the Love of God.
> Thus you know neither opposition, dislike, nor hatred, for every living creature is dear to you and the good of each is sought.
> These are perfect human sentiments and virtues. If a man has none of these, he had better cease to exist. If a lamp has ceased to give light, it had better be destroyed. If a tree bear no fruit, it had better be cut down, for it only cumbereth the ground.
> – 'Abdu'l-Bahá, *Paris Talks*, p. 36.

Such a strong exhortation! If you thought you weren't doing so well before, after reading that quote you might feel depressed. But that's not at all what the prophets and teachers mean, nor want.

Words such as the above give us a prescription for the illness that ails us all–finding our purpose and becoming a happy and joyful being under all conditions.

It's all about attitude:

> I myself was in prison forty years—one year alone would have been impossible to bear—nobody survived that imprisonment more than a year! But, thank God, during all those forty years I was supremely happy! Every day, on waking, it was like hearing good tidings, and every night infinite joy was mine. Spirituality was my comfort, and turning to God was my greatest joy. If this had not been so, do you think it possible that I could have lived through those forty years in prison?
> Thus, spirituality is the greatest of God's gifts, and "Life Everlasting" means "Turning to God."
> – 'Abdu'l-Bahá, Ibid., p. 35.

"Turning to God" can be the most fulfilling act a human can make, for one gives up their will and moves in accord with God's will, whatever that is. That's not to say we give up the freedom of our will completely. [We] are continually tested and faced with choices in developing our own perfect virtues. But like a radio, if the knob is turned "off" we can't hear the music.

So why, despite the similarities to the same day last week, is today different and potentially more fulfilling and meaningful than yesterday? [Our] capacity is only limited by perfection itself. Each day brings a new opportunity to move forward and improve both our lives and the lives of those around us. Every day—and this one in particular—stands unique.

Here's the question:

Is today just another day, or is it an opportunity?

#

How to Change the World in 3 Easy Steps

Culture

All things being equal, we love to do what we love and dislike doing what we don't love. So how do we find our passions in life?

Although interests can be as varied as the millions of colors on a PC's palette, it may take time to find and develop your true passions. If you're really blessed, you're not only interested in the job or work you perform, but you're passionately tied to promoting good outcomes in some significant and meaningful area of life—you have a passion for something!

Interests can be fleeting; passions are more substantial. If you care deeply about something, and want to exert time, energy, and effort toward it, you've found your passion. In today's world, we're lucky—we have plenty to be interested in, and plenty to be passionate about, too.

Beyond being simply interested, opportunities exist if one can afford the time and the energy to pursue them. Whether attending yoga, tai chi or gym classes, healthy living and exercise offer inner and outer benefits none can deny. Whether having your voice heard in small conference rooms or huge assemblies, we can all decide to participate in life, rather than playing the role of a couch-potato or an observer from the sidelines. Whether your concerned about animals or children or the elderly or the civil and human rights of everyone, groups exist that would welcome your help and support.

That's the marvel of today's world: a huge array of choices for many of us to express ourselves using our own unique style and voice to add to the success of any endeavor.

So, once you've found your passion, what comes next? Move on to the second step by doing your homework.

Just like those millions of colors on your PC's palette, innumerable professions, endeavors and causes exist. We may spend four or five years and a hundred thousand dollars for a college to prepare us for a profession, or simply fall into a career by chance and the seat of our pants, but either way, given a fair chance and opportunity, we can make something of ourselves.

But any endeavor we undertake usually requires careful planning and preparation to succeed. So, too, does any passionate social cause we become a part of require immersion in its premises, ideals, and actions before we can truly understand its big picture and goals.

Do you want to work for the good of humanity? Do you want to promote a civilized, orderly and peaceful society? Depending on where you live, local organizations can use your help.

Your local library, the ASPCA shelter or the local food bank and homeless shelter all need volunteers. You can join the non-profit organizations that offer social, helpful programs to all classes of society and all kinds of people. On a regional or national level, tens of thousands of charities promote some social good, from curing disease, to changing unjust laws, to providing mother and infant care or old age care, and on and on.

With the internet, it shouldn't be difficult to find out pertinent information on anything that inspires you to feel passionately about a cause. TheMuse.com lists 20 questions you can use to investigate before becoming involved in the workings of a socially redeeming effort.

The Bahá'í teachings offer a simple test for deciding between what produces true unity, peace and security and what may not: do your efforts bear fruit?

Existence is like a tree, and man is the fruit. If the fruit be sweet and agreeable, all is well, but if it be bitter it were far better there were none. Every man who has known the celestial bestowals is verily a treasury; if he remain ignorant of them, his non-existence were better than his existence.

The tree which does not bring forth fruit is fit only for the fire.

Strive night and day to change men into fruitful trees, virgin forests into divine orchards and deserts into rose gardens of significance. Light these lamps, that the dark world may become illumined.
– Attributed to 'Abdu'l-Bahá, *Divine Philosophy*, p. 110.

Once you've done your homework and tested the fruitfulness of your passions, met the people involved and seen the work they do, it's time to commit and lend them a hand. It's been said over and over —nothing in this existence can satisfy more than easing someone else's pain, or making another person feel happy or content. Whether it's the skills you have to offer, your mere presence and time, or your energy and commitment, it will be appreciated by those you serve.

Without doubt you will also feel fulfilled.

#

[**Author's Update:** Join the millions of Bahá'ís working in tens of thousands of communities using love and cooperation to achieve their primary goal--a unified planet on every level.

Check us out at www.bahai.org]

#

What's the Difference Between an Error and a Sin?

Culture

We commit errors all the time—it's part of being human. Are those errors sins, or simply mistakes?

Take my favorite example, driving a car. Pulling out into a small opening in oncoming traffic instead of waiting for a larger one might be considered rude but may have been a mistake in judgment or depth perception. Speeding—although most drivers exceed the speed limit—is considered an error worthy of a traffic ticket from the authorities.

Is speeding a sin against the law, a deliberate breaking of it?

A little definition work here might help.

An error implies a mistake. Whether conscious or unconscious, inconsequential or severe, it's in the eye of the beholder. We all make mistakes—that's normal and natural.

The Bahá'í teachings say **"mortal man is prone to err:"**

He [God] is closer to him than his own self.

He will, indeed, so remain forever, for, whereas the one true God knoweth all things, perceiveth all things, and comprehendeth all things, mortal man is prone to err, and is ignorant of the mysteries that lie enfolded within him ....

– Bahá'u'lláh, *Gleanings from the Writings of Bahá'u'lláh*, p. 186.

Webster's Dictionary defines sin as "the willful breaking of any moral or religious law." When we err, it may be out of ignorance or inattention. When we sin we usually know what law what we're breaking, but we break it anyway.

Interestingly, the word *sin* comes from the original Hebrew word *hata*, an archery term that literally means to miss the bullseye—but still hit the target.

We've had hang-ups about sin since the earliest times. The Seven Deadly Sins, codified in the 4th century, are: greed, sloth, pride, lust, envy, gluttony, and wrath. Comparatively, behavioral psychologists have catalogued a list of over six hundred human virtues.

Simply put, we acquire virtues by doing the right thing, and commit "sins" by doing the wrong thing—or sometimes by refusing to do the right thing. If you're attempting to become a better person, you strive to acquire virtues and eliminate sins.

But unlike some of the religions of the past, the Bahá'í teachings don't emphasize or belabor the concept of sin.

Instead, they define [sin] very differently than you may have heard it defined in the past: as the **"attachment of spirit and self to the material world ..."**

– 'Abdu'l-Bahá, *Some Answered Questions*, newly revised edition, p. 140.

All sin, the Bahá'í writings say, comes from our lower, animal nature; the ego; the insistent self:

God has created all in His image and likeness.

Shall we manifest hatred for His creatures and servants? This would be contrary to the will of God and according to the will of Satan, by which we mean the natural inclinations of the lower nature. This lower nature in man is symbolized as Satan—the evil ego within us, not an evil personality outside.

– 'Abdu'l-Bahá, *The Promulgation of Universal Peace*, p. 286.

Bahá'ís view sin as a personal matter, not a public one. For Bahá'ís there is no confession of sins, only a humble request for forgiveness made entirely, prayerfully and privately between each person and God. The Bahá'í teachings advise us to conceal the sins of others, and to lovingly help those who miss the bullseye in life:

If ye become aware of a sin committed by another, conceal it, that God may conceal your own sin.

– Bahá'u'lláh, *Epistle to the Son of the Wolf*, p. 55.

When we find a person fallen into the depths of misery or sin we must be kind to him, take him by the hand, help him to regain his footing, his strength; we must guide him with love and tenderness, treat him as a friend not as an enemy.

We have no right to look upon any of our fellow-mortals as evil.
– 'Abdu'l-Bahá, *Paris Talks*, p. 150.

We must look upon our enemies with a sin-covering eye and act with justice when confronted with any injustice whatsoever, forgive all, consider the whole of humanity as our own family, the whole earth as our own country, be sympathetic with all suffering, nurse the sick, offer a shelter to the exiled, help the poor and those in need, dress all wounds and share the happiness of each one.
– 'Abdu'l-Bahá, *Divine Philosophy*, p. 41.

We humans, the Bahá'í teachings say, have a natural inclination toward the good.

We're spiritual beings who temporarily live in a material world, and all of us struggle to fulfill our essentially spiritual nature and overcome our animal traits.

Bahá'u'lláh compares our tender hearts to mirrors that reflect what we point them towards:

Wert thou to cleanse the mirror of thy heart from the dust of malice, thou wouldst apprehend the meaning of the symbolic terms revealed by the all-embracing Word of God made manifest in every Dispensation, and wouldst discover the mysteries of divine knowledge.
– Bahá'u'lláh, *The Book of Certitude*, p. 68.

Bahá'ís consider humans to be naturally good, fundamentally spiritual beings.

Yes, we can all sin, by turning the mirrors of our hearts away from the sun—but because the sun is the source of all light and life, its rays can warm even the coldest heart.

#

To Everyone on the Planet: Have a Great Day!

Culture

As I sat on a bench outside our free public library, a young Latino man said, "Have a great day!" What a surprise!

I definitely felt pleasantly surprised, me, a stranger sitting on a bench. Oh, I didn't ignore him or his passing, in fact, I immediately noticed the lifting of his right arm and index finger as he pointed at me and nodded his greeting.

"Ah, you too!" I quickly replied, smiling.

I thought: How nice! This stranger said hello to me, to another stranger! Now wouldn't it have been even nicer if I had said something first?

We have maybe dozens of opportunities to uplift a person's spirit every day in our normal activities. Yet I remember lunch times in downtown Trenton, New Jersey, where I worked for decades, most people absorbed in thought, not looking into my face for either recognition or a nod or a simple "Hello." I wish I could say I was always ready with a smile or a nod or "Hello" myself.

We should all have a Great Day—that's why it was a revelation when I was a young Bahá'í to learn that this was "The Great Day of God," meaning, the day of a new messenger from God, who brought teachings of peace, love and unity. It took longer for me to realize that every age in which a new messenger of God appears is a "Great Day." What makes it "Great?"

Imagine a prize or an award waiting for you, and one day the Publisher's Clearing House crew knocks on your door with flowers in their arms and a big banner saying, "You've won!"

That's what it felt like for me to realize that Bahá'u'lláh, a Persian nobleman and prophet imprisoned for most of his life, had a message that could utterly change humanity's fortunes, if only we heeded his advice and exhortations.

In this God-given drawing, everyone on Earth wins:

The world of being shineth in this Day with the resplendency of this Divine Revelation. All created things extol its saving grace and sing its praises. The universe is wrapt in an ecstasy of joy and gladness. The Scriptures of past Dispensations celebrate the great jubilee that must needs greet this most great Day of God.

Well is it with him that hath lived to see this Day and hath recognized its station.
– Bahá'u'lláh, quoted by Shoghi Effendi in *The World Order of Bahá'u'lláh*, p. 106.

This is truly, as my new friend suggested, a great day—a shining, glorious, all-encompassing Day, in which we can all love and respect each other, honor and show kindness to each other, to a degree and on a scale humanity has yet to experience.

That is the hope of all Bahá'ís the world over—that everyone on this planet will recognize this great day. "Have a Great Day," never meant so much, because it is not only a hope, but also a promise and a divine reality:

Great and blessed is this Day—the Day in which all that lay latent in man hath been and will be made manifest. Lofty is the station of man, were he to hold fast to righteousness and truth ...
– Bahá'u'lláh, *Tablets of Bahá'u'lláh*, p. 219.

You see, in this contest, everyone has a voice, a ticket, a part to play in the peaceful unification of the world.

According to the Bahá'í teachings, every person is a child of God, every person has a God-given right to peaceful living and prosperity, a job, education, love and respect and living in harmony with one's fellows, in cooperation and peace rather than disagreement and hatred.

That's what I love about the writings of the Bahá'í Faith: they renounce division and disagreement and focus on unity and love. That's why I share these beliefs with all who read them, and then acknowledge, profoundly, that [an] individual's choice and free will governs how they may react or not react.

For in this Great Day of God, as on every day, the choice, the wonderful choice, is always ours—to offer cheery "Hello's," to strangers, or to respond right back with, "You have a Great Day, too."

#

Courtesy: The Virtue that Precedes All Others
Teachings

You're probably familiar with the old saying "You catch more flies with honey than you do with vinegar."

The Bahá'í teachings offer a similar but much more poetic aphorism:

A kindly tongue is the lodestone of the hearts of men. It is the bread of the spirit, it clotheth the words with meaning, it is the fountain of the light of wisdom and understanding.
– Bahá'u'lláh, *Epistle to the Son of the Wolf*, p. 15.

Both have to do with asking for what one wants or needs, and there's the rub. In our fast-paced Western cultures we're used to telling a clerk, "Medium hot coffee, black," and getting it for a few dollars and no more words, except perhaps a perfunctory "Thanks"—if we're in a good mood.

We're rushed, and we want service with few words and even fewer delays. We want our order right the first time with no mistakes, no matter how clear or unclear we've been in our request, and we want a full refund, no questions asked, if the smallest thing is wrong.

Demanding, aren't we?

Sadly, we go through the motions without understanding that an actual human exchange could be the cause of our happiness.

Attitudes of superiority and elitism like these begin in childhood. We all know that most human personalities are formed by the age of five (some say as early as three).

The importance of modeling by our parents or guardians is paramount to our future dealings with people. If our parents are unable to educate us, provide for us, teach us morals, we are bereft of the human emotion of empathy, and later that may become lack of sympathy, lack of remorse, or even sociopathic behavior.

Those tendencies all lead to demanding and telling others what to do, instead of realizing that life is a two-way street, and we are [obliged] to give understanding and empathy to others in return. The Bahá'í teachings say that only education—moral and spiritual as well as academic—can polish the gems of our inner beings:

Man is the supreme Talisman. Lack of a proper education hath, however, deprived him of that which he doth inherently possess. Through a word proceeding out of the mouth of God he was called into being; by one word more he was guided to recognize the Source of his education; by yet another word his station and destiny were safeguarded.
The Great Being saith:
Regard man as a mine rich in gems of inestimable value. Education can, alone, cause it to reveal its treasures, and enable mankind to benefit therefrom.
– Bahá'u'lláh, *Tablets of Bahá'u'lláh*, p. 162.

Educating our children through their teenage years to become wholesome, considerate, thoughtful, kind and wise adults is difficult enough.

Yet we often spend more of our money, time and resources learning about those physical things that support our bodies and minds than we do the spiritual things that support our true identities as creatures of a loving and magnanimous Creator.

Based on my wife Janet's knowledge of child development as a fifth-grade teacher, raising our children properly was much easier. One of the earliest concepts we taught was courtesy, which paved the way to other virtues. Courtesy encouraged sharing toys and playing with other children well, waiting to let others fully speak and not interrupting, being polite with friends and strangers and taking an interest in what they had to say. In other words, that initial virtue of courtesy led directly to mutual respect of persons and things.

Part of that respect involved learning how to courteously ask for things, for we fully believed Jesus Christ when he said, "Ask and you shall receive, knock and the door shall be opened." As older **Bahá'ís** we knew that also meant God, but it was very applicable to the catching flies with honey quote as well. As we taught our children courtesy, we realized, too, that it adorned every other human virtue:

We, verily, have chosen courtesy, and made it the true mark of such as are nigh unto Him. Courtesy is, in truth, a raiment which fitteth all men, whether young or old. Well is it with him that adorneth his temple therewith, and woe unto him who is deprived of this great bounty.
– Bahá'u'lláh, *Epistle to the Son of the Wolf*, p. 50.

What we ask for is important of course, but it's the "How" that makes all the difference in the world—it's the courtesy of the request that determines the response.

At work, when going to my own staff, I always started with one, their name, and two, the phrase, "Can you please…?" We mutually agreed on a time to complete the task. I tried to stay cognizant that they were doing other things as well.

To me, it was always a two-way street. Of course, there were times when I had to ask in a more forceful way, change priorities, and reassign projects, just as in any organization. But I always started with "Can you please…?" or at least tried to.

The modern advice to "Think before you act" is justified in all our relationships. To me, as I tried to explain to my children, it's all an outgrowth of simple courtesy.

#

Water, Water Everywhere, but Nary a Drop to Drink

Spirituality

Any seafaring person knows what this old saying about water refers to—not being able to use all that salty seawater to quench your thirst.

If you've ever been out in the middle of the ocean without anything to drink, you can relate. We all saw what Tom Hanks had to do for four years as a castaway on his remote island, cupping leaves in the rain and drinking the runoff. For too many in today's world, without access to proper sanitation and clean water, the hard life of a castaway seems tame by comparison.

Yet in developed countries we sell water like it's, well, water, and the water with fancy labels isn't that cheap. The advertising claims for spring water—Pure! Natural!—can seem ridiculous, as if all water doesn't come from rain in some fashion, especially the natural water in aquifers.

I remember at the office when the director learned that our large-bottled water fountains were fed by those dubious claims. He had me ask the bottling company in fact, whose ultimate reply was. "It's guaranteed natural," as if all water wasn't natural.

So out went the big water coolers!

We all need water to survive. Just like our natural need for water, though, we all have an innate thirst for the water of spirituality, the water of love, the water of life.

In this day, as in every day of past ages, the prophets have rained down the fresh water of the word of God on everyone on Earth. The water of the spirit quenches the thirst of souls of all ages, backgrounds, cultures, creeds and beliefs.

[Their] Words created civilizations that have, in many ways, elevated humanity's condition on this planet—and in other [ways] have set us back to the stone ages before the Word could be fully understood or properly implemented.

The Bahá'í teachings consistently ask us to drink this pure water of the soul, which comes from the divine rain of revelation, those "life-giving showers" of faith:

Now, the reality of prophethood, which is the Word of God and the state of perfect divine manifestation, has neither beginning nor end, but its radiance varies like that of the sun.

For example, it dawned above the sign of Christ with the utmost splendour and radiance, and this is eternal and everlasting. See how many world-conquering kings, how many wise ministers and rulers have come and gone, each and all fading into oblivion—whereas even now the breezes of Christ still waft, His light still shines, His call is still upraised, His banner is still unfurled, His armies still do battle, His voice still rings sweetly, His clouds still rain down life-giving showers, His lightning still streaks forth, His glory is still clear and indisputable, His splendour is still radiant and luminous; and the same holds true of every soul that abides beneath His shade and partakes of His light.

– 'Abdu'l-Bahá, *Some Answered Questions*, newly revised edition, pp. 173-174.

Sometimes, though, we don't welcome the rain; it interferes with the outdoor wedding we planned that day, or the summer picnic.

The rain of the word of God can be like that, the admonitions and laws guiding mankind's behavior toward his brother and sister sometimes seemingly restrictive, a nuisance, unwelcome and inconvenient.

Usually we accept the rain, making do with our umbrellas and rubber boots until it ends, understanding that it gives everything life. What else can we do?

We realize we have no control over the weather, the clouds, the system of causes that create precipitation in one town and not the next town over. But sometimes the rain causes floods and damage, even death to those caught unaware.

The rain of the words of the Prophets can be like those hard, physical rains, sweeping away and drowning out ignorance, untruth, hate and cruelty. The rain of the word of God can expose them for what they are—man-made not God-made constructs, deeply flawed and based on faulty and specious ideas. That spiritual rain sweeps away the detritus of winter and brings us a new springtime.

Rain gives life. Without water we will die. Without the word of God, we would have died—literally have destroyed ourselves—already. Yet it seems we have not yet decided to drink from the clear spring of the word of God and refresh and cleanse our bodies of all infirmities:

Ye are even as saplings in a garden, which are near to perishing for want of water. Wherefore, revive your souls with the heavenly water that is raining down from the clouds of divine bounty.
– Bahá'u'lláh, *Tabernacle of Unity, p. 69.*

It's easy to teach the Word of God to those who want to hear it, just as it is to rain on those who face a drought. But depending on what you're drinking, and its source, the taste and contents can enlighten or mask the realities we face today,

[Try it]—take a sip of the clearest, freshest water [physically and spiritually,] and feel it quench your soul's deepest thirst.

#

Do You Believe in Angels?

Spirituality PART 1 IN SERIES: THE DAWNING POINTS OF GOD'S SPIRITUAL BESTOWALS

Do you believe in angels? They certainly have figured prominently throughout humanity's religious history.

In Judaism, the archangels Michael and Gabriel play significant roles in the Torah. The Mormon Church began under the direction of the angel Moroni, who showed young Joseph Smith in 1827 where the golden plates were buried in [a hill in] New York State. In Christianity, the Archangel Gabriel visits the Virgin Mary and predicts the birth of Jesus Christ. Later, in the Qur'an, that same Archangel Gabriel commanded Muhammad to read. Although illiterate and frightened, he did, changing the history of the planet even today.

The serpent in the Garden of Eden who tempted Adam and Eve took on the guise of a disgraced Archangel known more commonly for ages as Lucifer.

The Bible is replete with appearances of angels:

Then I saw another angel flying in midair, and he had the eternal gospel to proclaim to those who live on the earth—to every nation, tribe, language and people.
– Revelation 14:6.

Forget not to show love unto strangers: for thereby some have entertained angels unawares.
– Hebrews 13:2.

We humans can act as "angels" with or without knowing it. When someone does something nice for us, in our best interests rather than their own, they become like an angel.

This harks back to the very essence of "good" and "evil;" concepts as old as people and their relationships with each other. In the ancient religions, angels represented goodness, kindness and altruism; while creatures like Satan represented selfishness, mean-spiritedness and evil.

Who are your angels?

My wife Janet is my angel in this world, although I know many. She is my guardian angel, a concept facilitated in Catholicism and elsewhere, one who watches over me and my doings for my own good.

My mother, 85, generous and kind, caring to a fault, sincere and concerned with her family's welfare and even that of strangers, personifies a living angel despite minor flaws.

When I sit outside on our patio on a breezy day enjoying the sun, I see the white-yellow cabbage butterflies flit about our gardens. [I]know that each one represents the spirit of my departed brother Stephen, watching over me, at least figuratively.

Angels appear in many shapes and guises, the shape of nature and the shape of man or woman or child, symbolizing all that we see as good, holy, and loving in the world.

Another example: all the people in my life, too numerous to mention, who have helped me advance in my various endeavors or careers. I would not be where I am today without the help and assistance of hundreds, perhaps thousands of "angels" who have made my journey through life easier, happier and more fulfilling. Because of their help I am able to leave the devils great and small far behind me and am filled with confidence, hope and joy:

Rejoice, for the heavenly table is prepared for you.
Rejoice, for the angels of heaven are your assistants and helpers.
Rejoice, for the glance of the Blessed Beauty, Bahá'u'lláh, is directed upon you.
Rejoice, for Bahá'u'lláh is your Protector.
Rejoice, for the everlasting glory is destined for you.
Rejoice, for the eternal life is awaiting you.

– 'Abdu'l-Bahá, *The Promulgation of Universal Peace*, p. 214.

When we do kind things, we're angels, too, especially when we give of ourselves, our time, our money, and our energy to selflessly help others. Whether helping those who are in need and charities, relatives or our children, doing volunteer work in the community, serving as educators in schools or working hard in worthwhile ways contributing to society, we all become angels in more ways than we realize.

I wish UNESCO would promote The Year of the Angel just as it has The Year of the Child and the Year of Women. Maybe that's not too far-fetched, since we are in the International Year of Light right now, and angels bring light not darkness, like Archangel Uriel carries the flame of God.

The world right now needs more angels and their unselfish, caring acts of generosity and love. We need angelic acceptance and not just tolerance. We need understanding and patience, and peaceful thoughts. We waste our energy acting out in frustration and rage against things we can only change by changing individual hearts and minds, thereby creating the positive power necessary to alter the systems and laws we abhor.

Want a good place to start? Try a few angelic smiles and kind gestures today.

#

Do Angels Really Exist?

Spirituality PART 2 IN SERIES: THE DAWNING POINTS OF GOD'S SPIRITUAL BESTOWALS

Growing up as a Catholic, I really believed in angels—until I reached adulthood. Now, though, I find myself believing in angels again.

No, I don't mean the kind of angels you see in the old paintings, with their halos, gauzy wings, beatific faces and diaphanous gowns. I've come to believe that those depictions were symbols for the human soul and all of its potential goodness and light.

The Bahá'í teachings define angels, and the angelic human behavior they represent, in a very different way than the old, traditional understandings would have you believe. People used to understand angels as disembodied spirits, metaphysical beings who could instantly protect our souls. Instead, the Bahá'í writings refer to angels as symbols of the confirmations of God—and as detached, spiritual people who act kindly, peacefully and positively in this world:

The meaning of 'angels' is the confirmations of God and His celestial powers.

Likewise angels are blessed beings who have severed all ties with this nether world, have been released from the chains of self and the desires of the flesh, and anchored their hearts to the heavenly realms of the Lord. These are of the Kingdom, heavenly; these are of God, spiritual; these are revealers of God's abounding grace; these are dawning-points of His spiritual bestowals.

– 'Abdu'l-Bahá, *Selections from the Writings of 'Abdu'l-Bahá*, p. 81.

This twofold definition of all things angelic—the confirmations and celestial powers of God; and those blessed souls who have detached themselves from the material things of this world—now informs my concept of angels. Let's explore both of these definitions.

First, what are the "confirmations of God and His celestial powers?"

We can get a clue from the Book of Revelation in the New Testament; and 'Abdu'l-Bahá's illuminating explanation of the meaning of one of its most famous passages:

And he carried me away in the spirit to a great and high mountain, and shewed me that great city, the holy Jerusalem, descending out of heaven from God, having the glory of God: and her light was like unto a stone most precious, even like a jasper stone, clear as crystal; and had a wall great and high, and had twelve gates, and at the gates twelve angels, and names written thereon, which are the names of the twelve tribes of the children of Israel:

On the east three gates; on the north three gates; on the south three gates; and on the west three gates.

And the wall of the city had twelve foundations, and in them the names of the twelve apostles of the Lamb. And he that talked with me had a golden reed to measure the city, and the gates thereof, and the wall thereof. And the city lieth foursquare, and the length is as large as the breadth: and he measured the city with the reed, twelve thousand furlongs. The length and the breadth and the height of it are equal. And he measured the wall thereof, an hundred and forty and four cubits, according to the measure of a man, that is, of the angel.
– Revelation 21:10-17.

St. John the Divine wrote the Biblical Book of Revelation, and here 'Abdu'l-Bahá reveals the true meaning of John's symbolic words:

Accordingly did Saint John the Divine tell of twelve gates in his vision, and twelve foundations. By 'that great city, the holy Jerusalem, descending out of heaven from God' is meant the holy Law of God, and this is set forth in many Tablets and still to be read in the Scriptures of the Prophets of the past ....

The meaning of the passage is that this heavenly Jerusalem hath twelve gates, through which the blessed enter into the City of God.

These gates are souls who are as guiding stars, as portals of knowledge and grace; and within these gates there stand twelve angels. By 'angel' is meant the power of the confirmations of God—that the candle of God's confirming power shineth out from the lamp-niche of those souls—meaning that every one of those beings will be granted the most vehement confirming support.

– 'Abdu'l-Bahá, *Selections from the Writings of 'Abdu'l-Bahá*, pp. 165-166.

We receive the confirmations of God, those heavenly angels, from the messengers of God, the prophets and founders of the world's great Faiths. Abraham, Krishna, Moses, Buddha, Zoroaster, Christ, Muhammad, the Báb and now Bahá'u'lláh—all have given humanity the laws of God, all have served as "portals of knowledge and grace," and all have shone as guiding stars to all humanity.

#

5 Ways to Become an Angel

Teachings PART 3 IN SERIES: THE DAWNING POINTS OF GOD'S SPIRITUAL BESTOWALS

While we're on the subject of angels, here's an age-old question: How can we humans become angelic?

In other words, how do we use our limited energy, resources, or even just the inner resolution [our inner resolve] to make the best of our own lives, to bring about the changes we want to see in ourselves and in the world? How, in other words, do we go about becoming angelic beings?

In the previous essay in this series, we learned that the Bahá'í teachings define angels as:

… blessed beings who have severed all ties with this nether world, have been released from the chains of self and the desires of the flesh, and anchored their hearts to the heavenly realms of the Lord.
– 'Abdu'l-Bahá, *Selections from the Writings of 'Abdu'l-Bahá*, p. 81.

Let's start with a principle as old as life itself: to first fill a cup, the old dregs [must] be discarded—then we can pour the new life in gradually and completely, renewing the essence of love and happiness. No one can fill a cup that's already full. We need clean pure water to live, and we need clean, pure motivations to release ourselves "from the chains of self" and become angelic souls:

Like this cup, you are full of your own opinions and speculations. How can I show you wisdom unless you first empty your cup? – Nyogen Senzaki

The whole duty of man in this Day is to attain that share of the flood of grace which God poureth forth for him. Let none, therefore, consider the largeness or smallness of the receptacle.

The portion of some might lie in the palm of a man's hand, the portion of others might fill a cup, and of others even a gallon-measure.
– Bahá'u'lláh, *Gleanings from the Writings of Bahá'u'lláh*, p. 8.

If we hold onto our old ways without emptying our cup, we will never receive that flood of grace Bahá'u'lláh describes. So first, if you want to become angelic, you must believe in yourself and in others to do the right thing and do the thing right. You must empty your cup. We're all angels here, remember?

Pray to God that He may strengthen you in divine virtue, so that you may be as angels in the world, and beacons of light to disclose the mysteries of the Kingdom to those with understanding hearts.
– 'Abdu'l-Bahá, *Paris Talks*, p. 55.

Second, you can't change the world if you are not willing to change yourself. To do that you must know that you are a powerful creation of God. You must recognize and nurture your inner angel:

O Son of Spirit! I created thee rich, why dost thou bring thyself down to poverty? Noble I made thee, wherewith dost thou abase thyself? Out of the essence of knowledge I gave thee being, why seekest thou enlightenment from anyone beside Me? Out of the clay of love I molded thee, how dost thou busy thyself with another? Turn thy sight unto thyself, that thou mayest find Me standing within thee, mighty, powerful and self-subsisting.
– Bahá'u'lláh, *The Hidden Words*, pp. 6-7.

Third, make a start, small or big, but it's easier to start small and build upon that. This means starting on your own behaviors and thoughts too. Pray. Often. Sincerely. Take the time needed to write down a plan of action, then follow it through. Make a strong inner commitment to develop your highest and best self, and to adopt and strengthen the angelic spiritual qualities of kindness, peace and unity:

… the sublime achievements of man reside in those qualities and attributes that exclusively pertain to the angels …
Therefore, when praiseworthy qualities and high morals emanate from man, he becometh a heavenly being, an angel of the Kingdom, a divine reality and a celestial effulgence.
On the other hand, when he engageth in warfare, quarrelling and bloodshed, he becometh viler than the most fierce of savage creatures …
– 'Abdu'l-Bahá, *Selections from the Writings of 'Abdu'l-Bahá*, p. 287.

Fourth, don't try to force your point of view on others.

Listen and research first, deeply, intently, caringly, as if you were paying attention to your best friend. Mull over what they tell you or show you. Don't discount their experiences just because they may be different than your own. Integrate them with your own thoughts and feelings. Empathize. Be angelic.

Fifth, and here's where we mostly fail—we don't give the process of change enough time to change! We are impatient and pushy. We want instant and immediate change, without having prepared a carefully thought-out replacement. This is where a plan of action is critically important. Learn to cooperate and work with others, not against them. Bend as the branch and be firm as the trunk when it comes to universal principles and truths. Recognize that we all have a lower and a higher nature, and invite all people, yourself included, to incline toward the divine and the spiritual:

Man has two aspects: the physical, which is subject to nature, and the merciful or divine, which is connected with God.

If the physical or natural disposition in him should overcome the heavenly and merciful, he is, then, the most degraded of animal beings;

and if the divine and spiritual should triumph over the human and natural, he is, verily, an angel.

– 'Abdu'l-Bahá, *The Promulgation of Universal Peace*, p. 41.

We actually—physically, mentally, spiritually and in all ways known to man—cannot succeed alone. We are an army of angels, cohort upon cohort in fact and in reality. We rely on the other angels in our lives to help us become as angelic as we can possibly be.

Let's join our arms and hands in solidarity and change the loathsome parts of existence into the heavenly realms of Paradise.

Here on earth.

Now.

Millions of angels out there can use our help.

#

Why Do We Do Bad Things?

Teachings

The Sisters of Mercy hated liars, and we were good liars. "I don't know who did that, Sister," we'd say, when we knew full well who had fired those spitballs.

Of course, when the Sisters caught us in some minor or major infraction, such as cursing aloud or having a fistfight on the playground, we were punished. My ears [were] pulled and my palm smacked more times by those Sisters than by my own mother.

But none of that stopped us. Smoking was cool. Being a tough guy, a hood, was cool. Cursing was cool. Owning a blade was cool. Casual sex was cool. Drugs were cool. Whatever we wanted to do was cool, and what others told us to do and how to be was uncool. We never cared enough to think about the consequences and disappointments we caused.

All behaviors, even mine back in grammar school, were [measured] with a simple reward and punishment model, one my mother and the Sisters tried unsuccessfully to use on me. We, in our headiness to grow up and be cool, never considered the risk of punishment because we never thought we'd get caught.

Catholic Grammar School graduation 1964

Besides, back then we confessed our sins on Saturday, knelt on the pew and said ten Our Father's in our mind, and all was forgiven anyway.

Then onto the next Saturday confession and the next, as if a man wearing a black cassock had the ability to absolve our souls of all sins. Even if you believe such things, it had no effect on us rebellious boys.

I finally did learn, though, that [repeating] bad behavior develops bad attitudes and bad habits—just like good attitudes develop good behaviors and their repetition develops good habits. Perhaps if I had understood, really understood the words and meanings of the Lord's Prayer back then, I might have grown up a better person sooner, or maybe even avoided jail twice.

Luckily, I did gradually learn those meanings after I accepted the Bahá'í teachings at age 20. I finally learned a simple lesson: that the world would reward me for good actions and punish me for the bad ones—and if the world didn't, God eventually would.

On this topic Bahá'u'lláh wrote:

Justice, which consisteth in rendering each his due, dependeth upon and is conditioned by two words: reward and punishment. From the standpoint of justice, every soul should receive the reward of his actions, inasmuch as the peace and prosperity of the world depend thereon, even as He saith, exalted be His glory:

"The structure of world stability and order hath been reared upon, and will continue to be sustained by, the twin pillars of reward and punishment."
– *The Tablenacle of Unity*, p. 40.

We all want justice—that all evildoers be found, punished, and put away from society, from harming others. Yet if one grows up with no real fear of lasting punishment, or ignores the punishments he receives, or doesn't learn life's lesson, he may want justice for others, and believe he can avoid it for himself.

The only lasting, long-term cure for that attitude is a belief in something larger and more powerful than the individual will.

'Abdu'l-Bahá, put it this way:

The tent of the order of the world is raised and established on the two pillars of "Reward and Retribution."

In despotic Governments carried on by men without Divine faith, where no fear of spiritual retribution exists, the execution of the laws is tyrannical and unjust.

There is no greater prevention of oppression than these two sentiments, hope and fear. They have both political and spiritual consequences.

If administrators of the law would take into consideration the spiritual consequences of their decisions, and follow the guidance of religion, "They would be Divine agents in the world of action, the representatives of God for those who are on earth, and they would defend, for the love of God, the interests of His servants as they would defend their own."

If a governor realizes his responsibility, and fears to defy the Divine Law, his judgments will be just. Above all, if he believes that the consequences of his actions will follow him beyond his earthly life, and that "as he sows so must he reap," such a man will surely avoid injustice and tyranny.

– *Paris Talks*, p. 157.

Bad behaviors are learned just like good ones are.

Punishment may help correct or stem bad behavior, but punishments have to go beyond the merely physical, because nothing short of an inner revelation on the part of a bad actor can change their soul and spirit to do good. For that we need religion, faith, and a just society—and the spiritual love of doing the right thing.

#

Why Do We Think of People as Strangers?

Culture

Tell me, how many people do you know?

All told, with my large family, long career in [state] government, Facebook friends, Linked-In contacts, blog followers, people I've met, even those reading this article, I may "know" a few hundred people—or at least, they know who I am.

That is, I might know their name, or face, or maybe a few tidbits about them. But in most cases I really don't know them well. I don't know the names of their children or where they live exactly. I don't know their deepest wishes or their most cherished goals. I don't know their hearts.

This anonymity, where I only know a little about my friends and nothing about the tens of thousands of people, millions and billions of people who will never know me, can be a great comfort sometimes.

If you think about it, people are all "strangers" at one point. Which is strange—especially because the word *strange* comes from the Latin *extraneus*, which means foreign. When you first met your spouse or your best friend or your closest colleague, were they foreign to you? No, probably not—you just hadn't gotten to know them. It's that way with everyone, really.

The poet William Butler Yeats said it this way: **"There are no strangers here—only friends you haven't met yet."**

We think of someone strange or foreign as a person with different customs, different clothing, a different language, or different perspectives. When we encounter foreignness, we can have two very divergent reactions: an interested curiosity or a disinterested aversion. We can be open or closed.

I'm here to tell you that life can be so much more interesting and exciting when we're open to new experiences, new ways of thinking and new friends.

The Bahá'í teachings ask everyone to be open, and never closed.

… do not consider anyone a stranger, for it is said by Bahá'u'lláh "Ye are all the rays of one sun; the fruits of one tree; and the leaves of one branch."
– 'Abdu'l-Bahá, *'Abdu'l-Bahá in London*, p. 80.

This advice, common to the great Faiths, challenges us to look for the good in all people, no matter their culture, country or color. It makes a simple request directly to our hearts: don't close up. Stay open, and receptive, and ready, to make a new friend, anyplace and at any moment. Be friendly. Share your smile. Think about strangers as friends you haven't met yet:

When a man turns his face to God he finds sunshine everywhere. All men are his brothers.

Let not conventionality cause you to seem cold and unsympathetic when you meet strange people from other countries.

Do not look at them as though you suspected them of being evil-doers, thieves and boors. You think it necessary to be very careful, not to expose yourselves to the risk of making acquaintance with such, possibly, undesirable people.

I ask you not to think only of yourselves. Be kind to the strangers, whether come they from Turkey, Japan, Persia, Russia, China or any other country in the world.

Help to make them feel at home; find out where they are staying, ask if you may render them any service; try to make their lives a little happier.

In this way, even if, sometimes, what you at first suspected should be true, still go out of your way to be kind to them — this kindness will help them to become better.

After all, why should any foreign people be treated as strangers?

Let those who meet you know, without your proclaiming the fact, that you are indeed a Bahá'í.

Put into practice the Teaching of Bahá'u'lláh, that of kindness to all nations.

Do not be content with showing friendship in words alone, let your heart burn with loving kindness for all who may cross your path.
– 'Abdu'l-Bahá, *Paris Talks*, pp. 15-16.

After immersing myself in Bahá'í culture and writings, mingling with the Bahá'ís and many others, I too came to realize that there are no strangers, not really. My wife-to-be and I were total strangers in high school art class, until one day Janet said to me, "Oh, I like your sculpture!" (It was flat and terrible)

That was the tiny opening that began our journey together for 47 years.

We are all strangers at one time, and just going out of our way a little bit can make all the difference—the difference between shunning a soul and missing out on love, or loving that soul and being fulfilled mentally, spiritually, even physically.

As I look back and ask my wife Janet what could have possibly attracted her to me, her answer was short. "You seemed like you had a good heart." I certainly fell in love with her good heart.

The vast majority of the human beings on the planet have good hearts, if we give them a chance or two.

Reach out to a stranger sooner rather than later.

It might just change your life.

#

Last Essay:
Why Do We Need Religion?

Religion

We all know from the moment we're born that everyone is different.

We have different speaking voices, different colored eyes and hair and skin, different-shaped faces and bodies, fingerprints, gaits, opinions, abilities and talents, dreams and much more. So why do we insist on labeling anyone the same as anyone else? Why do we categorize people?

We label people primarily because our brains naturally try to create order out of chaos. The human brain innately categorizes everything. That's why we have, in every language on Earth, a noun form for every individual entity. For example—I have a birth name and surname that identifies me and distinguishes me from you. Even though hundreds or thousands of people might have the same name, Rodney Richards, we are each still different.

No one can deny that fact. Try searching for your own name online, and you'll see what I mean. I've found doctors, sports team coaches, chemists, Ph. D's, and many more, all named Rodney Richards. I am not them.

Yes, some of us are twins, yet we are unique no matter how identical our physical traits may seem. You might share a skin color with some people, but the human hues number in the millions. Many of us believe in one religion or another, but we all worship in our own ways. No question about it—from our fingerprints to our philosophies, every individual is completely unique.

So how can we be the same and be so different at the same time? Because we are, in the reality of the spirit, **"one soul in one body:"**

He Who is your Lord, the All-Merciful, cherisheth in His heart the desire of beholding the entire human race as one soul and one body.
– Bahá'u'lláh, *Gleanings from the Writings of Bahá'u'lláh*, p. 214.

The Bahá'í teachings make it clear: we're all unique, but we have something deep within us that gives us a common identity, a universal purpose, a shared reality. 'Abdu'l-Bahá explains:

The phenomenal beings, which are captives of limitations, are ever subject to transformation and change in condition. How can such phenomenal beings ever grasp the heavenly, eternal, unchanging reality?

Assuredly this is an absolute impossibility, for when we study the creational world, we see that the difference of degree is a barrier to such knowing. An inferior degree can never comprehend a higher degree or kingdom.
– *The Promulgation of Universal Peace*, p. 172.

The creational world—what we call "life," existence, physical things—sucks us into believing that all is physical. Yet the wise know that life consists of other equally important, non-physical realities. The purpose of religion is to educate us and open our beings to these other truths.

That's exactly what religion and the Bahá'í Faith does: it fills our hearts, souls and minds with the reality of the mystical.

It allows us to see beyond nature and the purely physical world to an entirely different realm—one that suffuses life with a higher sense of meaning.

It tells us, without equivocation, that despite our individual and human differences we are one human race:

The tabernacle of unity hath been raised; regard ye not one another as strangers. Ye are the fruits of one tree, and the leaves of one branch.
– Bahá'u'lláh, *Gleanings from the Writings of Bahá'u'lláh*, p. 218.

Think about it.

Religion, and the spiritual reality of oneness it promotes, is one of the essential forces that keeps the human race together.

Governments at all levels try to unify us, and hardly succeed.

If it weren't for the teachings of religion, which give us our early moral training whether our families profess a faith or not, we would have no functioning society on Earth. Laws would be ignored. No standards of conduct would exist. Individuals would pursue their own animalistic inclinations without check. Society would become chaotic.

It's time [humanity] recognized the contributions and assets religion offers.

It's the only hope we have of unifying the world and achieving peaceful and productive coexistence.

It's the only hope we have for resolving differences of opinion that produce hate and disruption and war.

Religion is the only hope we have for understanding our true inner, spiritual, unified and unifying nature.

[The Bahá'í Faith is the Word of God renewed for this day and this age.

It doesn't claim to be final, but it does claim to have solutions to humanity's pressing problems.

It does claim that only belief in God and adhering to His Plan for this day can save us from destroying ourselves.

It only asks that every person investigate its claims for him or her self.

That is all Bahá'ís ask.]

#

Closing Remarks
THE MEANING OF TRUE RELIGION

"Should the lamp of religion be obscured," Bahá'u'lláh asserts, *"chaos and confusion will ensue, and the lights of fairness, of justice, of tranquility and peace cease to shine."*[3]

The lamp of religion is obscured and as a result people struggle. All levels of society are struggling. Many believe all bets are off whether we'll make it or not.

There can be no doubts whatsoever that the lamp of religion has been obscured for a long time. The lamp of religion was meant to shine forth unity and peace, cooperation and felicity amidst all mankind. Yet religious strife has become an impediment to the very unity religion is meant to establish and sustain.

Inasmuch as human interpretations and blind imitations differ widely, religious strife and disagreement have arisen among mankind, the light of true religion has been extinguished and the unity of the world of humanity destroyed. "[4]

Historically, the light of religion dimmed greatly with the passing of its Founders, those Gems of divine Holiness, as the question of rightful successorship dogged their expansions and later authority. Subsequent misinterpretation and misapplication of those founders' teachings split their unity and purpose, until innumerable sects now inhabit the globe. No single leader or council speaks for 100% of the followers of any major faith today – except the Bahá'í Faith.

Many religious leaders claim to be the final word of God's Will. In the Bahá'í Faith no one person holds such power. God's Will is expressed through elected councils from among all adult believers at multiple levels of society.

Considered discourse and consultation, with the freedom to express one's opinion, governs all council deliberations. The foundation for their proclamations and pronouncements is the reveled text of the extensive Bahá'í Writings beginning with those of the Báb, some written in His own hand.

At their very core is the basic tenet reiterated over and again by the Báb and Bahá'u'lláh:

"All the Prophets of God, abide in the same tabernacle, soar in the same heaven, are seated upon the same throne, utter the same speech, and proclaim the same Faith."[5]

To separate Them as has been done and to elevate one over another has been the cause of untold ills:

From the "beginning that hath no beginning," these Exponents of the Unity of God and Channels of His incessant utterance have shed the light of the invisible Beauty upon mankind, and will continue, to the "end that hath no end," to vouchsafe fresh revelations of His might and additional experiences of His inconceivable glory.

To contend that any particular religion is final, that "all Revelation is ended, that the portals of Divine mercy are closed, that from the daysprings of eternal holiness no sun shall rise again, that the ocean of everlasting bounty is forever stilled, and that out of the Tabernacle of ancient glory the Messengers of God have ceased to be made manifest" would indeed be nothing less than sheer blasphemy.[6]

Yet faithful promoters of religion preach the incomparable potency and finality of their faiths to this day, ignoring the similarities of their prophet-founders' lives and teachings with other Holy Ones, and thereby separating and removing themselves from closeness to others.

Too many followers have forgotten the purpose of their religion:

"The purpose of religion as revealed from the heaven of God's holy Will is to establish unity and concord amongst the peoples of the world; make it not the cause of dissension and strife."[7]

Further, followers of some past religions have gone to extreme, even deadly extents, to maintain their own superiority at all costs.

But superiority by force is anathema to true religion.

The religion of God and His divine law are the most potent instruments and the surest of all means for the dawning of the light of unity amongst men.

The progress of the world, the development of nations, the tranquility of peoples, and the peace of all who dwell on earth are among the principles and ordinances of God.

Religion bestoweth upon man the most precious of all gifts, offereth the cup of prosperity, imparteth eternal life, and showereth imperishable benefits upon mankind. 8

The struggles and travails of this world will be abolished when the unity of the Prophets and Their messages are realized, and blind imitation and error thrown aside:

The Prophets of God voiced the spirit of unity and agreement. They have been the Founders of divine reality. Therefore, if the nations of the world forsake imitations and investigate the reality underlying the revealed Word of God, they will agree and become reconciled. For reality is one and not multiple. 9

All religions have forever been geared towards the betterment of all humankind at whatever stage of their development, whether tribe, city, city-state, or nation.

The foundation for organic and wide-sweeping change has always been enshrined In ever progressive religions, as it is now proclaimed in the Bahá'í Writings and by Bahá'í institutions.

...the people of religions find, in the teachings of Bahá'u'lláh, the establishment of Universal Religion ---a religion that perfectly conforms with present conditions, which in reality effects the immediate cure of the

incurable disease, which relieves every pain, and bestows the infallible antidote for every deadly poison.[10]

Spiritual laws are universal and eternal, such as "love thy neighbor more than thyself." But social laws governing man's interaction with man are mutable. The old law of the Torah, "an eye for an eye" or cutting off the hand of a thief are no longer applicable in today's world. New religious and social laws in this global age are necessary even though eternal spiritual principles and tenets are immutable.

His Holiness Bahá'u'lláh has given instructions regarding every one of the questions confronting humanity. He has given teachings and instructions with regard to every one of the problems with which man struggles. Among them are (the teachings) concerning the question of economics that all the members of the body politic may enjoy through the working out of this solution the greatest happiness, welfare and comfort without any harm or injury attacking the general order of things. Thereby no difference or dissension will occur. No sedition or contention will take place.[11]

Baha'u'llah has written and revealed new social laws and ordinances for this modern age while simultaneously renewing and extending eternal spiritual laws and precepts.

Therefore I end where I began, especially noting the first five essays (pp 1-20), with my ultimate theme of Religion as the only sure source of humanity's unity, dignity, happiness and peace.

The Books of God are wide open and no longer closed thanks to Bahá'u'lláh.

The answers have been provided.

No matter the Prophet or Founder's name or titles, Their lives and miracles, the doings of Their followers, nor the Holy Words and exhortations in Their Books, the light of these Holy Revelators has always revealed humanity's true spiritual nature – and be assured it is good.

To the soul informed of God's singular reality, all His Messengers and Prophets are One and the same, arise from the same Source, and proclaim the same Faith.

One Religion, divine and continuous, the Religion of God, is the last shelter for a tottering civilization.

Only a single unified human race will bring about a new era of peace and security for all people.

This is truly a New Age, when all good is not only possible, but probable, and only through the renewed Religion of God.

The purpose of all the divine religions is the establishment of the bonds of love and fellowship among men, and the heavenly phenomena of the revealed Word of God are intended to be a source of knowledge and illumination to humanity.[12]

I have faith and assurance that unity and cooperation are inevitable. I believe that the signs of unity, progress, love, empowerment, justice, mercy, kindness and generosity are everywhere. Humanity is learning to do that which is right.

<u>The question is, can we get it right in time.</u>

Finally, 'Abdu'l-Bahá, the son of Bahá'u'lláh, made an astounding statement about the Eternal Covenant between God and Humanity:

"If it is considered with insight, it will be seen that all the forces of the universe, in the last analysis serve the Covenant."[13]

The Ancient Covenant still lives.

<u>God has not left us alone and will never do so.</u>

In this age, He has given us Bahá'u'lláh and His Teachings.

— Rodney Richards

APPENDIX

The Seven Candles of Unity

These prophetic words of "Abdu'l-Bahá, the Master, who passed away in 1921, describe conditions in the world to which we will no doubt attain. They are often referred to as signs of the lesser peace to be achieved in the Century of Light. Each one has come to pass in various aspects and in greater or lesser degrees. It is a vision of a time we can all ascribe to and either knowingly or unwittingly are bringing about.

The ultimate goal is the Most Great Peace.

"The first candle is unity in the political realm, the early glimmerings of which can now be discerned.

"The second candle is unity of thought in world undertakings, the consummation of which will erelong be witnessed.

"The third candle is unity in freedom which will surely come to pass.

"**The fourth candle is unity in religion which is the cornerstone of the foundation itself,** and which, by the power of God, will be revealed in all its splendor.

"The fifth candle is the unity of nations—a unity which in this century will be securely established, causing all the peoples of the world to regard themselves as citizens of one common fatherland.

"The sixth candle is unity of races, making of all that dwell on earth peoples and kindreds of one race.

"The seventh candle is unity of language, i.e., the choice of a universal tongue in which all peoples will be instructed and converse.

"Each and every one of these will inevitably come to pass, inasmuch as the power of the Kingdom of God will aid and assist in their realization."[14]

#

ENDNOTES

1. Statistic from David Langness, Managing Editor of BahaiTeachings.org, circa May 2017

2. Shoghi Effendi, *World Order of Bahá'u'lláh,* Letter dated March 11, 1936, The Unfoldment of World Civilization http://www.bahai.org/r/872238973

3. Bahá'u'lláh, *Tablets of Bahá'u'lláh* The First Ishraq http://www.bahai.org/r/419760347

4. 'Abdu'l-Bahá, *Promulgation of Universal Peace*, #52, 22 May 1912 http://www.bahai.org/r/978143270

5. Bahá'u'lláh, quoted by Shoghi Effendi, *World Order of Bahá'u'lláh* http://www.bahai.org/r/798501323

6. Bahá'u'lláh, ibid

7. Bahá'u'lláh, *Tablets of Bahá'u'lláh*, The Ninth Ishraq http://www.bahai.org/r/694735299

8. Bahá'u'lláh, ibid

9. "Abdu'l-Bahá, op cit

10. "Abdu'l-Bahá, Selections from the Writings of "Abdu'l-Bahá, #227

11. "Abdu'l-Bahá (From a Tablet, 'Star of the West', vol. 13, no. 9, December 1922; and "Foundations of World Unity"; The Compilation of Compilations, vol. III, Economics, Agriculture, and Related Subjects)

12 "Abdu'l-Bahá, *Promulgation of Universal Peace* # 108 http://www.bahai.org/r/922132408

13 Selections from the Writings of 'Abdu'l-Bahá, #192 http://www.bahai.org/r/162163083

14 Selections from the Writings of 'Abdu'l-Bahá, #15 http://www.bahai.org/r/141202836

BIBLIOGRAPHY

The letter below from the Bahá'í Publishing Trust to an individual is applicable to using Bahá'í copyrighted sources:

Subject: Re: World Wide Web Publishing
Date: Tue Nov 26, 1996
From: United States Bahá'í Publishing Trust
To: Mr. S_____ F_____

Dear Bahá'í Friend,

Thank you for your message of November 24 regarding internet publishing. We are very grateful that you took the time to ask permission for posting materials from the U.S. Bahá'í Publishing Trust on the World Wide Web.

You may certainly post anything from the Holy Texts without requesting permission each time. Writings of the three Central Figures and Shoghi Effendi may be used freely. According to a letter from the Universal House of Justice dated 9/4/81 to the National Spiritual Assembly of the Bahá'ís of the United States, "...Spiritual Assemblies and individual believers are free to quote in their publications from any of the Writings of the three Central Figures of the Faith or from the writings of the beloved Guardian, whether in the original language or in translation, without obtaining clearance from the copyright holder, *unless* the copyright holder in the case of a translation is an individual or is a non-Bahá'í institution..."

When quoting from the Bahá'í writings, great care must be taken to make sure that the quoted passages are accurate and presented in a dignified way. The Research/Review Office at the Bahá'í National Center is able to answer questions concerning proper use of the Writings.

Please cite the sources of all quotations, using the original sources rather than secondary sources. Use the most recent printing of the source.

There are some sources that have out-of-date translations or unauthenticated sections and should not be used without checking the particular passages....

Please use the following citation for the Sacred Texts: (Author, Title, page number) For example: ('Abdu'l-Bahá, *Bahá'í Prayers,* p. 167) ....

We ask, as a courtesy, that you place the following notice on your website for any item published by the U.S. Bahá'í Publishing Trust: "This title and other related titles are available from the Bahá'í Distribution Service. E-mail: BDS@usbnc.org   Phone: (800)   999-9019."

We hope this information helps you in your efforts to disseminate the teachings of the Bahá'í Faith on the World Wide Web.

Warmest regards, for Bahá'í Publications [an arm of the National Spiritual Assembly of the Bahá'ís of the United States]

In addition, Author's note: Various editions of Bahá'í-published or Bahá'í-authored books have been used throughout these essays and book. Some quotations used in the original blog essays have been updated from newer revised sources, such as those from *Some Answered Questions* and others.

Practically all references, are obtainable from the online Bahá'í Reference Library at http://www.bahai.org/library/ or http://reference.bahai.org/en/ by searching keywords. The http:// addresses given at the end of certain citations refers to an online-available source.

The author's own library of materials was also consulted.

Other sources used:

Hoffman, Bruce. *Inside Terrorism* Columbia University Press, Copyright 2006 (p.92)

Riccards, Michael P., Draft, *Wilson as Commander-in-Chief* (p.124-125)

RESOURCES

For more information on the Bahá'í Faith, investigate www.bahai.org or call 1-800-22-UNITE and your needs will be met. There is never any obligation.

Wikipedia has hundreds of articles on Bahá'í including its history and historical figures, institutions, and current events and activities.

Bahá'í Distribution Service (U.S. Bahá'í Publishing Trust), offers Bahá'í books and related materials for a fee at www.bahaibookstore.com as do other Publishing Trusts around the world and other booksellers.

Subscribe (free) to the Bahá'í World News Service at news.bahai.org for events and news happenings around the world.

For local community contacts, information and meetings most likely you will find BAHAI listed under CHURCHES in any White Pages or Yellow Pages Directory.
There are thousands of local Bahá'í websites as well.

ABOUT ME

Rodney has been a business and technical writer for thirty years and now writes prose and poetry since retiring in 2009 after a thirty-nine-year career with the State of New Jersey. His story *Episodes A poetic memoir* on living with bipolar disease was self-published in 2012 (out of print). His blog *writewithauthority.blogspot.com* started in 2014.

Rodney's book *Solving the World's Titanic Struggles* Volume 1 was self-published in 2018. It contains one hundred essays of philosophical and spiritual slants published online by BahaiTeachings.org. Volume 2 is due out the second half of 2021.

He has facilitated over 3,000 writing and poetry critique sessions with local writers since 2012 and has assisted fourteen writers edit, polish, and publish their books of memoir, fiction, and nonfiction.

His short story *Bike Slide* was published in the March 2017 issue of the Kelsey Review. Two of his poems appeared online in *The Drunken Llama.* He also owns and operates his own consulting company ABLiA Media LLC which helps writers edit, format, polish, and publish their works. Fourteen books of his clients have been published with more following.

Rodney served on the Rutger's Writing Conference Advisory Board for three years, 2017-2019, and introduced such notables as TV and movie critic David Bianculli, poet Mark Doty, author Mary Bly (pen name Eloisa James), publishing authorpreneurs Arielle Eckstut and David Henry Sterry and others at the annual conferences attended by two hundred.

His philosophy is that every person has a story to share and a unique voice with which to share it.

CONTACT ME

Email me at **1950ablia@gmail.com** or write c/o:

ABLiA Media LLC
P.O. Box 2536
Trenton NJ 08619

 Email is preferred. Please include your full name and email address. You can investigate my manuscript editing, revising, formatting, polishing, and publishing services for writers through my website at *rodneyrichards.info/*

Thanks for reading!
 I'd be grateful if you'd post a review on Amazon or another venue for your feelings and thoughts on the content or issues brought up in this book. Your show of interest or Likes make a difference. I read all reviews personally so I can appreciate your feedback and respond when practical.
 You can also find me on Facebook at **rodneywriter** *or Instagram at* **rrichardswriter.**
 Thanks for your support!

Rod

PS: And write your story! I hope to read it someday and learn from your experiences. It's easier now to self-publish or hybrid-publish for next to zero or little cost. Do it!

www.ingramcontent.com/pod-product-compliance
Lightning Source LLC
LaVergne TN
LVHW051110080426
835510LV00018B/1972